History

for the IB Diploma

Nationalism and Independence in India (1919–1964)

Jean Bottaro

Series editor: Allan Todd

CAMBRIDGE
UNIVERSITY PRESS

University Printing House, Cambridge CB2 8BS, United Kingdom

Cambridge University Press is part of the University of Cambridge.

It furthers the University's mission by disseminating knowledge in the pursuit of education, learning and research at the highest international levels of excellence.

Information on this title: education.cambridge.org

© Cambridge University Press 2016

First published 2016

Printed in Poland by Opolgraf

A catalogue record for this publication is available from the British Library

ISBN 9781316506486 Paperback

Dedication
In memory of Doug (1942-2016), whose support made this possible.

Contents

Introduction

1

1

Overview

This book is designed to prepare students for *Nationalism and Independence in India (1919–1964)*. This is Topic 10 in HL Option 3, History of Asia and Oceania for Paper 3 of the IB History examination. It focuses on the growth of the nationalist movement in India from the outbreak of the First World War in 1914 until the achievement of independence in 1947. It also looks at political and constitutional developments during this period, as well as the main campaigns in the independence struggle, and examines the role of key groups and individuals in this struggle. Particular attention is paid to the factors that led to the partition of the South Asian subcontinent into two separate states, India and Pakistan. Lastly, this book examines post-independence developments in India under its first prime minister, Jawaharlal Nehru, until his death in 1964. During this time India emerged as a united, secular democracy.

Figure 1.1: Indian citizens celebrating the independence of their country from British rule in 1947.

Themes

To help you prepare for your IB History exams, this book will cover the main themes and aspects relating to *Nationalism and Independence in India*, as set out in the IB *History Guide*. In particular, it examines the growth of the nationalist movement in India and the achievement of independence from Britain in terms of:

- the impact of the First World War and demands for Home Rule
- the significance of key political and constitutional developments between 1919 and 1935: the Amritsar Massacre, the 1919 Government of India Act, the Simon Commission, the Round Table Conferences, and responses to the 1935 Government of India Act
- the role and importance of key groups and figures: the Indian National Congress, the All-India Muslim League, Gandhi, Nehru and Jinnah
- the struggle for independence: the Non-Cooperation movement, the Salt March, the Civil Disobedience campaign and the 'Quit India' campaign
- the growth of Muslim separatism: the 'Two Nation' theory and the Lahore Resolution
- the impact of the Second World War: Bose and the Indian National Army, the Cripps Mission and the weakening of British power
- the achievement of independence: the role of Mountbatten; the reasons for the partition of the subcontinent
- post-independence India: ethnic and religious conflicts, the princely states, conflict over Kashmir, the successes and failures of Nehru's domestic policies.

Key Concepts

To perform well in your IB History exams, you will often need to consider aspects of one or more of six important key concepts as you write your answers. These six key concepts are:

- change
- continuity

- causation
- consequence
- significance
- perspectives.

To help you focus on the six key concepts, and gain experience of writing answers that address them, you will find a range of different questions and activities throughout these chapters.

Theory of Knowledge

In addition to the broad key themes, the chapters contain Theory of Knowledge links, to get you thinking about aspects that relate to history, which is a Group 3 subject in the IB Diploma. The *Nationalism and Independence in India* topic has several clear links to ideas about knowledge and history. Aspects of the subject are much debated by historians – especially where it concerns responsibility for the partition of India into two separate – and often antagonistic – states.

At times, the controversial nature of this topic has affected the historians writing about these states, the leaders involved, and their policies and actions. Questions relating to the selection of sources, and the way historians interpret these sources, have clear links to the IB Theory of Knowledge course.

For example, when trying to explain aspects of colonial policies, the motives of political leaders, and the significance of various developments, historians must decide which evidence to select and use to make their case, and which evidence to leave out. But to what extent do the historians' personal political views influence them when selecting what they consider to be the most important or relevant sources, and when they make judgements about the value and limitations of specific sources or sets of sources? Is there such a thing as objective 'historical truth'? Or is there just a range of subjective historical opinions and interpretations about the past, which vary according to the political interests of individual historians?

You are therefore strongly advised to read a range of publications giving different interpretations of British policies and actions, the aims – both stated and hidden – of political leaders, the effectiveness of features of the nationalist struggle, and the significance of different historical events during the period covered by this book, in order to gain a clear understanding of the relevant historiographies (see Further information).

IB History and Paper 3 questions

Paper 3

In IB History, Paper 3 is taken only by Higher-level students. For this paper, it specifies that three sections of an Option should be selected for in-depth study. The examination paper will set two questions on each section – and you have to answer three questions in total.

Unlike Paper 2, where there were regional restrictions, in Paper 3 you will be able to answer *both* questions from one section, with a third chosen from one of the other sections. These questions are essentially in-depth analytical essays. It is therefore important to study *all* the bullet points set out in the IB *History Guide*, in order to give yourself the widest possible choice of questions.

Exam skills

Throughout the main chapters of this book, there are activities and questions to help you develop the understanding and the exam skills necessary for success in Paper 3. Your exam answers should demonstrate:

- factual knowledge and understanding
- awareness and understanding of historical interpretations
- structured, analytical and balanced argument.

Before attempting the specific exam practice questions that come at the end of each main chapter, you might find it useful to refer first to Chapter 10, the final exam practice chapter. This suggestion is based on the idea that if you know where you are supposed to be going (in this instance, gaining a good grade), and how to get there, you stand a better chance of reaching your destination!

Questions and mark schemes

To ensure that you develop the necessary skills and understanding, each chapter contains comprehension questions and examination tips. For success in Paper 3, you need to produce essays that combine a number of features. In many ways, these require the same skills as the essays in Paper 2.

However, for the Higher-level Paper 3, examiners will be looking for greater evidence of *sustained* analysis and argument, linked closely to the demands of the question. They will also be seeking more depth and precision with regard to supporting knowledge. Finally, they will be expecting a clear and well-organised answer, so it is vital to do a rough plan *before* you start to answer a question. Your plan will show straight away whether or not you know enough about the topic to answer the question. It will also provide a good structure for your answer.

It is particularly important to start by focusing *closely* on the wording of the question, so that you can identify its demands. If you simply assume that a question is *'generally about this period/leader'*, you will probably produce an answer that is essentially a narrative or story, with only vague links to the question. Even if your knowledge is detailed and accurate, it will only be broadly relevant. If you do this, you will get half-marks at most.

Another important point is to make sure you present *a well-structured and analytical argument* that is clearly linked to all the demands of the question. Each aspect of your argument/analysis/explanation then needs to be supported by carefully selected, precise and relevant own knowledge.

In addition, showing awareness and understanding of relevant historical debates and interpretations will help you to access the highest marks and bands. This does not mean simply repeating, in your own words, what different historians have said. Instead, try to *critically evaluate* particular interpretations. For example, are there any weaknesses in some arguments put forward by certain historians? What strengths does a particular interpretation have?

Examiner's tips

To help you develop these skills, most chapters contain sample questions, with examiner's tips about what to do (and what *not* to do) in order to achieve high marks. Each chapter will focus on a specific skill, as follows:

- Skill 1 (Chapter 2) – understanding the wording of a question
- Skill 2 (Chapter 3) – planning an essay
- Skill 3 (Chapter 5) – writing an introductory paragraph
- Skill 4 (Chapter 6) – avoiding irrelevance
- Skill 5 (Chapter 7) – avoiding a narrative-based answer
- Skill 6 (Chapter 8) – using your own knowledge analytically and combining it with awareness of historical debate
- Skill 7 (Chapter 9) – writing a conclusion to your essay.

Some of these tips will contain parts of a student's answer to a particular question, with examiner's comments, to give you an understanding of what examiners are looking for.

This guidance is developed further in Chapter 10, the exam practice chapter, where examiner's tips and comments will enable you to focus on the important aspects of questions and their answers. These examples will also help you avoid simple mistakes and oversights which, every year, result in some otherwise good students failing to gain the highest marks.

For additional help, a simplified Paper 3 mark scheme is provided in Chapter 10. This should make it easier to understand what examiners are looking for in your answers, and therefore help you reach the higher bands. The actual Paper 3 IB History mark scheme can be found on the IB website.

This book will provide you with the historical knowledge and understanding to help you answer all the specific content bullet points set out in the IB *History Guide*. Also, by the time you have worked through the various exercises, you should have the skills necessary to construct relevant, clear, well-argued and well-supported essays.

Background to the period

The area where India, Pakistan and Bangladesh are situated today is usually called the Indian subcontinent or South Asia. Until 1947 it was ruled as the British colony of India. This book covers the struggle of the Indian people to gain independence from Britain. However, it is important to have some knowledge of Indian history before this. It is also useful to see colonialism in India in the broader context of European imperialism in Asia.

The land and the people

The South Asian subcontinent has distinctive geographic features that have helped to shape its history. There is a chain of high mountains across the north, separating India from Central Asia, but they did not prevent trade and interaction. The vast fertile plains of the Indus and Ganges rivers in the north of India attracted settlers and invaders and became the sites of dense human settlement. The long coastline bordering the Arabian Sea in the west and the Bay of Bengal in the east provided opportunities for fishing and trade for coastal communities, and later became sites of European trade and settlement.

The history of India stretches back thousands of years, with evidence of the Indus Valley civilisation going back further than 3000 BCE. Over the centuries, many different people invaded the region, including the Greeks under Alexander the Great, Huns, Arabs, Mongols, Afghans and Turks. They were attracted by the fertile land, the opportunities for trade, and the natural wealth of India – spices, silks, gold and precious stones. As a result, South Asia contained a rich mixture of people, cultures, languages and religions.

At first the main religion was Hinduism, and Hindu princes ruled most of the region. From about 1200, Turkish invaders brought Islam to India and established the Delhi Sultanates in the northern part of the subcontinent. These in turn were conquered by the Mughals, a Muslim dynasty originally from Persia (now Iran). The Mughals gradually extended their empire until, by 1700, it included most of present-day India, Pakistan and Bangladesh. The Mughal rulers were dependent on the support of local rulers – usually Hindu – who remained in power but paid taxes and tribute to the Mughal emperor. Some people adopted Islam as their religion, especially in the northern part of the subcontinent, but many remained Hindu. The two religions co-existed in India for many centuries. The Sikh religion, which contained elements of both Islam and Hinduism, also emerged.

Figure 1.2: The Taj Mahal in Agra was built by one of the Mughal emperors, Shah Jahan, as a tomb for his wife, Mumtaz Mahal. It combines Muslim and Hindu architectural styles and is one of the most famous buildings in the world because of its beauty and perfect proportions.

Colonialism in Asia

European interest in Asia was sparked by the spice trade. In 1498, the Portuguese were the first to find a sea route to the Indian Ocean, followed by the Dutch, the Spanish, the French and the English. The English East India Company (EIC) was established by royal charter in 1600 to trade with India. It set up trading posts along the coast but gradually expanded its control until, by the middle of the 19th century, it ruled over large parts of India and even had its own army. Although there was still a Mughal emperor, based in Delhi, he had no real power. However, after an uprising against EIC control in 1857 to 1858, the British government sent troops to crush the uprising and took over most of India as a British colony.

Other parts of Asia became European colonies as well. The Dutch East India Company established its headquarters for trade with Asia in Batavia (in northern Java). From there the Dutch gradually extended their control over other Indonesian islands, which they called the Dutch East Indies. France, encouraged by French missionaries and traders,

13

extended control over Southeast Asia and took over the Saigon delta region (Cochinchina) and the kingdoms of Annan, Cambodia, Tonkin and Laos. They called their vast empire French Indochina. Portuguese colonies in Asia were limited to small coastal enclaves, such as Macau in China and Goa in India. As well as India, Britain took over Malaya, Singapore, Hong Kong and the island of Sri Lanka (parts of which had previously been colonised by the Portuguese and the Dutch). Although the kingdom of Burma was determined to remain independent, it too became a British colony.

It was not only European powers which colonised Asia. In 1898, the USA took over the Philippines, which had previously been a Spanish colony. The Russian empire expanded eastwards into Siberia, where it took over the province of Amur from China and built the port of Vladivostok, giving Russia access to the Pacific Ocean. It also expanded southwards in Central Asia and took over the previously independent Islamic khanates (Kazakstan, Uzbekistan, Turkmenistan, Kyrgyzstan and Tajikistan). The Ottoman empire controlled most of West Asia (often referred to as the Middle East). Japan also became an imperialist power and took over Korea and the island of Taiwan.

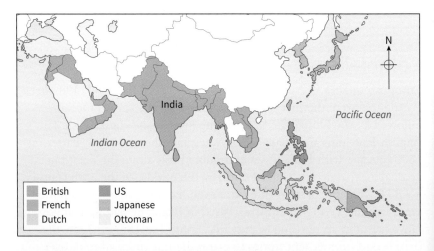

Figure 1.3: Colonial empires in Asia after the First World War.

The only large Asian countries which retained their independence were Japan, Thailand and China. However, although China remained politically independent, it was not economically independent; European powers occupied areas of Shanghai and Beijing and dictated trade terms to the Chinese, seriously weakening China, both economically and politically.

British India must be seen therefore in the context of a wider pattern of European domination of large parts of Asia, which intensified in the late 19th century. Similarly, the growth of a nationalist struggle for independence in India was mirrored by anti-colonial struggles in other European colonies in Asia, such as the resistance against French rule in Indochina. However, the scale and effectiveness of the nationalist movement in India made it unique in many ways, and its success in achieving independence in 1947 served as an inspiration to anti-colonial struggles in Africa and other parts of Asia.

Terminology and definitions

In order to understand this period of Indian history, you will need to be familiar with a few basic terms:

Caste

Traditional Hindu society was divided into a hierarchy of levels called castes. Status, occupation, rights, privileges and opportunities in life were all determined by the caste into which someone was born. Outside the caste system were the 'untouchables' who suffered various forms of exclusion and discrimination. After independence, the government outlawed 'untouchability' and introduced measures to improve these people's situation, but the tradition was difficult to eradicate.

Civil disobedience

Civil disobedience describes refusal to obey certain laws or government regulations which are considered to be unjust. Such actions are non-violent and visible, and done as a form of protest, with the expectation of being punished. Protestors seek to draw attention to the unjust law or policy which they hope to end. Many actions of the nationalist movement are seen as acts of civil disobedience, but the 'Civil Disobedience campaign' refers specifically to the campaign led by Gandhi and the Indian National Congress between 1930 and 1932, which started with the Salt March.

Communalism

Communalism means promoting the interests of one ethnic, religious or cultural group rather than those of society as a whole, and was responsible for the tensions between Hindus and Muslims in pre-independence India. It was also responsible for the violence and bloodshed between Hindus, Muslims and Sikhs that accompanied partition in 1947.

Dalit

Meaning 'the oppressed', Dalit was the term used by untouchables to refer to themselves. In the 1970s they formed the radical Dalit Panther organisation to fight for their rights.

Dominion status

This gave colonies autonomy to run their own affairs. The dominions were linked to Britain as members of the empire but not ruled by Britain. The colonies in which large numbers of immigrants from Britain had settled – Canada, Australia, New Zealand and South Africa – were granted dominion status. But British colonies in Asia, the rest of Africa and the Caribbean, were not.

Harijans

Meaning 'children of God', this was Gandhi's term for the untouchables. He fought for greater rights and freedom for them, and opposed the 1932 Communal Award which proposed separate representation. He reached an agreement with Dr B.R. Ambedkar, the leader of the untouchables, about reserved seats rather than separate electorates.

Hartal

A *hartal* was a strike or work stoppage, the closing of shops in a market as a form of protest, or boycott of British goods. *Hartals* were a feature of the Rowlett *satyagraha* of 1919 and later used in other non-violent protest campaigns launched by Gandhi and the Indian National Congress.

Hindutwa

This was a politicised form of Hinduism; the promotion of Hindu values and the creation of a state based on Hindu beliefs and culture. Its emergence during the 1920s contributed to the growth of communal tensions. It was the ideology of the militant Hindu nationalist group, the Rashtriya Swayamsevak Sangh (RSS), which was strongly anti-Muslim. Gandhi's assassin was a member of the RSS.

Home Rule

This described the concept of self-government or independence from Britain, similar to the demands by Irish nationalists at the time. Support for Home Rule Leagues in India during the First World War helped to sustain the Indian nationalist movement and were a factor contributing to the British government's decision to introduce constitutional reforms in the form of the Montagu Declaration in 1917.

Jain

Jain was a small religious community based mainly in Gujarat and Bombay. Jains teach respect for all living things and are strict vegetarians. They believe that spiritual advancement can be achieved through five vows – of non-violence, truthfulness, avoiding greed and exploitation, chastity and detachment from the world. Gandhi, who grew up in Porbandar in Gujarat, was influenced by the ideas of Jainism, which helped to shape his later political and spiritual beliefs.

Khalifat

Caliph (which can be spelled in a number of ways, including kalif) is a term for a supreme spiritual and political leader in the Muslim world. The Khalifat movement among Muslims in India wanted to secure the position of the Ottoman sultan as the spiritual leader of all Muslims by putting pressure on the British. When the Ottoman Empire was broken up after the First World War and Turkey became a secular state, the movement lost its primary goal and became part of the wider nationalist movement. It played an important role in the Non-Cooperation movement of 1920 to 1922.

Mahatma

'Great soul': the name given to Mohandas Gandhi.

Non-Cooperation

This described a refusal to cooperate; a means of showing opposition to government policies by refusing to participate in official functions or government institutions or to obey government regulations. The 'Non-Cooperation movement' was the first mass movement of civil disobedience launched by Gandhi and the Indian National Congress between 1920 and 1922.

Satyagraha

Satyagraha means 'soul force' or 'truth force'; a quest for truth though mass political activity. This philosophy of non–violent resistance promoted by Gandhi was based on the belief that ordinary people can bring about political change by using peaceful means to fight for justice. It was seen as both a moral philosophy and a political weapon.

Secular

Secularism is the view that religion should be separated from government or public education. The Indian National Congress promoted secularism as its goal, and the constitution of independent India confirmed India's status as a secular state.

Swadeshi

This was the idea of indigenous self-sufficiency which was used by the nationalists to promote the production and use of products made in India. It was first used as a form of organised protest after the partition of Bengal in 1905. The boycott of British goods was effective in reducing imports from Britain and stimulating local industries. The strength of support for the *Swadeshi* movement contributed to Britain's decision to introduce the Morley-Minto reforms in 1909.

Swaraj

This is a term for self-government (self-rule), or independence from foreign rule. The Indian National Congress adopted *Purna Swaraj* (complete independence) as its goal at its 1929 Congress session in Lahore, and formed an All-India Congress Committee to coordinate protests in order to achieve it.

Place names

In recent years, many place names in India have been changed. In this book, we have used the names that were in use at the time of the historical events discussed. Among other changes:

- Bombay is now Mumbai
- Calcutta is Kolkata
- Madras is Chennai
- Poona is Pune
- Simla is Shimla.

History and changing perspectives

Historians often change their views of past events. This may occur as new primary sources come to light or simply because new perspectives emerge. An analysis of these changes (historiography) is a higher-level historical skill.

There are several different interpretations of modern Indian history. Imperialist historians focus on the role played by Britain in bringing about change, in the form of infrastructure such as railways and communications systems, as well as systems of administration and government. They also see Britain's role in the progress towards independence as positive. In this view, India gained its independence because Britain had committed itself to a gradual process of constitutional reform towards self-government. This school of historical writing is sometimes referred to as 'History from above' as it places great emphasis on the role of key individuals, especially British officials, such as Irwin and Mountbatten.

In the view of nationalist historians, Indians achieved independence through their own efforts. In this view, Britain left India because it could no longer hold back the tide of resistance led by the Indian National Congress. Nationalist historians place special focus on the role played by Congress and by prominent Indian leaders – such as Gandhi and Nehru – in the independence movement.

Historians of the more recent 'Subaltern Studies' group focus on the role played by ordinary people in this struggle, and how they too were agents of political and social change. The word 'subaltern' is a military term meaning someone of inferior rank, but in this context it is used to refer to anyone who holds an inferior position in society, in terms of race, class, gender, sexuality, ethnicity or religion. Historians of this school write 'History from below' and examine the views of ordinary men and women and their part in the independence struggle.

Historians writing from a Marxist perspective view British colonialism as exploitative. They also analyse the Indian nationalist movement from a class perspective, and see it as serving the interests of élite groups (the landowners and the educated middle class) rather than representing the Indian people as a whole. They question whether the process of decolonisation and subsequent independence was beneficial for the masses in postcolonial India.

Summary

By the time you have worked through this book, you should be able to:

- understand the impact of the First World War on India and the significance of the Home Rule movement
- explain the main political and constitutional developments between 1919 and 1935 and responses to them in India
- evaluate the role of key groups and individuals in the nationalist movement
- compare and contrast the main campaigns and strategies used in the nationalist struggle for independence

- account for the rise of Muslim separatism and support for the 'Two Nation' theory
- understand the impact of the Second World War on the independence movement and on British power in India
- understand and explain the situation in India after the war that led to independence and partition
- understand the challenges facing post-independence India and evaluate the effectiveness of domestic policies in addressing them.

2

Origins of Indian nationalism and impact of the First World War

Introduction

The development of the Indian nationalist movement and demands for independence developed as a reaction against British policies and actions during the period when India was a British colony. Before the First World War, two rival nationalist organisations were formed: the Indian National Congress, which pressed for greater Indian representation in government, and the All-India Muslim League, which represented the interests of the Muslim minority. This chapter will examine the origins of Indian nationalism before 1914, as well as the impact of the First World War on India. During the war, the nationalist movement was strengthened by the activities of the Home Rule Leagues, which called for self-government and dominion status for India.

TIMELINE

1857 Indian Uprising against the rule of the East India Company (EIC)

1858 Government of India Act: British government takes control

1885 First meeting of the Indian National Congress

1892 Limited representation of Indians on provincial legislatures

1905 Partition of Bengal; anti-partition protests; start of *Swadeshi* movement

1906 Simla Deputation

Formation of All-India Muslim League in Dhaka

1909 India Councils Act implements Morley-Minto reforms

1911 Capital of British India moved from Calcutta to Delhi

Reunification of Bengal

1914–18 First World War

1914–15 *Ghadar* movement

1914 **June:** Tilak released from prison

1915 **Jan:** Gandhi returns from South Africa

Mar: Defence of India Act

1916 **April:** Tilak forms Home Rule League in Poona

Sept: Besant forms Home Rule League in Madras

Dec: Lucknow Pact between Congress and Muslim League

Nationalism and Independence in India (1919–1964)

1917 June: Arrest of Besant and other Home Rule leaders

1918–19 Spanish Flu epidemic

1918 Aug: Announcement of Montagu-Chelmsford reforms

KEY QUESTIONS

- What were the origins of the nationalist movement in India?
- How did the First World War affect India?
- To what extent did the demands for Home Rule boost the nationalist movement?

Overview

- Until 1947 India was a British colony. Colonial rule was efficient but authoritarian, and Indians themselves had no meaningful representation in it. Britain applied a policy of 'divide and rule' which emphasised religious and other differences among the people of India.
- Britain derived great economic benefits from India, including raw materials and markets. Indian soldiers fought in Britain's colonial wars, and indentured workers from India provided labour in other British colonies.
- In 1885, educated Indians formed the first nationalist organisation – the Indian National Congress. It called for greater representation for Indians in government, rather than independence from British rule.
- Muslim leaders formed a separate organisation, the All-India Muslim League, in 1906, to protect and advance the interests of Muslims, who were a minority in a predominantly Hindu country.
- During the First World War, India provided troops and supplies for the Allied war effort on a huge scale. In return for their considerable contribution to Britain's victory over Germany, Indians hoped for self-rule after the war.
- The war caused widespread hardship for many Indians as a result of food and fuel shortages, higher prices and increased taxation.

These problems were aggravated in 1918 by a severe famine and the Spanish Flu epidemic which killed over 12 million Indians.
- During the war Home Rule Leagues were established, calling for self-government and dominion status for India. The movement gave a boost to Indian nationalism, especially after the Indian National Congress adopted Home Rule as a political goal.
- The popularity of the Home Rule movement, as well as India's contribution to the war effort, prompted the British government to introduce constitutional reforms, which were outlined in the Montagu-Chelmsford proposals of 1918.

2.1 What were the origins of the nationalist movement in India?

The nationalist movement in India began in the period of British colonial rule. The movement developed as a reaction against the policies and actions of the British government in India as well as the attitudes of the British towards the Indian people.

British rule in India

British interest in India began when the English East India Company (EIC) set up trading posts along the coast from the beginning of the 17th century. EIC rule gradually expanded into the interior, and by the middle of the 19th century the company controlled extensive parts of India and had a large private army. Although there was still a Mughal emperor, based at the 'Red Fort' in Delhi, he had no real power. However, an uprising against EIC control in 1857 and 1858 resulted in the intervention of the British government, which sent troops to crush the rebellion and take over control from the EIC. Both sides were responsible for atrocities during the uprising and its suppression, and this left a legacy of bitterness and distrust.

Theory of Knowledge

History, terminology and bias

Indian nationalists regard the 1857 uprising as the First War of Independence. The British, however, referred to it as the 'Indian Mutiny', because it started among *sepoys*, Indian soldiers serving in the Bengal army of the EIC. The uprising had broad-based support from a wide range of Indians, however, including peasants, workers, landlords and princes.

What would be a more neutral term to describe this event? Use this example, and others you can think of, to explain how terminology can reflect bias in History.

ACTIVITY

Use the internet to find out information about the 1857 uprising. Was it planned or did it arise spontaneously? What impact did it have on British policies and actions in India? How did it affect Indian attitudes towards the British?

The Mughal emperor had supported the uprising, and after its failure he was removed from power and sent into exile. In 1858 the British parliament passed the Government of India Act, making India part of the British Empire, and in 1876 Queen Victoria was declared 'Empress of India'. Large parts of the country were placed under direct British administration, but some areas remained under the control of hereditary Indian rulers, with whom the British signed treaties that recognised their autonomy over local affairs. However, a British official (called the 'Resident' in the larger states and a 'Political Officer' in the smaller ones) ensured that British interests were always upheld. There were over 550 of these 'princely states', as they were called. Some of these were extensive, such as Hyderabad and Kashmir, but others were very small.

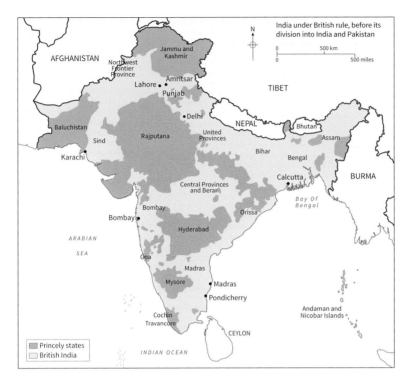

Figure 2.1: A map showing areas of India under British control until 1947 and the princely states.

The structure of British rule

After the harsh suppression of the 1857–58 uprising, British power in India seemed to be secure. The British referred to their empire in India as the 'Raj', a Hindi word for rule. The colonial administration was initially situated in Calcutta, which had been the centre of EIC control, although it was later moved to Delhi. The highest official was the viceroy who was appointed by the British government in London and ruled India on behalf of the British monarch. There was a great deal of status, material comfort and wealth attached to the position, and the salary of the viceroy was double that of the British prime minister. However, the viceroy had limited power to influence policy, which was decided by the British government in London and implemented by the Secretary of State for India, who was advised by a Council of India (none of whose members were Indian).

The administration was run by 5000 officials who formed the Indian Civil Service (ICS). They provided efficient, but authoritarian, government. Positions in the ICS were well-paid and highly prized among ambitious young Englishmen who had to sit competitive exams before they were accepted. Indians themselves had no meaningful representation in this government, although they later formed the bulk of the junior staff in the Indian Civil Service. British control over 300 million Indians was enforced by a large army, staffed by British officers and Indian troops. The administration and the army were financed out of taxes paid by Indians.

Economic and political benefits to Britain

The British viewed India as the most valuable possession in the British Empire and referred to it as the 'Jewel in the Crown'. They derived great economic benefits from it. Money, collected from peasants in the form of taxes, was transferred to London to fund the British government's purchase of EIC shares, finance capital investments (especially railways), and provide funds for the administration of India.

Critics felt that the money could have been better used for internal investments in India itself. Trade between Britain and India was facilitated by the opening of the Suez Canal in 1869, which drastically reduced the distance, time and costs of transporting goods.

Britain benefited from the balance of trade with India, which supplied raw materials – mainly cotton, jute, indigo, rice and tea – to British factories. In return, India bought manufactured goods such as textiles, iron and steel goods and machinery and, by 1914, was the biggest export market for British goods.

As a result, India under colonial rule was no longer an exporter of cloth to European markets. Instead it produced raw cotton that was manufactured into cloth in British factories and re-exported to Asia. Another disadvantage for India was that land formerly used to grow grains for staple foods was now used for commercial cash-crop production, making peasants dependent on foods grown elsewhere.

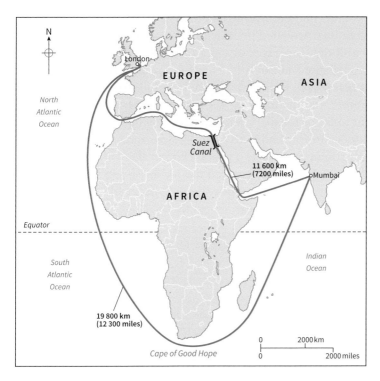

Figure 2.2: The routes between Britain and India via the Suez Canal and via the Cape of Good Hope.

India also served Britain's political and economic interests in other parts of the empire. Indian soldiers, paid for by Indian tax payers, were used to protect trade routes and serve British interests in China, East Africa and the Middle East. In the 20th century, large numbers of Indian soldiers provided military support for Britain in both world wars. India also served as a source of indentured labourers for British colonies in the West Indies, Africa and other parts of Asia.

By 1920, however, the system of indenture was stopped, partly as a result of criticism from Indian nationalists, who saw it as one of 'imperial exploitation that brought shame to India', according to Barbara and Thomas Metcalf. These historians also note that the plight of diaspora Indians was a 'critical stimulus to Indian nationalism'.

The nature of British rule

The British who went to live in India were predominantly men employed by the ICS or the army, sometimes accompanied by their wives and young children, who would then be sent back to England for their schooling. Attended by large numbers of Indian servants, most of these British residents experienced a far more luxurious lifestyle than they could afford in England. They lived mainly in the big cities, especially Calcutta, but moved to the cool foothills of the Himalayas in the hot summer months. Even the viceroy and his staff relocated the government to Simla for the summer. When the men retired they would inevitably return to England with their pensions funded by Indian taxes. The British in India were a ruling élite; an alien and in many cases arrogant minority, who regarded the Indians as subordinate and untrustworthy, and India as an exotic but uncomfortable place to live, as historian David Ludden explains:

SOURCE 2.1

South Asia was too hot, dirty, crowded, distant and alien to attract many British citizens. At the peak of their numerical strength, in 1911, British residents in British India numbered 185434, under one percent of Britain's population and about six one-hundredths of one percent (0.06%) of British India's population. These small numbers lived mostly in securely segregated British enclaves, doings their jobs and maintaining English-style households and communities, trying to live as comfortably as possible until they could go home, hopefully better off than when they arrived.

Ludden, David. 2014. **India and South Asia: A Short History.** *London. Oneworld Publications. p. 154.*

QUESTION

What message is conveyed by Source 2.1 about the attitudes of the British towards India?

The British believed that government should be firm and vigilant against the rise of any resistance to their rule. Above all, they wanted to prevent the formation of a united opposition movement. To this end, they stressed differences between people – significantly, differences of religion, and also of caste. They regarded caste as a form of fixed identity, instead of something that had developed and changed over time.

According to the historian Thomas Metcalf, the British saw caste as a 'concrete, measurable "thing" that could be fitted into a hierarchy able to be ascertained and quantified in reports and surveys'. The result of this colonial policy was to create and intensify existing differences in Indian society.

The British brought certain benefits to India. These included an efficient administration and judicial system, a good railway network and Western education for some. However, British rule was always based on an assumption of superiority.

SOURCE 2.2

We must rule our Asiatic subjects with strict and generous justice, wisely and beneficently, as their natural superiors, by virtue of our purer religion, our sterner energies, our subtler intellect, our more creative faculties, our more commanding and indomitable will.

A British official, quoted in James, Lawrence. 1997. **Raj: The Making and Unmaking of British India.** *London. Little, Brown and Company. p. 297.*

Indians resented the harsh realities of colonial control and the superior attitudes of the colonising power towards them. This view was later explained by Jawaharlal Nehru, who became a leading figure in the nationalist movement against British rule:

SOURCE 2.3

We in India have known racialism in all its forms since the beginning of British rule. The whole ideology of this rule was that of the master race, and the structure of government was based upon it; indeed the idea of the master race is inherent in (central to) imperialism. There was no subterfuge (nothing hidden) about it; it was proclaimed in unambiguous (direct) language by those in authority. More powerful than words was the practice that accompanied them and, generation after generation and year after year, India as a nation and Indians as individuals were subjected to insult, humiliation, and contemptuous treatment. The English were an imperial race, we were told, with the God-given right to govern us and keep us in subjection. As an Indian I am ashamed to write all this, for the memory of it hurts, and what hurts still more is that we submitted for so long to this degradation. I would have preferred any kind of resistance to this, whatever the consequences, rather than that our people should endure this treatment.

Nehru, J. 1946. **The Discovery of India.** *London. Meridian Books.*

QUESTION

Compare and contrast the views expressed in Sources 2.2 and 2.3.

With reference to their origin, purpose and content, assess the value and limitations of these two sources for a historian studying British attitudes towards Indians in the colonial period.

QUESTION

Discuss the structure and nature of British rule in India.

The birth of Indian nationalism

Towards the end of the 19th century, there was a growing feeling among educated Indians that there should be more Indian representation in government. In 1885, they formed a nationalist organisation called the Indian National Congress (INC, later referred to simply as Congress). It was not a political party and was, initially, simply a forum for discussion. The first meeting was held in Bombay and after that it met every year in late December in a different Indian city.

In its early stages, the Congress represented the interests of the wealthy middle class and it did not have mass support. Most of the founding members were graduates and all spoke English. They saw themselves as a bridge between the Indian masses and the colonial power. As a result, the existence of the Congress tended to limit the development of more radical nationalist groups.

The élitist nature of the early Congress made it very conservative in its goals, and it used petitions to try to achieve them. It did not question the continuation of British rule, but called rather for greater Indian representation in the legislative councils, easier access to the Indian Civil Service, reduced land taxes, less expenditure on the army and increased funding for Indian economic development. Although the early Congress was not at all radical in its goals or assertive in its actions, it laid the foundations of an organisation that later developed into a powerful political force.

Most of the Congress membership was Hindu, although it also had Muslim members. Right from the start, Congress leaders made explicit efforts to draw Muslims into their meetings, and members of the organisation believed that the interests of caste or religious affiliation should be secondary to the needs of the Indian nation as a whole. However, as you will read below, Muslims later established their own separate political organisation, the All-India Muslim League.

The growth of Indian nationalism before 1914

Serious nationalist opposition to colonial rule in India started when the British decided to partition the province of Bengal in north-eastern India. Bengal had been the first region to come under British control, and its main city, Calcutta, was the capital of British India. The province had a population of over 80 million people, the majority of whom were

Bengali-speaking Hindus. In 1905, the viceroy announced that the province would be divided into two: an eastern province with a Muslim majority, and a western part in which Bihari- and Oriya-speaking Hindus were in the majority. Ostensibly the partition was made in order to provide more efficient administration in a large and densely populated region.

Historians believe though that the real reason was to weaken the nationalist movement which had strong support in Bengal. At the time, Bengali-speaking Hindus saw the partition as a threat to their position in the region and a deliberate attempt by Britain to weaken Bengali nationalism.

Protests against the partition of Bengal

The partition sparked heated protests and opposition, ranging from acts of violence, such as the bombing of government buildings and an attempt to assassinate the governor of West Bengal, to more peaceful forms of protest. These included petitions, protests in the press, public meetings, pamphlets, posters and songs. Congress leaders also expressed their opposition to the partition, and the protests spread to other parts of India as well.

When all of these failed, protestors organised a boycott of British goods. This became known as the *Swadeshi* (self-sufficiency) movement. Protestors made public bonfires of manufactured goods from Britain and urged Indians to use local products instead.

The aims behind the movement were both to strike a blow at the British economy and also to revive indigenous industries. The boycott proved to be very effective. British imports into India dropped by 25%, and the economy of some areas – such as the city of Bombay on the west coast – expanded as Indian industries developed to take advantage of the gap. The British authorities reacted to the anti-partition protests with mass arrests, which had limited impact.

The events had significant results: Congress realised the political power of an economic boycott, and nationalists in other parts of India were united in support for the Bengali cause. Historian David Ludden explains the significance of this:

SOURCE 2.4

Events in Calcutta in 1905 changed imperial society for ever. They produced a new kind of politics that Congress delegates could not have imagined at their small, sedate meeting in Calcutta nine years before. Like the formation of the Congress itself, the new politics expressed public controversy over imperial policy. But now the drama moved into the streets and sometimes became violent. Calcutta was ground zero and centre stage for this radical innovation…

[T]he 1905 agitation against partition in Calcutta spread more widely than any before because Calcutta's stature as the imperial capital and as India's national city made Calcutta's public anger an expression of Indian national outrage. Calcutta's local Indian identities became national as agitation expressed Indian opposition to British domination.

Ludden, David. 2014. **India and South Asia: A Short History.** *London. Oneworld Publications. pp. 183–5.*

QUESTION

How and why, according to Source 2.4, was Calcutta central to the anti-partition protests?

The Simla Deputation and the Muslim League

In contrast to the opposition by Congress to the partition of Bengal, Muslims in Bengal supported partition in the belief that it would benefit them. Many of them became increasingly unnerved by the activities of the anti-partition movement, and by the appeals to Hindu nationalism made by some of the protestors. Support for the concept of a separate organisation to represent and safeguard Muslim interests began to grow. In October 1906 representatives of the Muslim community met with Lord Minto, the viceroy, at Simla and stressed the view that Muslims were a distinct community which needed separate representation for its own protection. This 'Simla Deputation' as it was called, received assurances from Minto that the political interests of Muslims would be safeguarded in any future constitutional reforms that were introduced, a move that had far-reaching and complex implications.

Nationalism and Independence in India (1919–1964)

In December 1906, Muslim leaders meeting in Dhaka formed the Muslim League, believing that this was the only way to protect the interests of the Muslim minority. At first the League was dominated by a similar middle-and upper-class leadership to the Congress. In spite of the apparent sympathy of the British towards their viewpoint expressed by Minto at Simla, many Muslims were alienated by the British government's reversal of the partition of Bengal in 1911. They were also angered by Britain's unwillingness to support the Ottoman Empire in the face of growing unrest in the Balkans and Russian expansionist ambitions in the region. At the same time, there was growing unity among Muslims, between conservative loyalists and a younger radical group who were more willing to seek an alliance with Congress. At its meeting in Lucknow in 1912 the Muslim League called for self-government for India.

KEY CONCEPTS QUESTION

Significance: Use the internet to do some research on the Simla Deputation. Discuss the significance of the agreement reached between it and the viceroy in 1906.

Differences that emerged in the Congress movement

The confrontation over Bengal created divisions in Congress between the 'Extremists' who supported public protests and the 'Moderates' who did not. The Moderates argued that it would be difficult for political leaders to control a mass popular movement where people might act unpredictably.

The Extremists, on the other hand, argued that mass public protests were the only way to put pressure on the British authorities. The Extremists formed a revolutionary wing, called the New Party, which had strong support in Calcutta, Poona and Lahore. This development was significant because it seemed that the more moderate leaders such as **Gopal Krishna Gokhale** were being marginalised in favour of radicals such as **Bal Gangadhar Tilak**, who urged more active opposition to British rule. Another more radical group even favoured assassination and sabotage as forms of protest against colonial policies and actions.

Gopal Krishna Gokhale (1866–1915):

Gokhale was a leading moderate figure in the Indian nationalist movement. In 1902 he gave up his position as head of History and Political Economy at Fergusson College in Poona to enter politics, and was president of Congress at the time of the anti-partition protests in 1905. He was a passionate supporter of non-violent and constitutional moves for reform and independence. He also believed strongly in social reform, such as the emancipation of women, and the extension of education. He founded the Servants of India Society, whose members took vows of poverty and service to the poor, especially among the 'untouchables' in Hindu society.

Bal Gangadhar Tilak (1856–1920):

Tilak was the first leader of the Indian National Congress to gain popular support. He was a lawyer and teacher and ran two nationalist newspapers. He opposed the call for constitutional reform advocated by the moderate Congress leaders and demanded self-rule – or *swaraj* – for India. When the movement split into two factions in 1907, he led the Extremists. The British saw him as a dangerous troublemaker, and in 1908 sentenced him to six years in prison for sedition (treason). He was released in 1914 and re-joined Congress.

The divisions in Congress came to a head in December 1907, at its meeting in Surat, when many Extremists left the party, leaving the Moderates in control. The government acted against the Extremists using harsh new measures introduced to crush the anti-partition protests. Tilak, the main Extremist leader, was sent to Burma to serve a six-year prison sentence for sedition. The split in Congress seriously weakened the nationalist movement in the years preceding the outbreak of the First World War.

Constitutional changes before the First World War

Although India was ruled as a colony, from as early as 1861, the Indian Councils Act gave wealthy Indians some limited representation in provincial legislatures, to which they were appointed by the British government in India. This representation was extended in 1892. However, the powers of the provincial legislatures were restricted to discussion about legislation, not the power to approve or enact it.

Further constitutional changes came after the British decision to partition the state of Bengal provoked such widespread protests. The strength of opposition to the partition plan forced Britain to reassess its policies in India. At first it tried to crush the protests, and by 1909 large numbers of Bengalis were in prison. However, many government officials, both in India and back in London, felt that the situation was running out of control. There were fears that Indian soldiers in the British army in Punjab were about to go on strike, and even rumours of another mutiny. The serving viceroy, Lord Minto, and the Secretary of State for India, John Morley, decided that concessions should be made to the nationalists so that Britain could maintain its control of the subcontinent.

ACTIVITY

Examine the short- and long-term consequences of the British decision to partition Bengal in 1905.

The Morley–Minto reforms were implemented in the Indian Councils Act of 1909. These reforms gave Indians some representation in government:

- They could elect representatives to sit on the viceroy's executive council.
- The provincial councils would be enlarged and given more powers.
- Two Indians were nominated to serve on the Council for India in London, the body which advised the Secretary of State.

In 1910 elections were held for the central and provincial legislative councils. Muslims were given separate representation – separate electorates and reserved seats – to ensure that the minority Muslims would have a voice in these councils. This significant (and contested) move established the principle of separate communal representation and shaped future political developments.

As a result of these changes, Indians now had the power to question the decisions of colonial officials and debate the budget for the country. Although the right to vote was always subject to various economic and educational qualifications, over the next decades these gradually became less restrictive with the result that the number of Indians entitled to vote slowly increased, although it always remained a small minority under British rule.

In addition to this, Bengal was reunited and the capital of India was moved from Calcutta, the site of anti-British activism, to the city of Delhi, which had been the capital of the Mughal empire, a move that pleased Muslims.

Figure 2.3: In an elaborate '*durbar*', incorporating many features of the Mughal past, the British king, George V, was crowned emperor of India in 1911.

KEY CONCEPTS QUESTION

Change and continuity: To what extent did the 1909 constitutional reforms represent continuity rather than change in the British administration of India?

The situation by 1914

The implementation of the Morley-Minto reforms in 1909 cooled the situation in India and restored the more moderate elements of Congress to power. However, although they welcomed the reforms, they regretted the recognition of separate minority interests. Extremists regarded the reforms as totally inadequate, because the right to vote was restricted to the wealthy élite, and seats on councils were reserved for landowners and business leaders. They continued to call for full self-government.

Indian national pride was strengthened when Rabindranath Tagore (1861–1941), a Bengali poet, novelist, musician and playwright was awarded the Nobel Prize for Literature in 1912, becoming the first Asian Nobel laureate. He was later knighted by the British king, but returned his knighthood in protest after the massacre of hundreds of unarmed civilians in 1919 by British troops at Amritsar (which you will read about in the next chapter).

DISCUSSION POINT

To what extent did British policies and actions contribute to the rise and growth of a nationalist movement in India?

2.2 How did the First World War affect India?

The First World War was essentially a conflict between European powers, but it involved their overseas empires as well. When war broke out in 1914, Britain expected support from its colonies, especially India, which supplied large numbers of soldiers, huge amounts of resources, and nearly 185 000 animals to the Allied cause.

Indian involvement in the war

There was a small group of Indians who saw the war as an opportunity to force the British out of India. Their leaders were based among Indian immigrants in California, where discrimination and poor working conditions had led to the emergence of the radical *Ghadar* movement. When war broke out they called on Indian workers abroad to return to India and start an armed uprising. Although about 8000 people responded to the call, the British authorities in India were prepared for them. Some were interned, and others were placed under restriction orders in their villages. The rest found little support for their cause in Punjab, where most of them had originated. Their efforts to get army units to mutiny met with little success, apart from a revolt by about 800 Indian troops in Singapore in February 1915. It was suppressed after five days during which 39 British officers and civilians were killed.

Although the *Ghadar* movement's radical plan for a mass uprising did not succeed, the British government was concerned about these anti-British actions and as a result passed the Defence of India Act in March 1915. This act suspended a wide range of civil rights, such as freedom of speech, of the press and of movement. According to Metcalf the purpose of this act was to have the powers to suppress 'presumed internal threats with extremely repressive measures'. The act also made provision for the establishment of special tribunals to try those suspected of acting against the interests of the British empire and for preventive detention of such suspects. The widespread use of the act to suppress any form of political activity made it deeply unpopular.

The actions of the *Ghadar* movement were an exception to what happened in the rest of India. When war broke out in August 1914, Indians of a wide range of political opinion expressed their willingness to support Britain, including the Muslim League even though Britain was officially at war with the Ottoman Empire from November 1914. Historian Lawrence James suggests that with the outbreak of war 'old tensions and animosities were suspended and representatives of every race, religion and caste publicly declared their loyalty to the King Emperor and their willingness to join in the struggle against Germany'. Even though some nationalists saw the war as an opportunity to press for greater independence, most Indians, including radicals like Tilak, urged support for Britain's war effort. **Mohandas Gandhi** who had recently returned to India from South Africa also supported the war effort, stating that if Indians expected to enjoy the privileges of belonging to the British Empire they should be prepared to share the responsibilities that this membership entailed. James suggests that the implications of this were clear: if India did its share of the war effort, then it would prove that it was worthy and ready for self-government.

Mohandas Gandhi (1869–1948):

Gandhi was born in Porbandar, one of the princely states, where his father was chief minister. He qualified as a barrister in London, and in 1893 he went to South Africa to represent a client in the large Indian community there. He stayed in South Africa for over 20 years and led the Indian community in a struggle against discriminatory colonial laws. It was during this period that he developed his philosophy of *satyagraha*, or soul force, which is sometimes interpreted as non-violent resistance. News of his activities in South Africa had reached India, but he was still relatively unknown when he returned there in January 1915.

One and a half million Indians volunteered to serve in the British army during the First World War, making it the largest volunteer army in history for the British empire. They fought on the Western Front and in East Africa against Germany, and at Gallipoli, in the Middle East and in North Africa against Turkey. Indian troops won 13000 medals for bravery, including 12 Victoria Crosses. About 65000 Indian soldiers were killed in the war, and an equal number wounded.

Figure 2.4: Indian soldiers served on the Western Front along with Allied soldiers from other parts of the British Empire.

The entry of the Ottoman Empire into the war on the German side created a conflict of loyalties for many Muslims in India. This was because the Ottoman Empire was the world's leading Islamic power, and the Sultan of Turkey was regarded as the caliph – the leader of Sunni Islam – which was the largest denomination within Islam, and to which most Muslims in India belonged. However, although many of them were reluctant to fight directly against Turkish troops, there were few serious mutinies among the Indian troops in the Allied armies. According to Metcalf, however, Britain feared a pan-Islamic conspiracy and so interned Muslim leaders such as **Shaukat Ali** and his brother **Muhammad Ali**, from the time that the Ottoman Empire entered the war until the armistice in 1918.

> ### Shaukat Ali (1873–1938) and Muhammad Ali (1878–1931):
>
> The Ali brothers were leading members of the Khalifat movement among Muslims in India who wanted to protect the Ottoman Empire by putting pressure on Britain. When the Ottoman Empire was broken up after the First World War, and Turkey became a secular state, the movement lost its primary goal and became part of the wider nationalist movement. Muhammad Ali served as president of the All-India Muslim League in 1918 and of the Indian National Congress in 1923.

By the end of the war it had become obvious to many Indians just how dependent Britain had been on their help to secure victory over Germany. Indian soldiers returning from Western Europe reported their experience of the high living standards and wealth of even the poorest classes in Britain and France compared with the people of India. Indians hoped that their sacrifices in the war would result in reforms that would give them greater representation in government.

The economic impact of the war on India

During the First World War, key industries in India, such as cotton textiles and iron and steel, experienced a boom as manufacturers took advantage of the increased demands caused by the war. A striking example of this expansion was the Jamshedpur works of the Tata Iron and Steel Company, where production increased dramatically.

Agriculture, however, remained the dominant sector of the economy, and the production of cotton and jute also expanded, leading to an overall increase in exports, especially to the United States and Japan. Before the war, Britain had been India's main trading partner, but this now began to change. Lawrence James suggests that the war 'fractured Anglo-Indian economic dependency' and that this became more even more pronounced after the war.

During the war there was opposition, supported by Congress, to the free trade policies which favoured Britain. Textiles manufactured in Britain were not subject to taxes when they landed in India, seriously undermining the profitability of local producers. In keeping with its earlier support for *swadeshi,* or economic self-sufficiency, Congress called for taxes on British imports to protect Indian industries. This call was partially implemented in 1917 when the Indian government agreed to take over £100 million of Britain's war debt in return for the right to tax manufactured cotton goods from Lancashire.

As the war dragged on, however, dissatisfaction grew, partly due to heavy wartime taxation and increased efforts at recruitment. For ordinary Indians, the war created rising food prices and shortages of fuel. An increase in taxes during the war created great hardships for poor peasant farmers, many of whom led a largely subsistence existence and who got increasingly into debt.

The situation was aggravated by food shortages and famine in large areas of India in 1918 when the monsoon rains failed. This coincided with the spread of the Spanish Flu epidemic. It was brought to India on returning troopships and spread rapidly along railway routes. It killed 12 to 13 million people within a year, most of them women between the ages of 15 and 50.

ACTIVITY

Use the internet to find out more about the Spanish Flu epidemic. Which countries were most severely affected? How was it linked to the First World War?

Discuss the positive and negative effects of the First World War on India.

Figure 2.5: The war created widespread hardship for many Indians, such as these water carriers in Agra circa 1917.

The political impact of the war on India

The Allies claimed that they were fighting to 'make the world safe for democracy' and they spoke of self-determination – the right of people to choose their own government. For Indian soldiers, fighting alongside other Allied troops, these claims created expectations that these concepts would be applied in India after the war.

The experiences of the war heightened nationalist sentiments and many hoped that the British would soon allow India a greater degree of independence. The wartime experiences of Indian soldiers influenced their thinking in other ways too, as did the situation they found back home in India, as Sources 2.5 and 2.6 show:

SOURCE 2.5

My own eyes have been opened since I came to Europe, and I have entirely changed my views which I had before…When I was in Hindustan and used to hear of anyone going to England for education…I used to say 'these people lose their religion and return as Christians'. Now that I have come here, I realise how wrong I was in my ideas. There is no question at all of religion – it is education alone which makes them wise, and teaches them to hate and abandon those habits and customs in our country which are improper, and to live according to their new ideas.

Samson, Jane. 2001. The British Empire. *Oxford. Oxford University Press p. 230–1; acknowledging, Omissi David (ed). 1999.* **Indian Voices of the Great War: Soldiers' Letters, 1914–1918.** *Houndmills. Macmillan. pp. 88–9, 324–5.*

SOURCE 2.6

Indian soldiers who returned home from various fronts at the turn of 1918 found a country in a state of flux. It was entering the first phase of an industrial revolution and was distressed by food shortages, inflation, high prices and a devastating epidemic. Alongside the hunger and sickness there were their offspring: discontent and restlessness. In turn, these generated a feeling that great, perhaps catastrophic events were just around the corner.

James, Lawrence. 1997. **Raj: The Making and Unmaking of British India.** *London. Little, Brown and Company. p. 463.*

QUESTION

What, according to Sources 2.5 and 2.6, was the impact of the war on people's attitudes in India? Source 2.5 is a primary source and Source 2.6 is a secondary source. Discuss the relative value and limitations of primary and secondary sources in historical research.

2.3 To what extent did the demands for Home Rule boost the nationalist movement?

The concept of 'Home Rule', or self-government, had become important in Ireland during this time, where Irish nationalists were demanding independence from Britain. The same call was made in India during the war and the Home Rule movement gave encouragement to Indian nationalism.

The origins of the Home Rule movement

The spread of the Home Rule movement was due largely to the efforts of two people – the radical Indian nationalist, Bal Gangadhar Tilak, and an Englishwoman, **Annie Besant**.

> ### Annie Besant (1847–1933):
>
> **Annie Besant** was a social reformer who had supported various causes in Britain before moving to India in 1893. She remained there for the rest of her life. She saw a Hindu revival as a means of creating national pride and self-esteem to counter the effects of British imperialism. Her book, *Wake Up India!*, published in 1913, was a blend of spiritual and secular ideas and appealed to a wide range of educated Indians. She promoted the idea that India should be granted self-government in the same way that the dominions (Canada, Australia, South Africa and New Zealand) had been. She went on lecture tours throughout India to spread this message. She was elected president of the Indian National Congress in 1917.

When Tilak was released from prison in June 1914, after serving six years for sedition, he focused on being readmitted to Congress. He adopted a conciliatory attitude to convince the Moderates that he no longer supported extremist measures and also to ensure that the authorities would have no cause to re-arrest him. At the same time, he began talking about Home Rule for India:

SOURCE 2.7

I may state once and for all that we are trying in India, as the Irish Home-rulers have been doing in Ireland, for a reform of the system of administration and not for the overthrow of Government; and I have no hesitation in saying that the acts of violence which have been committed in the different parts of India are not only repugnant to me, but have, in my opinion, only unfortunately retarded to a great extent, the pace of our political progress.

Quoted in Chandra, B. et al. 2012. India's Struggle for Independence **1857–1947.** *London. Penguin, Digital edition 2012, Chapter 13, Location 2727.*

QUESTION

With reference to its origin, purpose and content, assess the value and limitations of Source 2.7 for historians looking for evidence of Tilak's more conciliatory approach after his release from prison.

At the same time, Annie Besant was also energetically promoting the concept of Home Rule. She joined the Indian National Congress and worked hard to heal the rift between the Moderates and Extremists at the meeting of the Congress at Surat in 1915. Although she failed at this stage to convince Congress to adopt Home Rule as official policy, many Congress members were attracted to the idea.

In 1916 both Tilak and Besant set up Home Rule Leagues, Tilak in Poona in April and Besant in Madras in September. There was a great deal of cooperation between the two leaders, but the two movements did not unite. They focused their activities on different parts of India instead. Tilak's movement operated mainly in western India, and Besant's in the rest of the country. Both set up branches in towns and villages to promote political education through discussion groups, lectures, pamphlets and political meetings, and by setting up libraries and reading rooms. Within a year, 60 000 people had joined the Home Rule Leagues. As the movement gained increasing support, the authorities decided to act. Tilak's arrest and subsequent trial gained a great deal of publicity and support for the movement, especially when the case was thrown out by the High Court.

However, the turning point in the Home Rule movement came with the arrest and internment of Besant and some of her associates in June 1917. This sparked off wide condemnation, and many prominent Indian leaders, who until this point had not joined the Home Rule Leagues, did so now, including Mohammed Ali Jinnah. Tilak advocated the use of passive resistance, or civil disobedience, to put pressure on the government to release the detainees. At the same time, organisers collected the signatures of a million workers and peasants calling for Home Rule.

The mounting protests put pressure on Britain to reassess its policies in India and, in August 1917 the new Secretary of State, Edwin Montagu, announced that the government was willing to introduce changes. (See 2.3, Changes in British policy towards India, 1917–18, later in this chapter.) Annie Besant was also released in the following month, and, at Tilak's suggestion, was elected president of Congress in December 1917.

QUESTION

Examine the reasons why Britain saw the Home Rule movement as a threat to its position in India.

The achievements of the Home Rule movement

During 1918, the Home Rule movement gradually lost its influence and impetus. However, it had played a significant role in sustaining the Indian nationalist movement during the war years, especially after Congress adopted the concept of Home Rule as a goal. The Home Rule Leagues were not radical organisations: they essentially wanted autonomy rather than complete independence within the British Empire. However, they nudged the British government into introducing constitutional reforms, as announced in the Montagu Declaration in 1917.

SOURCE 2.8

The tremendous achievement of the Home Rule Movement and its legacy was that it created a generation of ardent nationalists who formed the backbone of the national movement in the coming years when, under the leadership of the Mahatma, it entered its truly mass phase. The Home Rule Leagues also created the organisational links between town and country which were to prove invaluable in later years. And further, by popularising the idea of Home Rule or self-government, and making it a commonplace thing, it generated a widespread pro-nationalist atmosphere in the country.

By the end of the First World War in 1918, the new generation of nationalists aroused to political awareness and impatient with the pace of change, were looking for a means of expressing themselves through effective political action. The leaders of the Home Rule League, who themselves were responsible for bringing them to this point, were unable to show the way forward. The stage was thus set for the entry of Mohandas Karamchand Gandhi… he was the rallying point for almost all those who had been awakened to politics by the Home Rule Movement.

Chandra, B. et al. 2012. India's Struggle for Independence *1857–1947. London. Penguin. Digital edition: Chapter 13. Locations 2913 and 2922.*

QUESTION

What, according to Source 2.8, was the significance of the Home Rule movement?

Nationalist politics during the war

The war also brought greater unity among the nationalists. A reconciliation between the Moderates and Extremists in Congress became possible after the adoption of a less radical position by Tilak, following his release from prison in 1914 and his subsequent support for Indian involvement in the Allied war effort. The death of the moderate leader Gokhale in 1915 gave Congress the opportunity to try to mend the division between the two factions. At the 1916 Congress meeting in Lucknow, the two factions put aside their differences. After that the reunited Congress had the confidence to make more assertive statements concerning self-rule for India.

The Muslim League too was ready to consider reaching an agreement with Congress. The reunification of Bengal in 1911 had made them fear that the British no longer regarded the issue of separate Muslim representation, as agreed in the Simla Accord, as important. Before the war they had relied on Britain to protect their minority rights, but with Britain at war with Muslim Turkey they no longer had the same confidence that this protection would continue. They decided therefore to move closer to the nationalist movement. A key figure in this was Mohammad Ali Jinnah, who was a member of both Congress and the League, as well as the Home Rule League. (You will read more about Jinnah in Chapter 4.) In both 1915 and 1916, the annual meetings of Congress and the League were held in the same city – Bombay in 1915 and Lucknow in 1916 – which facilitated greater cooperation between the two organisations.

In 1916, the Moderate and Extremists factions in Congress, as well as the Muslim League, signed the Lucknow Pact. In this it was agreed that Muslims would have a fixed proportion of seats in parliament, and extra seats in areas in which Muslims were in a minority. This meant that Muslims would be under-represented in areas with a Muslim majority (such as East Bengal and Punjab) and that in turn there would be Hindu under-representation in the other areas that were dominantly Hindu.

DISCUSSION POINT

Evaluate whether Congress or the Muslim League had more to gain from the Lucknow Pact. Before beginning your discussion, use the internet to find out further information about it.

Historians have interpreted the Lucknow Pact as an extremely important development. Crispin Bates sees its main significance in the fact that it was the first time that so many members of the Muslim League had sat at the same conference as prominent Hindu leaders in Congress, and that this groundwork was crucial to the launching of a nationwide movement by Gandhi after the war.

SOURCE 2.9

The Indian National Congress–All India Muslim League agreement, popularly known as the Lucknow Pact, can easily be considered one of the most important events in the trajectory of the nationalist movement in India. In the midst of the first world war, in 1916, both organisations presented a joint scheme of constitutional reforms to the colonial rulers with the expectation that this scheme would be implemented once the war ended. This marked the coming together of two major political organisations which hitherto had displayed a marked hostility to each other.

The significance of the Lucknow Pact lies in the fact that it was the first time that the Congress reached an agreement with an organisation which was explicitly a 'communal' one while the League, founded to counter Congress' claims to represent the whole of India, reached an agreement with the same organisation. The main feature of the pact was the demand for an expansion of the representative assemblies, both at the all-India and provincial levels, and appointment of Indians to the executive councils of the viceroy and the provincial governors. But more importantly, the Congress for the first time openly and explicitly conceded the principle of communal representation by accepting separate electorates for Muslims, something that it had grudgingly accepted as part of the Morley-Minto package of constitutional reforms.

Datah, Abhay. 2012. **'The Lucknow Pact of 1916: A Second Look at the Congress-Muslim League Agreement'** *in* **Economic and Political Weekly,** *Volume XLV11 No 10. March 2012. India. Sameeksha Trust. p. 65.*

Theory of Knowledge

History and significance

Who decides whether events are historically significant or not? To what extent is hindsight an advantage in determining this?

There are conflicting views of the Lucknow Pact. In the colonial period and immediately after independence, most historians cited it as a significant instance of cooperation between the two religious communities. Mukherjee (1989) claimed that, although the acceptance of separate electorates was a controversial decision, it was motivated by a 'sincere desire to allay minority fears about majority domination'.

Some historians took a more negative view: Mehotra (1979) suggested that, by signing it, Congress had surrendered to Muslim communalism and separatism. More recently, Robinson (2008) has argued that the Muslim leaders who signed the pact were not representative of the Muslim community as a whole but merely represented a small 'clique' of Young Party Muslims from the United Provinces. Historians such as Prasad (2009) have suggested that by signing it, Congress compromised its claim to represent all Indians by accepting the League's claim to represent Muslims.

KEY CONCEPTS QUESTION

Perspective: Explain why it is important to consider different interpretations and perspectives in history. Discuss the factors that influence the perspectives of historians.

Changes in British policy towards India, 1917–18

The contribution of India to Britain's war effort as well as the activities of the Home Rule Leagues brought about a change in British policy towards India. In August 1917, Edwin Montagu, the new Secretary of State, working together with Lord Chelmsford, the viceroy, announced the British government's intention to encourage 'the gradual development of self-governing institutions with a view to the progressive realisation of responsible government' in India. Historians Kulke and Rothermund believe that the term 'responsible government', rather than 'self-government' was a 'loaded phrase' which implied that in future the executive would be responsible to an elected parliament. This system went further than the Morley-Minto reforms of 1909 which had introduced a non-parliamentary system in which, these same historians suggest, the elected legislature 'acted as a kind of permanent opposition in the face of an irremovable executive'.

The British government also announced that Montagu would visit India to consult with the viceroy and Indian representatives. After a six-month fact-finding visit between November 1917 and May 1918, the Montagu-Chelmsford report was duly published in July 1918, outlining proposed reforms to the government of India, which were due to take effect the following year.

The report proposed a system of 'dyarchy' (or dual government) which theoretically divided power between the British and the Indians. Historians point out, however, that it was a very unequal division of power. The British-appointed central government in Delhi, in which Indians had advisory powers only, would be in control of key areas of government (such as foreign policy, defence and taxation). The elected provincial governments would only have control over aspects such as education, health and economic development. In addition, only 1.5 million of the wealthiest of British India's population of 300 million, would have the right to vote (although this number later increased to 5.5 million), and women were excluded from the franchise altogether. Historian Crispin Bates refers to the Montagu-Chelmsford proposals as 'a very mediocre experiment in democracy'.

Key features of the proposals were:

- elected provincial legislatures with control over education, health, agriculture and local government; however, the viceroy and provincial governors had the power to veto legislation
- an extension of the franchise, with property and income qualifications
- 'reserved' seats in the legislatures for different religious groups
- a council of six, three of whom would be Indian, to advise the viceroy
- the continuation of British control of security, foreign affairs, taxation, justice and communications.

ACTIVITY

Draw up a table to compare the main features of the Morley-Minto reforms of 1909 and the Montagu-Chelmsford proposals of 1918.

Historians Sugata Bose and Ayesha Jalal suggest that the intention behind these reforms was to 'divert Indian attention away from the centre and into provincial arenas' and the new franchise proposals were 'tilted in favour of the Raj's friends and not its critics'. Not surprisingly, the proposals were rejected by both Congress and the Muslim League as not going far enough. In London, however, critics of the proposals viewed them as dangerously liberal.

Then, in 1919, before these reform proposals could be implemented, the British government introduced a series of harsh repressive measures designed to crush opposition. These had far-reaching consequences, as you will read in the next chapter.

QUESTION

Discuss the impact of the First World War and the Home Rule movement on attitudes towards Britain in India as well as British policy towards India.

Paper 3 exam practice

Question

Discuss the **nature** of India's involvement in the **First World War** and the **extent** to which it **contributed** to the **rise of nationalism** in India. **[15 marks]**

Skill

Understanding the wording of a question

Examiner's tips

Although it seems almost too obvious to state, the first step in producing a high-scoring essay is to look **closely** at the wording of the question. Every year, students throw away marks by not paying sufficient attention to the demands of the question.

It is important to start by identifying the argument that the question requires you to address, and the **key or 'command' words** in the question. Here, you are being asked to explain how India was in involved in the war and to evaluate the impact that this had on the growth of Indian nationalism. The key focus of the argument is to explain and evaluate the link between the impact of the war on India and the growth of nationalism. The key words are as follows:

- nature
- First World War
- extent
- contributed
- rise of nationalism.

Key words are intended to give you clear instructions about what you need to cover in your essay – hence they are sometimes called 'command' words. If you ignore them you will not score high marks, no matter how precise and accurate your knowledge of the period.

For this question, you will need to take a balanced look at the following aspects of India's involvement in the war and the impact that each had:

- **India's military contribution:** How significant was it? Did wartime experiences affect attitudes?
- **The economic impact of the war:** How did it create hardships and dissatisfaction?
- **The political impact of the war:** How did it affect expectations? Did it heighten nationalist sentiments?
- **The Indian nationalist movement:** How strong was it before the war? What happened to it during the war?
- **Other factors:** What other factors may have contributed to rise of nationalism? The Home Rule movement? The Lucknow Pact?

You will need to start by explaining India's military and economic contribution to the war, and evaluating how it affected attitudes towards colonial rule as well as expectations about India's future after the war. You will also need to examine the nationalist movement itself at the start of the war, how it changed during the war, and whether it was stronger by the end of the war.

Then you need to evaluate the link between these two aspects. Was it India's involvement in the war which strengthened the nationalist movement? Or were other factors responsible? If the war was indeed a factor, how significant was it?

You need to decide which line of argument you will take (whether the war contributed to the rise of nationalism, or whether there were other factors that were equally or even more important). This will form your 'thesis', or view, which you should maintain throughout your answer. However, your essay needs to be structured to show that you understand both sides of the question, and that you can introduce relevant evidence for a variety of possible interpretations, while still showing that your view is the most convincing.

Common mistakes

Under exam pressure, a particularly common mistake would be to describe the economic and political impact of the war on India without relating it to the rise of nationalism, and explicitly addressing the issue of 'the extent to which…'.

Another common mistake is to write a one-sided essay – for example, to put forward a strong case for the war as the most significant factor, without examining other factors that may have played a role. You should also pay particular attention to the time frame of the essay. Dates are not specifically mentioned, but the question obviously refers to 1914 to 1918. Some candidates ignore these implied dates and include information on the origins and growth of the nationalist movement before the war.

Remember to refer to the simplified Paper 3 mark scheme in Chapter 10.

Activity

In this chapter, the focus is on understanding the question and producing a brief essay plan. Look again at the question, the tips and the simplified mark scheme in Chapter 10. Using the information from this chapter, and any other sources of information available to you, draw up an essay plan (perhaps in the form of a two-column chart) which has all the necessary information for a well-focused and clearly structured response to the question.

Paper 3 practice questions

1   Evaluate the significance of the Home Rule movement in India during the First World War.

2   Discuss the reasons for and consequences of the 1916 Lucknow Pact between the Indian National Congress and the All-India Muslim League.

3   To what extent is it accurate to say that the contribution of India to Britain's war effort brought about a change in British policy towards India?

4   To what extent was the Lucknow Pact a victory for the Muslim League and a surrender by Congress to Muslim communalism and separatism?

5   'British attempts to suppress the Home Rule movement served instead to strengthen its appeal'. To what extent do you agree with this statement?

Political developments between 1919 and 1935

3

3

Introduction

After the First World War, Britain introduced stricter measures of repression, resulting in the 1919 Amritsar Massacre. At the same time, Britain also introduced constitutional reforms in two Government of India Acts (in 1919 and 1935). However, neither of them satisfied the demands of Indian nationalists who saw the reforms as half-hearted and meaningless. This view was reinforced by the exclusion of Indian representation on the 1928 Simon Commission and by the inconclusive Round Table Conferences held in London between 1930 and 1932. This chapter provides the political and constitutional context in which the nationalist movement for independence operated in the period between the two world wars.

TIMELINE

1918 July: Rowlatt Commission presents its report

1919 Mar: Rowlatt Acts come into force

13 Apr: Amritsar Massacre

Nov: Appointment of two commissions to investigate Amritsar Massacre

Dec: Government of India Act passed by British parliament; Indian National Congress meeting in Amritsar

1920 Feb: Report of INC Commission

May: Hunter Report

Nov: First elections under new Government of India Act

1928 Simon Commission visits India

Aug: Nehru Report

1929 Oct: Irwin Declaration

1930 Nov: First Round Table Conference

1931 Mar: Gandhi-Irwin Pact

Sept: Second Round Table Conference

1932 Aug: Announcement of Communal Award

Nov: Third Round Table Conference

1935 Aug: Government of India Act

1937 Feb: General election in India

KEY QUESTIONS

- To what extent was the Amritsar Massacre a turning point?
- How did the Government of India Act (1919) affect India?
- What was the significance of the Simon Commission?
- How effective were the Round Table Conferences?
- What were the responses to the Government of India Act (1935)?

Overview

- At the end of the First World War, instead of anticipated reforms, Britain introduced stricter measures of repression to suppress dissent. These Rowlatt Acts resulted in widespread protests.
- In these circumstances, a meeting in Amritsar in the province of Punjab in 1919 had tragic consequences, when soldiers shot and killed nearly 400 unarmed civilians, and wounded over 1000 more. Subsequent measures of repression, as well as British reactions to the massacre, increased the tensions.
- The Amritsar Massacre and its aftermath were a turning point in Anglo-Indian relations and in the development of the Indian nationalist movement.
- The 1919 Government of India Act introduced a form of 'dyarchy' (dual government) in which a certain amount of power over local affairs was given to Indian legislatures in the provinces. However, Britain retained firm control over the central government and had the right to veto legislation.
- Opposition to British rule intensified with the exclusion of Indians from the Simon Commission, appointed by the British government in 1928 to make further constitutional recommendations. Indian political groups adopted the Nehru Report which called for dominion status for India.

- The British government held a Round Table Conference in London in 1930 which was attended by British politicians and a wide range of Indian representatives, but not the Indian National Congress, which boycotted it. In the absence of Gandhi and other Congress representatives, the conference lacked credibility.
- Further Round Table Conferences were held in 1931 and 1932, but no meaningful progress on the issue of constitutional reform was made, despite Gandhi's presence at the 1931 conference.
- In 1935, the British government went ahead and introduced further constitutional changes in another Government of India Act. It gave greater powers to elected provincial legislatures and extended the right to vote to more people, including women. However, Britain still retained ultimate control over key aspects of government.
- Indian political groups condemned the changes as inadequate but nevertheless participated in provincial elections in 1937, in which the Indian National Congress emerged as the strongest political movement.

3.1 To what extent was the Amritsar Massacre a turning point?

As you saw in Chapter 2, the contribution of India to Britain's war effort during the First World War, as well as the activities of the Home Rule Leagues, brought about a change in British policy towards India. The result was the Montagu-Chelmsford Report which proposed constitutional changes to be enacted in 1919. Although Congress and the League had rejected the proposals as inadequate, at the beginning of 1919 there was an air of expectation that change was imminent and that India was moving closer towards self-government.

However, 1919 proved to be a watershed year for India, not on account of any moderate constitutional reform, but because of Britain's introduction of the repressive Rowlatt Acts and the reaction to them. This resulted in the Amritsar Massacre, which proved to be a turning point in relations between Britain and India as well as in the nationalist struggle for independence in India.

Increased repression after the war

Before the end of the war, the British authorities were keen to introduce legislation that would give them the power to suppress any political unrest after the war, especially in Bengal, Bombay and Punjab which they believed to be centres of potential revolutionary activity. They appointed a judge, Justice Rowlatt, to chair a commission to make recommendations in this regard. The Rowlatt Commission presented its report in July 1918 and it formed the basis for the Rowlatt Acts of March 1919.

The Rowlatt Acts

The Rowlatt Acts provided for the continuation of wartime controls over political activities, including detention without trial, censorship and house arrest. They also abolished normal judicial procedures for political offences, such as trial by jury. The burden of proof in these cases would be weighted in favour of the prosecution. The measures were rushed through the Imperial Legislative Council in spite of the unanimous opposition of the Indian members of the council, some of whom, like Mohammad Ali Jinnah, resigned in protest.

Historians offer different reasons for the hasty introduction of these acts. Metcalf suggests that they were a 'panic-stricken recourse to coercion' by the British authorities who feared 'the spectre of a revival of revolutionary terrorism, together with the uncertainties of post-war economic dislocation'. Kulke and Rothermund believe that they were simply measures that would enable the authorities to 'continue the wartime suppression of sedition'. Crispin Bates suggests that they were linked to the British government's fear of revolutionary Bolshevik activity after the Russian Revolution of 1917: 'The measure was introduced by the British partly as a response to their fear of the rising tide of Bolshevism in the Soviet Union. It also reflected their desire to hold on to the grip they had established over Indian politics during the war.'

James notes that the British government was influenced by the Rowlatt Commission's findings that an 'under-manned police force which had scarcely contained terrorism was bound to be overwhelmed once wartime legislation lapsed, detainees were released and large numbers of ex-soldiers returned home'.

ACTIVITY

Do some further research on the reasons for the introduction of the Rowlatt Acts. To what extent do the views of these historians contradict each other? Which argument do you find the most convincing? In what ways were the acts contradictory to the spirit of reform implied by the Montagu-Chelmsford proposals of 1918?

Reactions to the Rowlatt Acts

There was anger and indignation about the acts and they alienated a wide range of people including politically moderate Indians. They saw them as an insult after India's contribution to Britain's war effort and a sign that their loyalty was not respected or appreciated. Bates describes the acts as 'bewildering to even the most sympathetic politicians, being introduced in peacetime, without consultation, and with no major sign of dissent on the horizon, and at the same time as the government was proposing to introduce constitutional reform'. The Rowlatt Acts became a major source of widespread opposition. Critics summed up their rejection of them with the slogan 'No trial, no lawyer, no appeal', according to Kulke and Rothermund.

There were protest marches in major cities and opponents of the new measures organised two *hartals* (work stoppages) to be held on 30 March and 6 April. The suggestion for this form of protest had been made to Congress by Mohandas Gandhi. At this stage, Congress did not have the organisational structures to organise protests of this scale or nature, so members of the Home Rule Leagues and the Muslim Khalifat movement helped to organise the protests. According to historian Mridula Mukherjee, the protests were 'accompanied by violence and disorder' especially in the province of Punjab 'which was suffering from the after-effects of severe war-time repression, forcible recruitment, and the ravages of disease'. The cities where the anger was strongest were Lahore and Amritsar.

Although the Rowlatt Acts were hurriedly enacted, they were never properly applied because of the strength of opposition to them. They were officially repealed in March 1922.

ACTIVITY

Use the internet or any other sources of information available to you to find out more about the Khalifat movement. Why was it formed? What was its ultimate goal? What part did it play in the nationalist movement in India?

The Amritsar Massacre and its aftermath

In Amritsar the situation was tense and incidents of uncontrolled unrest occurred. Banks were stormed, buildings set alight, and a number of Europeans were physically attacked. Believing that this might be the start of a general uprising, the governor of Punjab province sent troops into the city to restore order, under the command of General Reginald Dyer. Determined to stamp out any further disturbances, Dyer issued an order prohibiting all public meetings and gatherings and imposed a curfew.

However, 13 April 1919 was the day of the Baisakhi festival, an important event in the Sikh religious calendar, and a large number of people from surrounding villages gathered in the Jallianwalla Bagh, a large square in the centre of Amritsar which was enclosed on three sides. Later investigations showed that most of the people were unaware of Dyer's order prohibiting all gatherings.

In a show of strength, Dyer brought his troops into the square and ordered them to open fire on the unarmed crowd. The soldiers killed 379 people and wounded over 1200 more within ten minutes. Many of those killed were women and children who had been trapped because soldiers had blocked the exits. Dyer and his troops then departed, leaving the wounded to fend for themselves.

Figure 3.1: An illustration from a German satirical magazine, 21 January 1920, showing British general Reginald Dyer surveying the aftermath of the massacre at Amritsar.

Dyer subsequently defended his actions that day in a report written for his superiors in the army:

SOURCE 3.1

I fired and continued to fire until the crowd dispersed, and I considered this the least amount of firing which would produce the necessary moral and widespread effect it was my duty to produce if I was to justify my action. If more troops had been at hand, the casualties would have been greater in proportion. It was no longer a question of merely dispersing the crowd, but one of producing a sufficient moral effect from a military point of view, not only on those present but more specifically throughout the Punjab. There could be no question of undue severity.

Quoted in Bates, Crispin. 2007. **Subalterns and Raj: South Asia since 1600.** *London. Routledge. p. 132.*

Dyer then imposed extremely oppressive measures of martial law in Amritsar. These included public floggings and other arbitrary punishments designed to humiliate the population and demonstrate

British power. The most hated of these was the 'Crawling Order' which forced any Indian who passed down the street where a British woman missionary had been attacked, to crawl on their stomachs.

QUESTION

What message does Source 3.1 convey about Dyer's attitude towards the events at Amritsar? Consider how the publication of this report would have increased tensions in India at the time.

Theory of Knowledge

History and ethics

The actions of Dyer in Amritsar would be condemned today as totally unacceptable and would probably be considered war crimes. What is the role of historians in reporting events such as these? To what extent should they make moral judgements about the past, or should they report events in a totally neutral manner?

The commissions of inquiry

Two commissions were set up to investigate the massacre. In November 1919, the Punjab Sub-Committee of the Indian National Congress heard evidence from 700 witnesses and published its report in February 1920. It was uncompromising in its condemnation of Dyer's actions in Amritsar, calling the massacre a 'calculated piece of inhumanity towards utterly innocent and unarmed men, including children, and unparalleled for its ferocity in the history of modern British administration'.

The British government also appointed a commission of inquiry – called the Hunter Committee after its chairman. It began its meetings in Lahore in November 1919 and published its report in May 1920. It found that Dyer had 'acted beyond the necessity of the case' and that he 'did not act with as much humanity as the case permitted'. Although this was only a mild expression of censure, Dyer was forced to resign from the army. However, some British officials in India and in London expressed approval of his actions, many settlers in India regarded him as a saviour, and he was welcomed back in England as a conquering hero. The *Morning Post* called him 'the man who had saved India' and started a fund for him, which soon amassed over £26 000 in public donations – a substantial sum of money at the time. When the Hunter Report was debated in the British parliament, the House of Commons censured Dyer's actions, but the House of Lords took the opposite view and passed a motion approving of them and stating that Dyer had been treated unjustly.

DISCUSSION POINT

How do you think Dyer's supporters justified their support for him?

The significance of the Amritsar Massacre

The Amritsar Massacre caused heated debate in Britain, both in the press and in parliament, about British policy and actions in India. Although some prominent politicians expressed support for Dyer's actions, others were appalled, as this statement by Montagu, the Secretary of State for India, shows:

SOURCE 3.2

Once you are entitled to have regard neither to the intentions nor to the conduct of a particular gathering, and to shoot and to go on shooting, with all the horrors that were here involved, in order to teach somebody else a lesson, you are embarking upon terrorism, to which there is no end. I say, further, that when you pass an order that all Indians, whoever they may be, must crawl past a particular place, when you pass an order to say that all Indians, whoever they may be, must forcibly or voluntarily salaam any officer of His Majesty the King, you are enforcing racial humiliation. I say, thirdly, that when you take selected schoolboys from a school, guilty or innocent, and whip them publicly… and whip people who have not been convicted, when you flog a wedding party, you are indulging in frightfulness, and there is no other adequate word which could describe it… Are you going to keep your hold upon India by terrorism, racial humiliation and subordination, and frightfulness, or are you going to rest it upon the goodwill… of the people of your Indian Empire?

Part of a statement by Edwin Montagu, Secretary of State for India, in a House of Commons debate. 8 July 1920. HC Deb 08 July 1920 Vol. 131 cc1705–819.

Theory of Knowledge

Primary sources and bias

Records of parliamentary debates (such as Source 3.2) are important sources of information for historians. What does this suggest about the importance of keeping public records and allowing access to them? To what extent can a source like this be taken at face value? What are the values and limitations of primary sources such as these?

SOURCE 3.3

The enormity of the measures taken by the Government in the Punjab for quelling some local disturbances has, with a rude shock, revealed to our minds the helplessness of our position as British subjects in India. The disproportionate severity of the punishments inflicted upon the unfortunate people and the methods of carrying them out, we are convinced, are without parallel in the history of civilised governments… Considering that such treatment has been meted out to a population, disarmed and resourceless, by a power which has the most terribly efficient organisation for destruction of human lives, we must strongly assert that it can claim no political expediency, far less moral justification. The accounts of the insults and sufferings by our brothers in Punjab have trickled through the gagged silence, reaching every corner of India, and the universal agony of indignation roused in the hearts of our people has been ignored by our rulers… Knowing that our appeals have been in vain… the very least that I can do for my country is to take all consequences upon myself in giving voice to the protest of the millions of my countrymen, surprised into a dumb anguish of terror. The time has come when badges of honour make our shame glaring in the incongruous context of humiliation, and I for my part wish to stand, shorn of all special distinctions, by the side of those of my countrymen, who… are liable to suffer degradation not fit for human beings.

These are the reasons which have painfully compelled me to ask Your Excellency, with due reference and regret, to relieve me of my title of Knighthood…

Letter published in **Modern Review** *(Calcutta monthly), July 1919, from Rabindranath Tagore, Indian Nobel Laureate, to Chelmsford, Viceroy of India, 31 May 1919. Quoted in Krishna Dutta and Andrew Robinson, eds. 1997.* **Selected Letters of Rabindranath Tagore.** *Cambridge. Cambridge University Press.*

Nationalism and Independence in India (1919–1964)

At first, details about the massacre and subsequent developments in Amritsar were slow to circulate because martial law in Punjab prevented the distribution of news. But once details started to emerge, Indians were appalled at the news of the massacre, and more especially by British reactions to it.

QUESTIONS

- How effective do you think Tagore's action in returning his knighthood would be as a form of protest?
- Discuss the effectiveness of the language used by Tagore in his letter to the viceroy.
- Compare and contrast the views expressed in Sources 3.2 and 3.3 about the impact of the Amritsar Massacre and subsequent British actions on relations between India and Britain.
- With reference to their origin, purpose and content, assess the value and limitations of Sources 3.2 and 3.3 for historians researching the impact of the Amritsar Massacre.

After the massacre, many more people began to support Congress and its call for an end to British rule. Among the new supporters were moderate members of the Indian élite who until that point had considered themselves to be loyal British subjects. One of the Congress leaders who was outspoken in his condemnation of the Amritsar Massacre was Mohandas Gandhi. Historian Ian Copland suggests that the Amritsar Massacre was 'rendered infinitely more repugnant in Gandhi's eyes by the tacit endorsement of [Dyer's] actions by a large section of English opinion'. From this point, Gandhi emerged as the dominant figure in the nationalist movement (you will learn more about him in Chapter 4).

KEY CONCEPTS ACTIVITY

Cause and consequence: Discuss, in pairs, the main causes and consequences of the Amritsar Massacre. Then write a short newspaper article to explain which cause and which consequence was the most important.

QUESTION

Examine why the Amritsar Massacre is considered to be a turning point.

3.2 How did the Government of India Act (1919) affect India?

The Montagu-Chelmsford Report of July 1918 had committed Britain to the long-term goal of self-government for India. This was formalised in December 1919 with the passing of a Government of India Act by the British parliament which established the system of 'dyarchy' (dual government), dividing power between the central and provincial governments and between the British and the Indians. Key provisions of the act were:

* An Imperial Legislative Council to advise the viceroy (who was still appointed by the British government); most members of the council were to be elected, but with an advisory function only, giving the elected Indian representatives no real power.
* Central government control of foreign affairs, defence, communications and the collection of certain taxes (income tax, salt tax and customs duties).
* Provincial governors with appointed executive councils, with control of a 'reserved list' of certain government functions (law and justice, police, land revenue, labour and irrigation).
* Elected provincial legislatures and ministers with control of a 'transferred list' of government functions (such as agriculture, health, education, local government and local development).
* The right to vote for provincial legislatures extended to about 5.5 million men (less than 5% of the adult male population), based on property qualifications.
* Separate electorates for minorities.

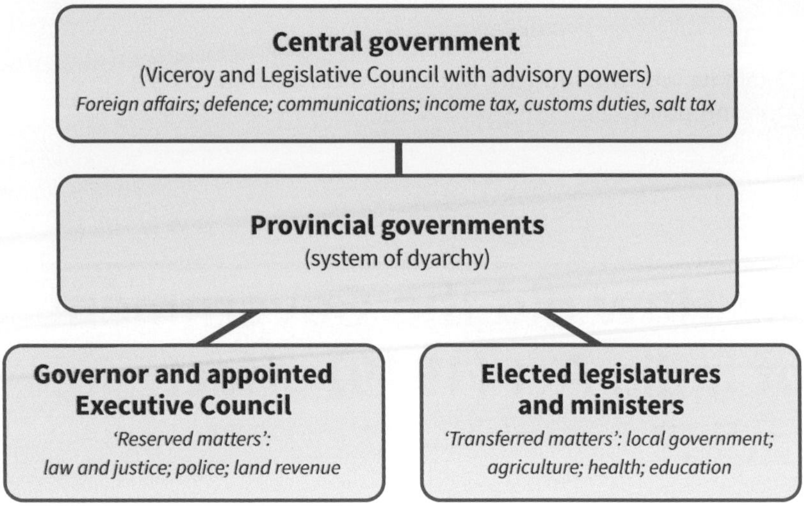

Figure 3.2: The division of powers as set out in the 1919 Government of India Act

QUESTION

Study the information in the text and the diagram. Explain which features of the Government of India Act ensured continued British control in India.

Historians analyse the implications of these constitutional changes. Bates explains that the elected provincial legislatures were given the task of collecting 'unpopular and antiquated taxes', such as the land tax, to fund any local development projects. The central government, on the other hand, got its revenues from customs duties, the salt tax and income taxes which were easier to raise.

SOURCE 3.4

The 1919 Act was thus hardly a radical step, but it was a crucial element in the British attempt to extend their control over India, and to increase its tax revenues without having to deal with the criticism that would inevitably result from this. In other words, they tried to seduce Indian collaborators, as in the past, into doing the unpopular and difficult business for them… However, from a British point of view the reforms were obviously a tremendous success because they clearly seduced a great many conservative politicians into once again co-operating with the British regime.

Bates, Crispin. 2007. **Subalterns and Raj: South Asia since 1600.** *London. Routledge. pp. 123–4.*

QUESTION

What, according to Source 3.4, were the advantages to Britain of the 1919 Government of India Act?

Another criticism of the act is that it reinforced separate identities and created divisions by recognising separate representation for different communities. Copland suggests that this encouraged 'political appeals to communal values' by politicians anxious to win support from their separate electorates. Bates asserts that the act 'encouraged communalism and perpetuated a policy of divide and rule'. He also suggests that it was 'cynical and undemocratic' because it left 'working–class, tribal and peasant groups almost wholly unrepresented'.

Referring to the fact that the Government of India Act came into force in the same year as the Rowlatt Acts and the Amritsar Massacre, historian David Ludden comments on the contradictory nature of British policies towards India in Source 3.5:

SOURCE 3.5

This two-handed imperial strategy – giving Indian politicians more power, but cracking down on dissent and agitation – launched decades of rancorous politics. For the next thirty years, British government would measure out increments of new power for elected governments in India with one half-open hand, and use the other hand as mailed fist to crush all opposition with constitutionally established emergency powers, soldiers, police, censors, and judges; all the while blaming nationalists for any disruptions of law and order.

Ludden, David. 2014. **India and South Asia: A Short History.** *London. Oneworld Publications. p. 200.*

QUESTION

Compare and contrast the perspectives of historians such as Crispin Bates, Ian Copland and David Ludden of the constitutional changes introduced in 1919.

The tentative steps towards self-government in the 1919 Government of India Act did not satisfy Indian nationalists. However, at its 1919 conference held in Amritsar a few days after the passing of the act, Congress leaders expressed formal thanks to Montagu for the constitutional reforms, a motion that was sponsored by Gandhi and Motilal Nehru, the father of independent India's first prime minister, Jawaharlal Nehru. It was only after the release of the Hunter Report into the Amritsar Massacre that attitudes hardened and Gandhi and other Congress leaders urged voters to boycott the first elections held under the new act in November 1920.

3.3 What was the significance of the Simon Commission?

One of the clauses in the 1919 Government of India Act committed Britain to reviewing the constitutional changes within ten years. In 1927, the Conservative government in power in Britain, concerned that Labour might win the next general election, decided to move this date forward while it was still in power. The Conservatives were afraid that a future Labour government would make too many concessions to Indian nationalists.

As a result, in 1927, the British government appointed a commission led by Sir John Simon to investigate how the current system was working and to make recommendations for further constitutional reform in India. However, no Indians were included in the commission which was composed entirely of British parliamentarians.

According to historian Crispin Bates, Birkenhead, the Secretary of State, had deliberately excluded Indians because he believed that they were 'quite incapable of agreeing on a workable political framework'. Other historians refer to this exclusion as a major blunder on the part of the British government. Metcalf suggests that the implications were that the Indians 'were still children who needed all-knowing parents to legislate for them'. When the members of the Simon Commission arrived in Bombay in 1928 they were met by protesting crowds. Everywhere they went in their travels around the country there were angry public demonstrations.

Congress and a large section of the Muslim League, as well as other political organisations, decided to boycott the commission and refused to give evidence before it. Even moderate politicians, who favoured dialogue with Britain, spoke out about the offensive implications of the exclusion of Indian representation on the commission.

Figure 3.3: Protesters march to express their opposition to the arrival of the Simon Commission, 1928.

Nevertheless, the commission later produced a two-volume draft report which recommended representative government at a provincial, but not national level. However, the report was overshadowed by two more significant developments – the Nehru Report of 1928 and the Irwin Declaration of 1929 – and so it was abandoned before it was even published.

The Nehru Report and the Congress resolutions

A range of Indian political groups organised a series of All-Parties Conferences in 1928 which were chaired by **Motilal Nehru**, the Congress president. The purpose of the meetings was to discuss the formation of a united front to oppose the Simon Commission. The meeting also discussed constitutional proposals drawn up by Nehru and representatives of other parties.

This 'Nehru Report' called for dominion status for India, along the same lines as that already granted to Canada, Australia, New Zealand

and South Africa. This gave these dominions full self-government although they remained linked to Britain as members of the British Empire. The report also called for a federal constitution for India, with a strong central government.

The Muslim League was concerned because, in terms of the constitutional proposals in the Nehru Report, Muslims would lose the separate electoral status which they had enjoyed since the Morley-Minto reforms of 1909. The Muslim League leader, Jinnah, tried unsuccessfully to negotiate a compromise with Hindu nationalists, and in December 1928 the Muslim League withdrew from the All Party Conferences. Many other parties adopted the Nehru Report, although the British government ignored it.

Motilal Nehru (1861–1931):

Nehru was an early leader of the Indian nationalist movement, a leader of the Indian National Congress, and founder of the influential Nehru-Gandhi family. His son, Jawaharlal Nehru, was independent India's first prime minister (1947–64); his granddaughter, Indira Gandhi, was prime minister from 1966 to 1977 and from 1980 to 1984; and his great grandson, Rajiv Gandhi, was prime minister from 1984 to 1989.

Not all members of Congress were satisfied with the call for dominion status within the British Empire. Younger members, notably Jawaharlal Nehru and Subhas Chandra Bose, wanted India to break all links with Britain. At the meeting of Congress held in December 1928 two motions were adopted:

- One proposed by Gandhi called for dominion status.
- The second, proposed by Jawaharlal Nehru and Bose, called on the British to leave India and set the end of 1929 as the deadline; failing which, Congress threatened mass civil disobedience.

When the British ignored the calls and instead made vague statements about future constitutional developments, impatience at the slow pace of reform increased.

The Irwin Declaration, 1929

To avoid an imminent showdown between the nationalists and the British authorities, the viceroy, Lord Irwin, proposed to the British government that an official statement should be made clarifying British support for dominion status for India. This suggestion was welcomed by the new Labour government and, in October 1929, the 'Irwin Declaration' (sometimes referred to as the 'Dominion Declaration') was published. As well as confirming British support for dominion status, it also proposed a Round Table conference in London to draw up a constitutional framework for a future Indian dominion.

Indian representatives would be invited to this conference which would be held independently of the Simon Commission, which at this stage had not yet produced its report. This meant that any recommendations that the commission made would be largely irrelevant. Metcalf suggests that the setting up of the Round Table Conference left 'the forlorn Simon to twist in the wind'.

3.4 How effective were the Round Table Conferences?

As a result of the lack of response to the demands by Congress that Britain should leave India by the end of 1929, Congress embarked on a mass civil disobedience campaign in 1930 (you will read more about this in Chapter 5). Thousands of Congress leaders, including Gandhi, as well as participants in the campaign were sent to prison. Congress rejected participation in the Round Table Conference, the first stage of which was planned for 1930.

The first Round Table Conference, 1930–31

The first Round Table Conference met in London between November 1930 and February 1931. It was attended by representatives from the three main political parties in Britain, leaders of some of the princely states, and 57 representatives chosen by the viceroy to represent Indian opinion. Congress was not represented because of its decision to boycott the conference. Nevertheless, the conference made some progress in reaching agreement on the form and powers of a new constitution. Copland comments that this agreement was 'despite, or perhaps because of, the absence of Congress'.

The broad agreements reached at the Round Table Conference were:

- A federal state which would include the provinces of British India as well as the princely states.
- Provincial autonomy instead of 'dyarchy' in the provinces.
- The franchise to be extended to about 10% of the population.
- This franchise to be based on property or education qualifications.
- Separate electorates to ensure due representation for workers and untouchables.

However, in the absence of Gandhi, and without the participation of Congress, many felt that the deliberations of the conference did not carry much weight. In January 1931, Irwin decided to release Gandhi from prison and to negotiate with him personally. The result was the Gandhi-Irwin Pact of March 1931:

- Gandhi agreed to end the civil disobedience campaign and to participate in the next Round Table Conference.

- In return, Irwin agreed to the release of the majority of political prisoners, the cancellation of fines, the unbanning of organisations and the relaxation of certain other emergency powers.

Although some people welcomed the pact, there was anger and criticism of it too. In Britain, Winston Churchill emerged as its most outspoken critic and he strongly condemned Irwin's action. He thought it was utterly wrong, and bad for British prestige, for the viceroy to negotiate on equal terms with someone whom Churchill regarded as a dangerous troublemaker. He formed the India Defence League which was supported by right-wing Conservative politicians and Lancashire cotton industrialists who feared the loss of markets in an independent India. The writer, Rudyard Kipling, was a vice-president of the league.

ACTIVITY

Use the internet and any other sources available to you to find out more about Churchill's attitude towards self-government for India. Explain the significance of it.

In India, many members of Congress were outraged at Gandhi's decisions and his lack of consultation with the organisation. According to historians Bose and Jalal, many ordinary Indians who had willingly joined in the civil disobedience campaign were 'dismayed that Gandhi was once again abandoning their struggle at the wrong moment and giving away too much for too little'. Kulke and Rothermund also note that 'Irwin gained much and Gandhi very little' from the pact, but suggest that Gandhi appreciated the pact for its 'symbolic significance rather than for its specific concessions'.

Historian Mridula Mukherjee sums up some of the criticisms of the Pact in Source 3.6. (Gandhiji is a term of respect sometimes used when referring to Gandhi.)

SOURCE 3.6

The terms on which the Pact was signed, its timing, the motives of Gandhiji in signing the Pact… have generated considerable controversy and debate among contemporaries and historians alike. The Pact has been variously seen as a betrayal, as proof of the vacillating nature of the Indian bourgeoisie and of Gandhiji succumbing to bourgeois pressure. It has been cited as evidence of Gandhiji's and the Indian bourgeoisie's fear of the mass movement taking a radical turn; a betrayal of peasants' interests because it did not immediately restore confiscated land, already sold to a third party, and so on.

Chandra, B., Mukherjee, M., Mukherjee, A., Mahajan, S. and Pannikar, K.N. 2012. India's Struggle for Independence 1857–1947. *London. Penguin. Digital edition: Chapter 22 'Civil Disobedience 1930–1'. Location 4913.*

QUESTION

Why, according to Source 3.6, did the Gandhi-Irwin Pact generate so much controversy and debate?

The second Round Table Conference, 1931

A direct outcome of the pact was Gandhi's attendance at the second Round Table Conference which met in London from September to December 1931. According to historian Bipan Chandra, the majority of delegates were 'loyalists, communalists, careerists and place-hunters, big landlords and representatives of the princes' who had been hand-picked by the government to justify the claim that Congress did not represent the interests of all Indians and to neutralise Gandhi and his efforts 'to confront the imperialist rulers with the basic question of freedom'. Gandhi attended the second conference as the sole representative of Congress. Kulke and Rothermund suggest that this was a mistake and point out some of the implications of this decision:

SOURCE 3.7

Gandhi insisted on being sent there as the sole representative of the Congress because he did not want to initiate discussions so much as simply to present the national demand. Once in London, however, he got involved in dealing with complicated issues like federal structure and the representation of minorities. He had never wanted to talk about all of this and was out of his depth. A couple of constitutional advisors should have accompanied him, given this agenda.

Gandhi was completely frustrated, but Irwin – who had got him into this fix and who had returned home by that time after finishing his term as viceroy – remained completely aloof from the conference… Had he also masterminded Gandhi's discomfiture at the conference? He could not, of course be blamed for the Congress decision to send Gandhi as its sole representative to the conference; but from a long-term perspective Irwin's success at getting Gandhi involved in the process of British-Indian constitutional reforms was of great importance.

Gandhi's participation in this conference tied the Congress down to British-Indian constitution-making in a way that was not yet obvious to the contemporary observers.

Kulke, Hermann and Rothermund, Dietmar. 1986. **A History of India.** **London.** *Routledge. pp. 292–3.*

QUESTION

What message is conveyed by Source 3.7 about the significance of Gandhi's involvement in the second Round Table Conference?

The conference did not succeed in making any real progress on constitutional reform. In Source 3.8, historian Lawrence James implies that the Indian delegates were to blame for this; while Crispin Bates suggests other reasons for the failure of the talks in Source 3.9.

SOURCE 3.8

It was derailed by bickering over the balance of electoral power, involving the reservation of seats for racial and religious minorities which was considered essential for stability.

This was already a well-chewed bone of contention which again led to divisions. Hindus and Muslims could not agree terms and Congress was apprehensive about the possible emergence of an axis between the Muslims and the princes.

James, Lawrence. 1997. **Raj: The Making and Unmaking of British India.** *London. Little, Brown and Company. p. 532.*

SOURCE 3.9

As Gandhi made his way to London in August, there was a change of government [in Britain] owing to the gathering financial crisis, and the Tory-dominated national government which took over from the Labour Party, had no interest in making concessions.

The talks therefore made little progress (from a nationalist point of view). Gandhi himself was the only INC representative, and Sarojini Naidu the only delegate sent by the Indian women's groups.

The other delegates, Indian princes (carefully nurtured by the British as an alternative political voice since the 1920s), representatives of the Indian Liberal Party, and members and representatives of 'minority groups', including women, were all chosen by the British.

Realising the inevitability of disaster, Gandhi sensibly distanced himself from the talks…

Bates, Crispin. 2007. **Subalterns and Raj: South Asia since 1600.** *London. Routledge. p. 148.*

QUESTION

Compare and contrast the reasons given in Sources 3.8 and 3.9 for the failure of the second Round Table Conference.

While he was in Britain, in many places Gandhi was met by cheering crowds who saw him as a champion of the underdog. Even unemployed workers in the textile towns in Lancashire turned out to cheer him, and his reception was especially warm in the working-class districts of east London.

Figure 3.4: Gandhi with cheering mill workers in Lancashire in 1931.

ACTIVITY

Use the internet and any other sources available to you to research information about Gandhi's visit to London in 1931. Then write a short report to explain:

- why he went to London
- how he was received – by official figures and by the general public
- what he achieved while he was there
- how successful the visit was.

No agreements were reached at this meeting and so Gandhi returned home politically empty-handed. In January 1932, he called for a resumption of civil disobedience, and soon he and thousands of other participants were imprisoned once again. In August 1932 the British government unilaterally announced the 'Communal Award' which was to be incorporated into any future Indian constitution. The award gave separate electorates to the 'depressed classes' as the British referred to 'untouchables', or lower-caste Hindus. According to Bose and Jalal, Britain was resorting to 'a new round of political engineering to divide and deflect the nationalist challenge'. Gandhi saw this as yet another attempt to create divisions in Indian society and he threatened to fast to death in his prison cell unless the decision was reversed. According to Kulke and Rothermund the fast had a great impact on public opinion: 'Temples were thrown open to the untouchables, [and] they were given access to wells which had been denied them before.' Gandhi called off the fast after an agreement with the leader of the 'depressed classes', **Dr B.R. Ambedkar**, in which it was agreed that there would be a larger number of reserved seats for the depressed classes rather than separate electorates. This agreement between them was referred to as the Poona Pact.

B.R. Ambedkar (1891–1956):

Ambedkar was a leading jurist, economist and scholar who had suffered from caste discrimination, inequality and prejudice as a child but went on to excel academically and gain doctorates from Columbia University in the US and the London School of Economics. He became a leading activist and social reformer who campaigned for the rights of Dalits (untouchables) and supported the principle of reserved seats in parliament for them. He later served as law minister in the first government of independent India and played a major role in drawing up India's constitution.

The third Round Table Conference, 1932

From November to December 1932, the third and last Round Table Conference was held. The Labour Party which had initiated the Round Table Conferences did not attend and neither did Congress. Although various constitutional issues were discussed, such as the franchise and the role of the princely states, the meeting did not make any significant progress. After this, constitutional changes were initiated by the British government in another Government of India Act. Many of the provisions of this act were issues which had been discussed at the three Round Table Conferences.

Examine what the Round Table Conferences were intended to achieve and evaluate whether they achieved their goals.

3.5 What were the responses to the Government of India Act (1935)?

As support for the nationalist movement grew, the British government was forced to accept that more meaningful constitutional change was necessary. These changes were enacted in the 1935 Government of India Act. It was the last constitution imposed on India by Britain, but some of the features in it formed the basis of independent India's first constitution adopted in 1950.

The Government of India Act (1935)

The main provisions included in the Act were the following:

- India was divided into 11 provinces, and voters in each province could elect the provincial government.
- The system of 'dyarchy' was abolished and the provincial governments controlled everything except defence and foreign affairs.
- Voting rights were extended to about 35 million people (which represented about one sixth of the adult population) and included women.
- The electorate was separated into religious, racial and 'special interest' constituencies: Muslims, Sikhs, Indian Christians, Eurasians and Europeans all had their own separate constituencies. The 'special

interest' constituencies were for universities, commerce and industry, landlords and organised labour.

- The act ensured that Britain retained control of the provinces through emergency powers, which could be imposed whenever it was deemed necessary.
- The British viceroy had ultimate power and was in charge of defence and foreign affairs. He was advised by an executive council which had separate representatives for Hindus, Muslims, Sikhs, Christians, Europeans and other minority groups.
- In the central legislature about 30–40% of the seats were taken by members nominated by the princely states. The act made provision for the formation of a future All-India Federation once more than half of the princes backed the idea, but this never happened as most of them were reluctant to lose any aspects of their independence and sovereignty in a federation.
- Burma, which until then had been ruled as part of British India, was given its own separate government.
- The act set no definite date for dominion status but made provision for further constitutional reforms in the future.

ACTIVITY

Design a diagram to illustrate the system of government introduced in the 1935 Government of India Act. (You can use Figure 3.2 as an example to base your one on.)

KEY CONCEPTS QUESTION

Change and continuity: Compare the 1935 Government of India Act with the 1919 Act. To what extent did the reforms represent change or continuity in British policies towards India?

According to historian Bipan Chandra, in introducing these reforms, the British hoped to win people over to constitutional struggle rather than mass civil disobedience. They also hoped to cause dissension and a split within Congress between the right- and left-wings, between those who were prepared to work within the new reform measures and those who rejected them outright.

Historians suggest that even though the act gave more power to Indians themselves, Britain was still reluctant to give up control. Copland comments, 'The British liberalised their governance of India grudgingly and with grave reservations.' Chandra quotes a statement from Linlithgow, Chairman of the Joint Parliamentary Committee on the Act of 1935, and viceroy of India from 1936, in which he stated that the act had been framed 'because we thought that was the best way… of maintaining British influence in India. It is no part of our policy… to expedite in India constitutional changes for their own sake, or gratuitously to hurry the handing over of the controls to Indian hands at any price faster than that which we regard as best calculated, on a long view, to hold India to the Empire.'

Bose and Jalal suggest that by 'bringing autocratic and subservient princes to redress the balance against the democratic and nationalist challenge in British India, the 1935 Act sought to safeguard British rule in India, not weaken it'. Commenting on all the constitutional reforms that had taken place since 1917, Robert Stern contends that throughout this period there was a 'persistent British unwillingness to part with the substance of power' and that the British government periodically 'delivered packages of constitutional reforms in which ostensible concessions to nationalist aspirations were wrapped together with insidious schemes to protect British power from what it conceded.'

ACTIVITY

Chandra, Copland, Bose and Jalal, and Stern are all sceptical about the constitutional reforms introduced by Britain in this period. Use the internet to do some research to find more positive views of historians about British policies towards India. Which viewpoint do you find the most convincing?

Responses to the act

Indian leaders condemned the proposals as too little too late. According to historians Sugata Bose and Ayesha Jalal, Jawaharlal Nehru called the act a 'new charter of slavery'; Bose dismissed it as a scheme 'not for self-government, but for maintaining British rule'; and Jinnah described it as 'most reactionary, retrograde, injurious and fatal to the interest of British India vis-a-vis the Indian states'.

Congress unanimously rejected the 1935 Act and called instead for the election of a Constituent Assembly to frame a constitution for an independent India. Congress was especially critical of the perpetuation of the concept of separate electorates.

SOURCE 3.10

Congressmen believed that the British were playing the 'communal card' to divide and rule: readily acceding to minority demands because it suited British interests to do so, trying to reduce the Congress to an organization of [high caste] Hindus, discrediting Indian nationalism, proliferating and politicizing communal divisions within the Indian middle classes in order to oppose them one to another and fragment their opposition to British rule. In a subcontinent of myriad ethnic diversities, it was a card that could be played again and again.

Stern, Robert. 1993. **Changing India: Bourgeois Revolution on the Subcontinent.** *Cambridge, Cambridge University Press. p. 145.*

QUESTION

What message does Source 3.10 convey about Congress perceptions of British rule in India?

However, although some members of Congress supported the concept of boycotting the forthcoming elections as an indication of their rejection of the act, others took a more pragmatic view. They thought that it would be better to participate and then work to change the system from within.

The 1937 elections

So, although both Congress and the League had condemned the 1935 reforms as inadequate, they decided to participate in the provincial elections held in 1937. The right to vote was based on a property qualification, and so was limited to 35 million of the wealthier part of the Indian population, including women. For the first time, wealthier peasants had the right to vote as well.

In the elections, Congress emerged as the strongest political force, with 70% of the popular vote. After some deliberation as to whether to accept office, they formed the provincial governments in seven (later eight) of the 11 provinces in India.

In stark contrast, the Muslim League did not do well in the elections, winning barely 5% of the total Muslim vote. Nevertheless, Jinnah hoped that the League could form part of coalition governments in the provinces with large Muslim minorities. However, having won the elections so convincingly, Congress was not prepared to compromise with the League in this way: it turned down Jinnah's offer of cooperation, although it did appoint some of its own Muslim members to the provincial governments. Historians such as Metcalf refer to the attitude and actions of Congress towards the League at this time as arrogant and 'high-handed', and say that they caused the League to strengthen its efforts to gain a mass following. In some provinces, Muslim leaders complained of favouritism towards Hindus, and the promotion of Hindu symbols and the Hindi language, although this was never Congress policy.

Between 1937 and 1939, elected provincial legislatures effectively governed India. But the outbreak of war in 1939 meant a postponement of further constitutional reforms laid out in the 1935 Government of India Act.

KEY CONCEPTS QUESTION

Significance: What was the significance of the 1937 election results?

Paper 3 exam practice

Question

To what extent was the nationalist movement in India strengthened between 1919 and 1935 by what it perceived as half-hearted attempts at constitutional reform by the British government? **[15 marks]**

Skill

Planning an essay

Examiner's tips

As discussed in Chapter 2, the first stage of planning an answer to a question is to think carefully about the wording of the question, so that you know what is required and what you need to focus on. Once you have done this, you can move on to the other important considerations:

- Decide your **main argument, theme or approach** *before* you start to write. This will help you identify the key points you want to make. For example, this question clearly invites you to make a judgement about whether Britain's attempts at constitutional reform were 'half-hearted', and whether these attempts had a direct impact on the growth of support for the nationalist movement. You will need to decide on an approach that helps you produce an argument that is clear, coherent and logical, by examining and evaluating each stage of constitutional change between 1919 and 1935.
- Plan the **structure of your argument:** the introduction, the main body of the essay (in which you present precise evidence to support your arguments) and your concluding paragraph.

For this question, whatever overall view you have about the nature and impact of the constitutional changes, you should try to present a **balanced** argument. You will need to critically examine each stage, explaining what changes it introduced and also what the British intended to achieve. Were the British committed to introducing gradual changes as a process towards self-government in India? Or were they designing the changes in such a way that they retained control? You will also need to examine the reaction and subsequent responses of the nationalist movement to each stage of constitutional reform.

3 Nationalism and Independence in India (1919–1964)

In any question, you should try to **link** the points you make in your paragraphs, both to the question and to the preceding paragraph, so that there is a clear thread that develops naturally, leading to your conclusion. Linking words and ideas help to ensure that your essay is not just a series of unconnected paragraphs.

You may well find that drawing up a spider diagram or mind map helps you with your essay planning. For this question, your spider diagram might look like this:

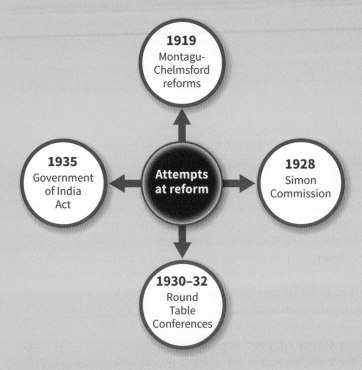

When writing your essay, include **linking phrases** to ensure that each smaller 'bubble' paragraph is linked to the 'main bubble' (the question). For example:

The Montagu-Chelmsford reforms gave limited powers to elected provincial legislatures in the first round of constitutional reform after the First World War. However, Britain retained control through…

In addition, Britain had committed itself to reviewing the constitutional changes within ten years, so in 1928 appointed the Simon Commission to propose the next stage of constitutional reform. However, …

Furthermore, after the angry reaction to the exclusion of Indian representation on the Simon Commission, Britain next proposed a series of Round Table Conferences to discuss constitutional reform…

After the failure of the Round Table Conferences to achieve agreement on constitutional reform, Britain went ahead and passed the Government of India Act in 1935…

There are clearly many factors to consider, which will be difficult under the time constraints of the exam. Producing a plan with brief details (such as dates, views and main supporting evidence) under each heading will help you cover the main issues in the time available. Your plan should enable you to keep your essay balanced, so that you do not spend too long on any one aspect. It should also ensure that you remain focused on the question and do not wander off into narrative description.

Common mistakes

It is very easy to look at questions and adopt a one-sided view in response to them. In this essay you need to analyse critically the British reform initiatives (and their motives) and the nationalist responses (and whether they were strengthened – or weakened – by each stage of reform). Linking different arguments can be difficult, but it is a good way of achieving the highest marks. Always consider the **full demands** of a question before you begin, and remember – your plan will help you to develop a convincing answer.

Activity

In this chapter, the focus is on planning answers. Using the information from this chapter and any other sources of information available to you, produce essay plans – using spider diagrams or mind maps – with all the necessary headings (and brief details) for well-focused and clearly structured responses to **at least two** of the following Paper 3 practice questions.

Remember to refer to the simplified Paper 3 mark scheme in Chapter 10.

3

Nationalism and Independence in India (1919–1964)

1 Examine the causes and consequences of the introduction of the Rowlatt Acts in 1919.

2 To what extent was the Amritsar Massacre a turning point in Anglo-Indian relations and in the development of the Indian nationalist movement?

3 'The exclusion of Indian representation on the Simon Commission was a political blunder which had far-reaching consequences.' How far do you agree with this statement?

4 Evaluate the reasons for the failure of the Round Table Conferences to produce any meaningful progress on negotiated constitutional reform.

5 Compare and contrast the constitutional reforms instituted in the 1919 and 1935 Government of India Acts and evaluate the reasons why Indian nationalist leaders rejected both of them.

The role and importance of key groups and individuals

4

Introduction

Accounts of this period of Indian history usually highlight the actions of key organisations and individuals. The Indian National Congress undoubtedly played a dominant role by organising mass non-violent protests, while the Muslim League played a smaller, yet critical, role in negotiations leading to partition and independence. There were many able leaders within the Congress movement, but Gandhi and Nehru are usually singled out: Gandhi as the inspiration behind the mass campaigns, and Nehru as the first leader of independent India. The emergence of the Muslim League as a crucial role-player was due to the efforts of Jinnah. This chapter will examine the role and significance of each of these groups and individuals in the nationalist struggle for independence.

TIMELINE

1869–1948	Life of Mohandas Gandhi
1876–1948	Life of Mohammad Ali Jinnah
1885	Formation of the Indian National Congress
1888–1964	Life of Jawaharlal Nehru
1906	Formation of the All-India Muslim League
1915	Return of Gandhi from South Africa
1920–22	Non-Cooperation movement
1930–34	Civil Disobedience campaign
1937	Provincial elections won by Congress
1942	'Quit India' campaign

KEY QUESTIONS

- What role did the Indian National Congress play in the nationalist movement?
- How important was the All-India Muslim League in the nationalist movement?
- Why was Gandhi so important to the nationalist movement?
- What was Nehru's contribution to the nationalist movement?
- How significant was Jinnah's role in the nationalist movement?

Overview

- The nationalist struggle for independence in India was dominated by the Indian National Congress. From a small élitist group, it developed into a powerful political force which organised mass non-violent non-cooperation and civil disobedience campaigns to force the British to leave India.
- It also used constitutional avenues to try to bring about change, and participated in provincial governments after winning the 1937 elections. However, it resumed civil disobedience protests during the Second World War.
- Muslims formed a separate organisation, the All-India Muslim League, to represent and safeguard their interests. There was early cooperation between the League and Congress in the Lucknow Pact of 1916 and many Muslims participated in the 1920–22 Non-Cooperation campaign organised by Congress. However, relations between the two organisations later deteriorated.
- The poor showing of the Muslim League in the 1937 elections provided a wake-up call to the movement and after that it worked hard to unite Muslims in India and promote recognition of Muslim rights. The League's support for Britain during the Second World War strengthened its position in postwar negotiations about independence.
- Mohandas Gandhi played a dominant role in the Indian National Congress. His tactic of non-violent civil disobedience mobilised millions of people throughout India and transformed the nationalist struggle into a mass movement with wide appeal.
- As the political and spiritual leader of a movement that successfully challenged a powerful colonial ruler, Gandhi became an inspiration to other nationalist and civil rights leaders and an icon of 20th century history. Nevertheless, there are many differing historical interpretations of Gandhi's role, some of them critical.
- Jawaharlal Nehru was Gandhi's close associate, confidante and successor and together they formed a powerful partnership. Nehru attracted the support of the educated middle classes, intellectuals and young people, and was a leader of the left-wing in Congress.
- Nehru's vision for India was of a tolerant, secular democracy. As India's first prime minister after independence, he played a dominant role in shaping the nature and structure of democracy in India.

- Mohammad Ali Jinnah was the most prominent leader of the All-India Muslim League. During the 1920s he tried unsuccessfully to promote a compromise solution between the viewpoints of the League and Congress on the issue of separate representation for Muslims in a future Indian constitution.
- After 1937, Jinnah built up support for the League as the sole representative of Indian Muslims, and tirelessly presented the League's demand for a separate Muslim state after independence. This resulted ultimately in the partition of India.

4.1 What role did the Indian National Congress play in the nationalist movement?

The nationalist struggle for independence in India was dominated by the Indian National Congress. The early Congress was not at all radical in its goals or assertive in its actions, but it laid the foundations of an organisation that later developed into a powerful political force.

The early years

As you read in Chapter 2, the Indian National Congress was formed in 1885 by a group of liberal nationalists. They met annually but initially had no permanent office and hardly any contact between their annual meetings. However, in the early decades they set up a network of branches throughout India. The early Congress leaders supported constitutional reform within the framework of British rule and called for greater Indian representation in government. In its early stages, the Congress represented the interests of the wealthy middle class and it did not have mass support. Most of the founding members were graduates and all spoke English.

They believed that the interests of region, caste or religious affiliation should be secondary to the needs of the Indian nation as a whole.

The early leaders saw themselves as a bridge between the Indian masses and the colonial power, and they supported gradual constitutional change. However, by the beginning of the 20th century some younger members of Congress were becoming critical of the ideas and methods of the older conservative leaders. They advocated instead the adoption of more assertive methods of promoting Indian identity and nationalism.

Figure 4.1: The first meeting of the Indian National Congress, 1885.

The partition of Bengal in 1905 and the *Swadeshi* movement that developed in reaction to it made Congress aware for the first time of the political power of an economic boycott. The confrontation over Bengal also aggravated tensions in Congress between the 'Extremists', led by Bal Gangadhar Tilak, who supported more active opposition to British rule, and the 'Moderates', led by Gopal Krishna Gokhale, who did not. The tensions came to a head at the annual Congress meeting held in Surat in December 1907, when many Extremists left the party, leaving the Moderates in control. The split in Congress seriously weakened the nationalist movement in the years preceding the outbreak of the First World War.

During the First World War the activities of Congress were eclipsed by the Home Rule Leagues which gained popular support. Although many Congress members were attracted to the concept of Home Rule, Congress did not initially adopt it as official policy. The split in Congress was mended when Tilak was readmitted in 1916 and the two factions signed the Lucknow Pact. After this the reunited Congress had the confidence to make more assertive statements concerning self-rule for India.

By the end of the war, Congress was developing into a truly national organisation. However, according to Guha it had two serious weaknesses: it was active only in the major cities, and its proceedings were conducted exclusively in English. As a result, the British were able to dismiss it as an organisation representing only middle-class professionals who did not speak for the people of India as a whole.

India's substantial contribution to Britain's war effort led many moderate Congress leaders to expect that Indians would be rewarded with Home Rule after the war. As a result, they were disappointed when the Montagu-Chelmsford reforms of 1918, and the subsequent Government of India Act, did not meet these expectations. Wartime hopes were shattered even more in March 1919 with the introduction of the repressive Rowlatt Acts, the massacre at Amritsar and British reactions to it. But in the protests in the immediate aftermath of the Amritsar Massacre, Congress was 'conspicuously absent', according to historians Bose and Jalal, because it 'had no organizational machinery for agitational politics' at that stage.

DISCUSSION POINT

Discuss the effects of the Montagu-Chelmsford reforms, the 1919 Government of India Act and the Rowlatt Acts on India.

The Indian National Congress in the 1920s

During the early 1920s the Indian National Congress expanded into a mass movement. It was Mohandas Gandhi who transformed it from an élitist moderate organisation representing the English-educated middle class into a mass-based nationalist movement. (You will read about the role and importance of Gandhi later in this chapter, and more about the nationalist struggle in Chapter 5.) Also under Gandhi's influence, Congress in the 1920s expanded its appeal to a wider section of Indian society by forming provincial committees that operated in local Indian languages instead of English. This measure helped forge links between the cities and the countryside. Bose and Jalal suggest that the reorganisation of provincial congresses along linguistic lines was done because 'Gandhi knew well that the emotive power of anti-colonial sentiment often sprang from linguistic nationalisms'.

At its annual meeting in Nagpur in December 1920, Congress adopted Gandhi's proposal of a campaign of non-violent non-cooperation as its main strategy against British rule. In this it was supported by the Khalifat movement which was outraged by Britain's treatment of the Ottoman Empire at the end of the war. This cooperation between Congress and the Khalifat movement in the campaign created a degree of Hindu-Muslim unity at the time. But this unity was threatened by communal tensions and even violence, such as the Moplah rebellion in 1921, in which several hundred people died in communal attacks.

ACTIVITY

Use the internet and any other sources that are available to you to find out what happened to the Ottoman Empire after the First World War. Examine how these developments affected the Khalifat movement.

The Non-Cooperation campaign lasted from 1920 to 1922, when Gandhi called it off because of incidents of violence. But during this time the membership of Congress grew substantially from about 100 000 to 2 million members. Many of the new supporters were businessmen and richer peasant farmers, but it also attracted poorer peasants and railway workers. However, not all members of Congress supported the campaign of defiance, and some conservatives left to join other political groups, such as the Liberal Party. After 1922, the leadership of Congress passed to moderates, such as C.R. Das and Motilal Nehru. They supported working within the parameters set out in the 1919 Government of India Act and formed the *Swaraj* (Home Rule) Party to contest local elections. The new party remained part of the Congress movement. However, younger, more radical members of Congress, such as Jawaharlal Nehru and Subhas Chandra Bose, grew increasingly impatient with this strategy and pushed for renewed action.

The exclusion of Indian representation on the Simon Commission galvanised moderates and radicals in Congress to work together once again. Congress paid a key role in organising the 1928 All-Parties Conference and a dominant role in formulating the Nehru Report which called for dominion status – a call which did not satisfy the more radical members of Congress. At its annual meeting held in Calcutta in December 1928 they proposed a motion, which was adopted by Congress, calling on Britain to leave India by the end of 1929, failing which Congress threatened mass civil disobedience. Historians suggest that the decision by Congress to adopt this more radical proposal was influenced by a wave of labour strikes and student protests at the time which made Congress moderates realise that they risked losing control of the nationalist movement.

A significant feature of the Nehru Report was its rejection of separate electorates for Muslim voters (which Congress had agreed to in the 1916 Lucknow Pact with the Muslim League). Some historians are critical of the refusal of Congress to compromise on this issue with Jinnah. Bose and Jalal suggest that 'The absence of generosity in the part of Congress augured poorly for the future of Hindu–Muslim compromise and, by extension, for the anti-colonial struggle.'

The election of Jawaharlal Nehru as Congress president in 1929 and 1930 preserved the unity of the movement. Under Nehru's leadership, Congress adopted *Purna Swaraj* (complete independence) as its goal at its 1929 Congress session in Lahore, and formed an All-India Congress Committee to coordinate protests in order to achieve it.

ACTIVITY

Compare the differences between dominion status and complete independence.

The Indian National Congress in the 1930s

In 1930 Congress launched a mass Civil Disobedience campaign, during which thousands of Congress leaders, as well as participants in the campaign, were sent to prison. Congress also boycotted the Round Table Conference held in London that year. Many members of Congress were later angered by Gandhi's decision to call off the Civil Disobedience campaign after the Gandhi-Irvin Pact of March 1932. When – despite Congress participation – the second Round Table Conference made no significant progress, Congress resumed the Civil Disobedience campaign, and as a result, thousands more participants and Congress leaders were jailed once again. However, the sustained protests forced the British government to accept that more meaningful constitutional change was necessary.

Figure 4.2: This Indian National Congress poster called 'The Right Path to Liberty' shows Indians from all communities climbing the road towards freedom. But the bridge is broken and Gandhi, Nehru and other Congress leaders are in prison. The Hindu god, Krishna, tells Mother India that with a little more sacrifice the bridge will be mended and freedom gained.

The result was the 1935 Government of India Act. Historian Bipan Chandra suggests that the British government was hoping to cause a split within Congress between the right and left wings, between those who were prepared to work within the new reform measures and those who rejected them outright. Congress unanimously rejected the act and called instead for the election of a Constituent Assembly to frame a constitution for an independent India. However, while the radicals wanted Congress to boycott the forthcoming elections as an indication of their rejection of the act, the moderates took a more pragmatic view. They thought that it would be better to participate and then work to change the system from within. The moderate viewpoint prevailed, and Congress participated in the 1937 provincial elections. Its success in them demonstrated that it was by far the strongest political force, with 70% of the popular vote. After some deliberation as to whether to accept office, it formed the provincial governments in seven (later eight) of the 11 provinces. Historians such as Metcalf are critical of the subsequent refusal by Congress to reach a compromise agreement with the Muslim League by including some of its members in coalition governments in the provinces with large Muslim minorities.

Between 1937 and the outbreak of war in 1939, Congress ran most of the provincial governments in India. Historians suggest that this had a significant impact on Congress. Stern claims that, after 1937, Congress 'became what it was to become: a moderate, reformist party that played to the accompaniment of radical, leftist rhetoric'. Metcalf states that during this period Congress began transforming itself from a mass movement into a political party, and comments on the nature of Congress rule:

SOURCE 4.1

In office the Congress did few of the things it had said it would do. It did not subvert the 1935 Act, but rather cooperated amicably with the British provincial governors, and enforced law and order much as its predecessors had done. An organization of commercial and professional élites and substantial peasants, it did not, apart from measures to relieve indebtedness, enact extensive agrarian reforms. The Congress was also caught up in an enduring tension between its India-wide structure, with a High Command dictating policy, and the increasing importance of the provinces, where local leaders pursued their own interests supported by their own followers. Nevertheless, the long-term effects of the Congress ministries were immense. One was simply the training Congress politicians, used only to agitation and opposition, received in the practice of government. By the time war broke out in 1939, capable and experienced, they were well prepared to take up the reins and themselves rule India, as they were to do only a few years later.

Metcalf, Barbara and Metcalf, Thomas. 2006. **A Concise History of Modern India (Second Edition).** *Cambridge. Cambridge University Press. p. 196.*

QUESTION

How, according to Source 4.1, did the provincial Congress ministries act once they were elected to office? To what extent would this have contributed to the dissension between the left and right wings in Congress?

By the late 1930s there was continuing dissension between the left and right wings in Congress. Left-wing leaders such as Jawaharlal Nehru and Bose were impatient with the cautious and conservative approach advocated by Gandhi and moderate leaders who dominated Congress. Gandhi tried to heal the rift by ensuring that first Nehru (1936–37) and then Bose (in 1938) served as President of Congress.

In 1939, Bose was re-elected as president in the first contested election in the history of the movement. He was supported by the youth, trade union and peasant wings of the party. It seemed that elements within Congress had run out of patience and were moving towards support for a more radical revolutionary – and potentially violent – solution to British domination of India. However, Bose's re-election was opposed by many of the most powerful figures in Congress, and the election threatened to split the party in two, weakening the nationalist movement.

When Bose realised he would not have the cooperation of the moderates in Congress, he left to form the revolutionary Forward Bloc Party. These developments showed that, despite the emergence of radical forces, the moderates managed to maintain control of Congress.

KEY CONCEPTS ACTIVITY

Change and continuity: Compare the goals and actions of Congress during the 1920s and 1930s. Then write a short paragraph to explain whether you think they represented change or continuity.

4 Nationalism and Independence in India (1919–1964)

When the Second World War began in 1939, the viceroy committed India to fighting on the Allied side, without consulting the elected Indian representatives. As a result, the provincial Congress ministries resigned *en masse*.

The 1940s and beyond

During the war, Congress organised a 'Quit India' campaign to put pressure on Britain, and in response the British imprisoned hundreds of Congress leaders for the duration of the war. At the same time, however, Britain committed itself to independence for India after the war.

Between 1945 and 1947, in the heated discussions preceding independence, Congress vigorously opposed the concept of partition, proposed by the Muslim League and supported by Britain, and called for the creation of a single, secular state. But in the atmosphere of escalating violence, Congress leaders reluctantly came to accept that partition was the only viable solution and that British India would be divided into two separate states.

In the first election in independent India in 1952, the Congress Party won an overwhelming majority of seats. It had enormous prestige as the leader and heir of the nationalist movement and its links with Gandhi. As such, its supporters came from a wide range of social, economic and regional backgrounds. It appealed to landowners and capitalists, as well as to the urban and rural working class.

These supporters represented a range of political opinion, giving the party the character of a broad coalition, with the ability to include and reconcile different and sometimes competing points of view. (See Chapter 9 for more details about the role of the Congress Party in post-independence India.)

SOURCE 4.2

The Indian National Congress is one of the great political parties of the modern world. It has a lineage and record of achievement comparable to that of the Labour Party in Great Britain, the Social Democratic Party in Germany, and the Democratic Party in the United States. From its beginnings in 1885 its ambitions were immense, these contained in its very title, with the last, definitive word indicating that it would not be sectarian, but embrace Indians of all shapes and sizes, or castes and communities.

To be sure, there was often a slippage between the ideal and the practice. Dalits and Muslims did not always feel at home in the Gandhian Congress –hence the appeal of rival leaders like B.R. Ambedkar and M.A. Jinnah. While emphasizing freedom, the Congress did not lay adequate stress on equality –industrial workers and agricultural labourers did not feature strongly in its programmes. Among the Congress leaders in the Gandhian era were some Hindu conservatives, who were deeply unsympathetic to the idea that Dalits and women could enjoy the same rights as upper caste men.

Withal, despite its failures and inconsistencies, the Congress that brought India freedom was a party of distinction and achievement… Across the colonised countries of Asia and Africa, the party of Gandhi and Nehru acted as a beacon of hope and inspiration.

Guha, Ramachandra, 'The Past and Future of the Indian National Congress', published in **The Caravan: A Journal of Politics and Culture.** *1 March 2010. Delhi Press.*

QUESTION

Using Source 4.2, and your own knowledge, evaluate the role and significance of the Indian National Congress in the nationalist movement.

4.2 How important was the All-India Muslim League in the nationalist movement?

The formation of the All-India Muslim League needs to be understood in the context of the demographic make-up and religious breakdown of the population of British India. Towards the end of the 19th century, Muslims formed just under 20% of the population, while the Hindu majority numbered about 75%. The formation of the Muslim League and its policies and actions need to be seen against this background.

> **DISCUSSION POINT**
>
> Why are the position and rights of minorities such difficult issues to resolve? Can you think of examples, other than in India, where the subject of minorities has been an issue?

The early years

When the Indian National Congress was formed in 1885, most of its membership was Hindu, although it had Muslim members as well. Right from the start, Congress leaders made explicit efforts to draw Muslims into their meetings. Copland suggests that Muslim participation in Congress was 'initially quite robust at about 16%' but then dropped off dramatically. However, several prominent Muslims, such as Mohammad Ali Jinnah, joined Congress and three Muslims served as president of Congress in the early years. As you read in Chapter 2, in 1905 Muslims supported the British decision to partition Bengal, where Muslims formed 30% of the population, as they believed it would benefit them. They became concerned about the actions of the anti-partition protestors, especially the appeals to Hindu nationalism made by some of them. These concerns were addressed by the assurance of British support for Muslim interests given to the Simla Deputation by the viceroy. After this, support for the concept of a separate organisation to represent and safeguard Muslim interests began to grow. In December 1906, Muslim leaders meeting in Dhaka formed the All-India Muslim League, believing that this was the only way to protect the interests of the Muslim minority. At first the League was dominated by a similar middle-and upper-class leadership to Congress. Britain's reversal of the partition of Bengal in 1911 angered many Muslims and led to growing unity between conservative loyalists and a younger radical group. At its meeting in Lucknow in 1912 the Muslim League called for self-government for India. This more assertive approach attracted new members, among them Mohammad Ali Jinnah.

During the First World War, with Britain at war against Muslim Turkey, the Muslim League became concerned that Britain would no longer uphold the interests of the Muslim minority in India. As a result, it decided to move closer to the nationalist movement. In both 1915 and 1916, the annual meetings of Congress and the League were held in the same city – Bombay in 1915 and Lucknow in 1916 – which facilitated greater cooperation between the two organisations. In 1916, Congress and the Muslim League signed the Lucknow Pact. The League welcomed this assurance that Congress accepted the principle of separate representation for Muslims.

KEY CONCEPTS QUESTION

Significance: Assess the significance of the Simla Deputation and the Lucknow Pact.

The Muslim League in the 1920s

In the early 1920s, many Muslims supported the Khalifat movement, the aim of which was to support the Sultan of Turkey, who was regarded as the Caliph, the spiritual leader of Sunni Islam. The defeat of Turkey in the war and the break-up of the Ottoman Empire in the postwar peace settlements threatened this position. Gandhi expressed support for the Khalifat movement, and in turn its members provided substantial support for the Non-Cooperation movement of 1920 to1922. However, the Khalifat movement collapsed when Turkey itself abolished the position of the sultan in 1923 and became a secular republic.

Not all Muslims supported the Non-Cooperation movement. Many, like Jinnah, rejected the activism involved and preferred to use constitutional methods to bring about change. As a result, he resigned from Congress. Many Muslims were also uncomfortable with Gandhi's style of leadership, and in 1923 only 3.6% of Congress delegates were Muslim, a downward trend from the 10.9% of 1920. The cooperation between the League, the Khalifat movement and Congress began to disintegrate, especially after the suspension of the Non-Cooperation movement.

With the collapse of the Khalifat movement, the Muslim League emerged once more as the main representative of Muslim opinion. Jinnah, who served as president of the League on several occasions, continued to work to promote cooperation between Congress and the League.

At a meeting of the League held in Delhi in 1927, the League offered to end its support for separate electorates in exchange for an agreement that Muslims could fill one-third of the seats on the Central Legislative Council. Some historians suggest that this proposal represented a significant attempt at cooperation and reconciliation by the Muslim League, but, under pressure from Hindu nationalists, Congress rejected it.

The League made another attempt to reach an agreement with Congress in 1929 and presented a 14-point compromise plan drafted by Jinnah, which was also rejected by Congress. After this, there was very little cooperation between the League and Congress. Jinnah temporarily retired from politics and moved to London to work as a lawyer, referring to the situation as the 'parting of the ways'.

SOURCE 4.3

Was this, as Jinnah averred at the time, the 'parting of the ways' for India's Hindus and Muslims? In some ways the comment was prophetic. The Muslim League and the Indian National Congress would continue to negotiate right down to the eve of independence in 1947, but Congress would never receive a better offer for an amicable political settlement. Nor would there ever be a Lucknow-style rapprochement. After 1929 the two parties would never again work together for the national good. Yet in other ways, perhaps, the forecast was premature.

Copland, Ian. 2001. **India 1885–1947: The Unmaking of an Empire.** *Harlow. Pearson Education. p. 60.*

Use the internet and any other sources available to you to do further research on the events leading to this 'parting of the ways' in 1929. Discuss whether it could have been avoided.

The Muslim League in the 1930s

In the absence of Jinnah, the Muslim League did not play a very significant role in the early 1930s. Although large numbers of Muslims participated in the Civil Disobedience campaign, the Muslim League was not involved.

Like Congress, the Muslim League rejected the 1935 Government of India Act, but also decided to participate in the 1937 elections. Jinnah returned to India and became president of the Muslim League once again, this time on a permanent basis. Historian Ian Copland suggests that at this stage the League was in a state of decline: 'fragmented, demoralised and chronically short of funds'. Jinnah set about organising the League's campaign for the elections.

In the elections, the League won only 109 (out of a possible 482) Muslim constituencies, and under 5% of the total Muslim vote. Most of the votes in Muslim constituencies went to provincial Muslim parties. The poor showing of the League in these elections provided a wake-up call to the movement and after 1937 it worked hard to unite Muslims in India and promote recognition of Muslim rights.

According to David Ludden, the prospect of Hindu domination gave the League a strong argument for 'Muslim solidarity across regional and ethnic lines, to make the Muslim League the party of Indian Muslims'.

SOURCE 4.4

The League began in earnest the campaign after 1937 that it should have begun before: vote-getting, mobilizing support for the League among Muslim villagers. It was, however, a campaign of mobilization largely by propaganda that appealed directly to the religious and communitarian sentiments of ordinary Muslims. *Islam was in danger!* Political time was short in 1937. By and large, the League did not campaign to enlist peasants into its alliance. It was and remained an alliance of urban, educated professionals, landlords and a few industrialists… Under League auspices, reports were prepared after the 1937 elections which accused Congress ministries of being explicitly Hindu in their style and in their substance insensitive to Muslim sentiments and interests.

Stern, Robert. 1993. **Changing India: Bourgeois Revolution on the Subcontinent.** *Cambridge, Cambridge University Press. p. 148.*

DISCUSSION POINT

Why is religion sometimes such a divisive force in society? Can you think of other examples in history or in the contemporary world where religious differences have caused tensions and even violence?

The Muslim League in the 1940s

The war created political opportunities for the Muslim League. When the provincial Congress ministries resigned in 1939, the League declared it to be a 'day of deliverance' from the 'tyranny, oppression and injustice' of Congress rule. The following year, in a declaration made in Lahore, the Muslim League declared its support for the notion that India was a country of 'two nations' and called for the creation of a separate Muslim state. When Congress rejected the British government's offer of delayed independence and introduced its 'Quit India' campaign in 1942, the Muslim League continued to cooperate with Britain and, as a result, was able to operate openly and legally during the war years.

As the situation in India became increasingly tense and Congress became the target of British repression, the League moved to give full support to Britain's war effort. In return, Britain gave serious consideration to the Muslim League's demand for a 'two-state solution' in India after the war.

The League was consequently in a strong negotiating position at the end of the war: its support for Britain's actions in India would be a key factor in the emergence of a separate Muslim state of Pakistan after independence. (See Chapters 6 and 7 for more details about the role and importance of the Muslim League.)

ACTIVITY

Draw up a table to contrast the Indian National Congress and the Muslim League, using the following categories: support base; political aims; attitude towards the British; tactics and actions.

4.3 Why was Gandhi so important to the nationalist movement?

Mohandas Gandhi (1869–1948) is considered to be one of the outstanding figures of the 20th century, and was both the political and spiritual leader of the nationalist movement.

Theory of Knowledge

The 'Great Man' theory of history and objectivity

Many historians place great emphasis on the role played by Gandhi in the nationalist struggle for independence in India. Is it wrong to place too much emphasis on the role of one individual? What other approaches can historians take when they write about this period of history? How easy is it to view an iconic figure like Gandhi objectively?

4

Early life

Gandhi was born into a middle-class Indian family; his father had been a high-ranking official in Porbander, one of the princely states. Gandhi was brought up in the Jain religious tradition, which influenced his later political and spiritual beliefs. He trained as a lawyer at University College London.

One of his first legal positions was in South Africa, where he experienced racial discrimination at first hand. He also saw the British colonial authorities in South Africa use extreme violence to quell opposition to its rule, in the ruthless suppression of a Zulu rebellion in 1906. These formative years led Gandhi to reject racism and injustice, not only for Indians but for all people. He spent 21 years in South Africa, where he was involved in a struggle against discriminatory laws affecting the large Indian community there.

It was during this period that he developed the principles of *satyagraha* and the tactics of non-violent resistance. These experiences, together with his religious background, convinced him that the most effective way of fighting colonial oppression was by non-violent methods. He believed that any other strategy in India might lead to the same violent response by the British that he had seen in South Africa.

Gandhi returned to India in 1915, and spent over a year travelling around the country assessing local conditions. He also focused on issues of self-reliance and social mobility, encouraging the building of schools, hospitals and clean water facilities. From this early period there was a combination of Western liberal thought and an Indian approach to non-violent protest in his actions.

Gandhi championed a form of non-violent resistance, or civil disobedience, to colonial rule that stemmed from an Indian concept called *satyagraha,* or soul force. It was based on the belief that ordinary people can bring about political change by using peaceful means to fight for justice. Bose and Jalal explain *satyagraha* as a quest for truth though mass political activity and suggest that Gandhi saw it as a political weapon rather than a moral philosophy. This is how Gandhi explained *satyagraha*:

SOURCE 4.5

Soul force, or the power of truth, is reached by the infliction of suffering, not on your opponent, but on yourself. Rivers of blood may have to flow before we gain our freedom, but it must be our blood… The government of the day has passed a law which I do not like. If, by using violence, I force the government to change the law, I am using what may be called body-force. If I do not obey the law, and accept the penalty for breaking it, I use soul force. It involves sacrificing yourself.

Quoted in Bottaro, J. and Calland, R. 2001. **Successful Human and Social Sciences Grade 9.** *Cape Town. Oxford University Press. p. 45.*

Satyagraha involved a campaign of non-cooperation with the British administration, boycotts of British schools, universities and law courts and, critically, boycotts – called *hartals* – of British goods. Gandhi consciously rejected Western values and adopted the dress and lifestyle of a simple peasant. He established an *ashram,* or community, committed to non-violence and self-sufficiency using traditional methods. This appeal to traditional cultural values allowed him to connect to the masses of the Indian peasantry. He also identified with the problems of specific groups and earned their respect and support: tenant farmers exploited by landlords, industrial workers involved in disputes with factory owners, and poor farmers unable to pay taxes after bad harvests.

By 1918, Gandhi had led the first non-violent acts of non-cooperation in the 'Champaran agitation' where he supported the cause of peasant farmers in the Champaran district of Bihar, who were being forced to grow indigo for British planters, instead of food crops for their own use. He also successfully mediated a conflict between workers and industrialists in textile mills in Ahmedabad, and supported protest actions against government plans to increase the land tax, by peasant farmers in the Kheda district of Gujarat. The success of these events won Gandhi support and admiration through his identification with peasant struggles. They also established his reputation as an effective leader of mass civil disobedience. The strategy was very effective when used against a liberal democracy like Britain, where suppressing such protests was a difficult public-relations problem for the British government to solve.

Figure 4.3: Gandhi at his spinning wheel; his promotion of spinning had symbolic significance rather than practical use – hand-woven cloth (*khadi*) symbolised a rejection of foreign manufactured goods and the promotion of self-reliance; the spinning wheel (*chakra*) became the symbol of the Indian nationalist movement.

Involvement in the nationalist movement

Gandhi became a national figure following the Amritsar Massacre in 1919, after which he launched his first all–India Non–Cooperation campaign. Through this and later campaigns, which mobilised millions of people throughout India, he was able to transform the nationalist struggle into a mass movement with wide appeal.

Gandhi also proved to be adept at propaganda. The Salt March of 1930 is an excellent example of this. By marching hundreds of kilometres in full view of the international media to collect salt illegally, Gandhi made an extremely effective political statement. (You will read more about the Salt March and other protest actions in Chapter 5.)

Gandhi was imprisoned several times during the independence struggle and, both inside and outside prison, he used hunger strikes as a form of political and social protest.

Gandhi can be seen as a social liberal. He wanted reform of the Indian caste system to create greater equality, and his liberal attitude also extended to the emancipation of Indian women. He was partly successful on both counts, which is significant given the deeply rooted cultural attitudes that he was challenging. His firm commitment to liberal democratic principles, the emancipation of women and a reform of the caste system had a deep influence on the kind of democracy that India became.

Although he was a Hindu, Gandhi was committed to the belief that India should be a unified and secular state. He devoted much time to trying to create greater understanding and tolerance between the Hindu and Muslim communities. He fought hard to maintain the unity of India, and he deplored the violence that accompanied partition. He saw communalism as one of the greatest threats facing India, and ironically it was this force that resulted in his assassination.

ACTIVITY

Compare the concepts of 'communalism' and 'secularism' in the context of Indian history at that time.

Gandhi took advantage of Britain's involvement in the Second World War to increase the pressure for independence in the 'Quit India' campaign. He has been criticised for this because of his failure to take a stand against Nazism. He was, however, quite correct in pointing out the inconsistencies of the British position in fighting Nazism without giving self-determination to the Indian population. The events of the First World War period had also taught him that British promises could not necessarily be relied upon.

Gandhi has been criticised too for his attitude to the form of the postcolonial state in India. India was a diverse society, but over 75% of the population was Hindu.

Many of the ethnic and religious minorities – especially Muslims – genuinely feared Hindu domination in an independent India. Gandhi has been accused of not fully understanding the depth of Muslim fears. This arguably contributed to the final division of the subcontinent into India and Pakistan, an event that was accompanied by considerable bloodshed.

SOURCE 4.6

Gandhi never claimed to speak for Hinduism, and he did not seek an avowedly Hindu India... [He] sought an India built on a coalition of religious communities, not one of Hindu dominance. Nevertheless, Gandhi's entire manner, dress, and vocabulary were suffused with Hinduism. Religion, in his view, formed the binding glue of the nation. Even as he reached out to other communities, this 'mahatma' inevitably embodied a deeply Hindu sensibility. As the years went by he shrewdly turned it to political advantage. The costs, however, were substantial.

Metcalf, Barbara and Metcalf, Thomas. 2006. **A Concise History of Modern India Second Edition.** *Cambridge: Cambridge University Press. p. 174.*

QUESTION

What, according to Source 4.6, were the apparent contradictions in Gandhi's views and actions regarding religion?

Gandhi was assassinated in 1948 by a Hindu extremist, Nathuram Godse, who felt that Gandhi had weakened India by upholding secular rather than Hindu nationalist values. (You will read more about this in Chapter 9.)

In India, Gandhi is seen as the father of the nation. Although he was not the originator of non-violence as a means of political action, he was the first to apply it successfully on a large scale. He became the pre-eminent independence politician of the day, and a great spiritual and moral leader. He became known as the 'Mahatma' – a semi-religious term meaning 'great soul'.

Search for the BBC news report published on 29 January 1998, the 50th anniversary of Gandhi's death. To what extent are the criticisms of Gandhi from left- and right-wing perspectives valid? Examine whether he deserves the title of 'Father of the Nation'. Discuss the suitability of the title of this article ('The Lost Legacy of Mahatma Gandhi').

Views of Gandhi

Gandhi was such a dominant figure in Indian as well as 20th-century world history that it is difficult to evaluate objectively his impact on the nationalist movement and India's final transition to independence. Nationalist historians have emphasised the heroic nature of his role and stress his importance to the movement.

Marxist historians have viewed his role more critically and seen him as an instrument of conservatism and middle-class dominance. Historians of the Subaltern Studies group stress the role played by millions of ordinary people in the nationalist movement and believe that, without their involvement, Gandhi would not have achieved the prominence that he did. Revisionist historians take a more rounded view and, while noting Gandhi's undoubted achievements, they are also critical of some of his decisions and actions as well as his authoritarian style of leadership.

Some are also critical of what they perceive as his unrealistic vision of an idealised pre-modern rural-based society and his rejection of modern industrial technology.

Historian David Arnold, in his biography of Gandhi, explains another way in which interpretations of Gandhi can be classified.

SOURCE 4.7

Interpretations of Gandhi have varied widely but they have followed three main lines of discussion. Firstly, Gandhi is represented as a man who exercised the power of a saint rather more than that of a politician... Gandhi is seen not only to have had a deep spirituality, but to have possessed great moral and physical courage and an unwavering commitment to non-violence that transformed the lives of those around him... His saintly adherence to non-violence and self-suffering is seen as having enabled Gandhi to transform India's nationalist struggle from a narrowly focused and élitist political campaign into a mass-based moral crusade, enabling him to take on, and ultimately undermine, the authority of the British Empire...

Second only to the saintly image of Gandhi is his reputation as the 'father' or 'maker' of modern India. Such an idea was common during the later stages of the Indian nationalist movement and has been widely held in India and elsewhere since Independence... Such an idea rests on Gandhi's perceived centrality and dominant role in the anti-colonial struggle from 1919 onwards... Perhaps even more than his political leadership, Gandhi's wide-ranging programme of social reform stamped an indelible mark on modern India...

Thirdly, the idea of Gandhi has constantly moved between the perception of Gandhi as a revolutionary and as a traditionalist, even as a downright reactionary... By combining social with political change and devising new means to reach these goals, Gandhi might appear to deserve the title of revolutionary which many of his enthusiasts have awarded him. And yet it can be argued that the 'people' Gandhi empowered in India... were not in fact the lowest of the low, but those who, for all their grievances, were more comfortably ensconced in the social hierarchy and for whom Gandhi's non-violence conveniently by-passed more threatening forms of revolutionary upheaval.

Arnold, David. 2001. **Gandhi.** *Harlow. Pearson Education. pp. 5–9.*

4.4 What was Nehru's contribution to the nationalist movement?

Another key leader in the Indian National Congress was Jawaharlal Nehru (1889–1964). Although he was 20 years younger than Gandhi, Nehru became his close associate, confidante and successor. The son of the prominent Congress leader, Motilal Nehru, Jawaharlal Nehru came from a wealthy family, and was educated in England, at Harrow School and at Trinity College at Cambridge University. Like Gandhi, he qualified as a lawyer in London. Together with many educated Indians of his generation, he deeply resented British attitudes, policies and actions in India. He joined the Indian National Congress in 1919, and devoted the rest of his life to politics. He was attracted by Gandhi's philosophy of active yet peaceful civil disobedience, and yet, at the same time, according to Metcalf, he was committed to a modern India on a par with the industrialised West, rather than being attracted to 'Gandhi's utopian pastoralism or in his moralising asceticism'. He was jailed many times because of his role as a Congress leader working for the independence of India, and he spent a total of nine years as a political prisoner.

As the general secretary of Congress during the 1920s, Nehru travelled widely around India and saw at first hand the conditions of poverty and oppression under which millions of people lived. This gave him a driving determination to improve the position of the peasants. In 1927 he attended the Congress of the Oppressed Nations in Brussels where he was exposed to radical ideas. He wanted the socio-economic emancipation of India as well as political independence. He also travelled to the Soviet Union, where he came to believe that some form of socialism, in the form of central planning, would be the solution to India's social and economic problems, as is evident in this address that he made to Congress in 1936:

SOURCE 4.8

I am convinced that the only key to the solution of the world's problems and of India's problems lies in socialism, and when I use this word I do so not in a vague humanitarian way but in the scientific, economic sense. I see no way of ending the poverty, the vast unemployment, the degradation and the subjection of the Indian people except through socialism. That involves vast and revolutionary changes in our political and social structure, the ending of vested interests in land and industry, as well as the feudal and autocratic Indian States system. That means the ending of private property, except in a restricted sense, and the replacement of the present profit system by a higher ideal of cooperative service… If the future is full of hope it is largely because of Soviet Russia and what it has done.

Address by Jawaharlal Nehru to the Indian National Congress, Lucknow, April 1936. Printed in **The Labour Monthly,** *Vol. 18, May 1936, No. 5, pp. 282–305.*

QUESTION

With reference to its origins, purpose and purpose, assess the value and limitations of Source 4.8 to historians researching Nehru's role in the nationalist movement.

At the same time, Nehru valued liberal and humanist ideas, and had a vision of India as a tolerant secular democracy. He became the leader of the left wing of the Congress, and was regarded by some of the more conservative members as a militant revolutionary. With Gandhi's backing, Nehru became president of Congress in 1929. There were other more experienced politicians who were rivals for this position, but Gandhi saw qualities in Nehru that other Congress leaders lacked.

Gandhi believed that Nehru would be able to draw in the youth who were attracted to more extreme left-wing causes. As Congress president, Nehru called for complete independence from Britain, rather than simply dominion status. He served a further two terms as Congress president in 1936 and 1937 and campaigned vigorously for the 1937 provincial elections, contributing in this way to the impressive Congress electoral victories.

Nehru became Gandhi's political heir and was recognised as such from 1942 onwards. Together they formed a powerful partnership. While Gandhi mobilised the masses, Nehru attracted the support of the educated middle classes, intellectuals and young people. He became head of the interim government in 1946 and as such played an important role in the negotiations leading to independence and partition.

Figure 4.4: Jawaharlal Nehru and Mohandas Gandhi.

A strong supporter of democracy and secularism, Nehru advocated socialist central planning to promote economic development in India. He served as India's first prime minister, leading the Congress Party to victory in India's first three general elections. He played a dominant role in shaping the nature and structure of democracy in India between 1947 and 1964. (You will read more about the role and importance of Nehru after independence in Chapter 9.)

4.5 How significant was Jinnah's role in the nationalist movement?

Mohammad Ali Jinnah (1876–1948) – known to his followers and in Pakistan today as *Quaid-i-Azam* or 'Great Leader' – was an important figure in the Indian independence movement. Like many other leaders in the nationalist movement, he had a Western education. After studying at Bombay University, he trained as a lawyer in London in the 1890s where he was influenced by British liberal ideas. As a result, he came to believe that the Indian independence struggle should use constitutional methods. He was a member of the Indian National Congress from 1896, but only became active in Indian politics after defending the leading nationalist Tilak who was arrested and charged with sedition at the time of the protests in Bengal in 1905.

In 1913, Jinnah joined the Muslim League and in 1916 became its president for the first time. He believed that India had a right to independence, and argued that Indians were entitled to agitate for this goal. However, he also recognised the benefits that British rule had brought to India in the form of law, culture and industry. In many ways these were the views of most Indian nationalist leaders at the time. At the same time, Jinnah was also a member of the Home Rule League which wanted dominion status for India. This would give India autonomy rather than complete independence within the British Empire. Initially Jinnah was a moderate liberal Anglophile, but Britain's failure to give independence to India after the First World War caused him to adopt more radical views.

In 1920, when the Indian National Congress launched a Non-Cooperation campaign, Jinnah resigned from Congress. He thought that Gandhi's tactics of non-cooperation could destabilise the political structure. He was also uneasy about Gandhi's public image as a traditional Hindu holy man. But the key difference between Jinnah and the leaders of Congress was his promotion of separate electorates for Muslims.

At the time of the Nehru report in 1928, Jinnah made concerted efforts to promote a compromise solution between the viewpoints of the League and Congress on this issue. Bates suggests that it is important to note the efforts made by Jinnah to bring about compromise because 'he is often unfairly described in later years as the architect of partition'.

Other historians believe that Congress should share the blame for the partition of India. They argue that Jinnah never really wanted partition but used the concept of it as a means to try to force Congress to share power with the Muslim League and in this way get political rights for Muslims, but that Congress leaders would not accept this.

KEY CONCEPTS ACTIVITY

Perspective: Discuss why it is important to consider a range of historical perspectives when studying a controversial topic such as the partition of India.

Under Jinnah, the Muslim League became an alternative pressure group that the British sometimes played off against Congress. Throughout the 1920s and 1930s Jinnah campaigned for independence, but he became disillusioned at the slow pace of reform. He fought successfully for separate Muslim representation in elections, but was bitterly disappointed about the poor performance of the League in the 1937 elections.

From then on, he set out to build up support for the League as the sole representative of Indian Muslims. He claimed that, in a single postcolonial state, Muslims would be swamped by the Hindu majority.

SOURCE 4.9

Undoubtedly, an important factor in the League's revival was the astute, visionary and at time ruthless leadership of Jinnah himself, who, in comparison to his Congress opposite numbers, had the further advantage of being virtually a one-man band. Learning from the party's abysmal showing in the 1937 elections, Jinnah set about re-building the League by reducing membership fees…, opening new branches, and recruiting a crop of energetic and talented professionals…to staff the party organisation. Within two years, these measures had swelled the League's membership at least tenfold, a good proportion of this growth occurring in regions where, hitherto, the League had been weak or non-existent… In turn, the League's evolution into a mass party made it a more saleable asset, allowing Jinnah to secure valuable financial backing from wealthy Muslim businessmen…

But the march of events during this decade also favoured the League. Congress provincial rule alienated many Muslims. This made them easy targets for Jinnah's recruiting drive.

Copland, Ian. 2001. India 1885–1947: The Unmaking of an Empire. *Harlow. Pearson Education. pp. 70–1.*

QUESTION

What, according to Source 4.9, were the reasons for revival of the Muslim League after 1937?

ACTIVITY

Use the internet or any other sources available to you to do some research on the Congress provincial governments which ruled much of India between 1937 and 1939. To what extent were Muslims justified in feeling 'alienated' by their policies and actions, as Source 4.9 suggests they were?

During the Second World War, Jinnah astutely supported the British, and this strengthened the position of the League in later negotiations. In 1941, he started a newspaper, *Dawn*, to spread the League's views, and he put considerable pressure on Cripps during the British representative's visit to accept the concept of a separate Muslim state. During this period, Gandhi tried unsuccessfully to come to an agreement with Jinnah, but there were fundamental differences in their ideas about partition.

Figure 4.5: This photograph of Jinnah (left) with Gandhi (right) gives no indication of the fundamental differences between them in their views about partition.

In the tense period after the war, Jinnah took advantage of the confusion to continue to demand a separate Muslim state. On 16 August 1946, he instructed his followers to engage in 'Direct Action'. This led to strikes and protests and, eventually, communal violence on a large scale.

Some historians believe that it was Jinnah's call for direct action that caused much of the violence and bloodshed that followed. Others however believe that that it would have happened anyway, given the tensions at the time. Metcalf believes that, perhaps unintentionally, Jinnah's call precipitated the 'horrors of riot and massacre that were to disfigure the coming of independence'. Ramachandra Guha states that Jinnah was deliberately trying to 'polarise the two communities further, and thus force the British to divide India when they finally quit'. However, other historians, including Bose and Jalal, believe that Jinnah's intentions have been misinterpreted and that he was merely trying to ensure 'an equitable share of power for Muslims' in a united India, and not the creation of a separate Islamic state.

> DISCUSSION POINT
>
> **Discuss the conflicting views about Jinnah's role in the independence movement and the partition of India into two separate states.**

Eventually the British and Congress leaders accepted the partition of India, with Pakistan as a separate Muslim state. Jinnah became its first leader, but died of tuberculosis within a year. The new state of Pakistan, for which he had fought so hard, was a fragile political entity, with its West and East zones separated by 1500 km (930 miles) of Indian territory.

There is some debate about whether Jinnah wanted a secular or an Islamic state in Pakistan. He died before he could put policy into action. Many scholars believe that he wanted a state similar to modern Turkey.

It is interesting to note Jinnah's comments on the nature of the state he envisaged for Pakistan in Source 4.10, in an address he made to the first meeting of the Pakistan Constituent Assembly, on 11 August 1947.

SOURCE 4.10

You are free; you are free to go to your temples; you are free to go to your mosques or to any other places of worship in this State of Pakistan. You may belong to any religion, or caste or creed – that has nothing to do with the business of the State.

Now I think we should keep that in front of us as our ideal and you will find that in course of time Hindus would cease to be Hindus and Muslims would cease to be Muslims, not in the religious sense, because that is the personal faith of each individual, but in the political sense as citizens of the State.

Mohammad Ali Jinnah's address to the Constituent Assembly of Pakistan, 11 August 1947. Quoted in Copland, Ian. 2001. **India 1885–1947: The Unmaking of an Empire.** *Harlow. Pearson Education. p. 117.*

With reference to its origin, purpose and content, assess the value and limitations of Source 4.10 to historians researching the reasons for the partition of India and the establishment of the state of Pakistan.

Paper 3 exam practice

Summary activity

Copy the following spider diagram to show the contribution of key groups and individuals in the struggle for independence in India. Then, using the information in this chapter and any other sources available to you, complete the diagram. Make sure that you include, where relevant, brief comments about different historical debates and interpretations.

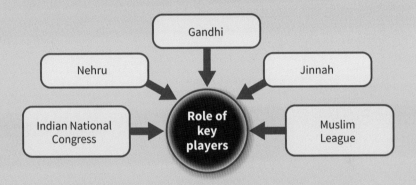

Paper 3 practice questions

1   Examine the evolution of the Indian National Congress from a small élitist organisation to a powerful political force which posed a serious challenge to British rule in India.

2   Discuss the reasons for the transformation of the Muslim League from a position of political weakness in 1937 to a situation where it was a key player in negotiations about India's future by 1945.

3   To what extent has Gandhi's role in the struggle for independence struggle been over-emphasised by historians?

4   Discuss the extent to which Nehru played a complementary role to Gandhi and helped in this way to strengthen support for the Indian National Congress.

5   Evaluate the attempts made by Mohammad Ali Jinnah to promote cooperation between the Indian National Congress and the All-India Muslim League between 1916 and 1937.

The struggle for independence

5

Introduction

The Indian nationalist movement developed a unique form of protest against British rule: mass non–violent campaigns of civil disobedience. They were based on Gandhi's philosophy of *satyagraha*. The aim was to force the British government to withdraw from India and grant independence. Between 1920 and 1942, the Indian National Congress launched three major campaigns: the Non–Cooperation movement (1920–22), the Civil Disobedience campaign (1930–34) and the 'Quit India' campaign (1942). Although thousands of participants were jailed, the British authorities could not stop the momentum of the protests. This chapter examines the context, nature and significance of these three campaigns in the struggle for independence.

TIMELINE

1919 **Mar:** Rowlatt Acts

Apr: Amritsar Massacre

1920 **Dec:** Congress adopts Gandhi's proposal for Non-Cooperation campaign

1922 **Feb:** Violence at Chauri Chaura; Gandhi calls off Non-Cooperation campaign; arrest of Gandhi

Mar: Gandhi sentenced to six years in prison

1929 **Dec:** *Purna Swaraj* resolution by Congress

1930 **Jan:** 'Independence Day'

12 Mar–6 Apr: Salt March

May: Arrest of Gandhi; march on Dharasana salt works

1931 **Mar:** Gandhi-Irwin Pact and suspension of Civil Disobedience campaign

1932 **Jan:** Civil Disobedience campaign resumed

Gandhi re-arrested

1934 **Apr:** Suspension of Civil Disobedience

1937–39 Provincial Congress ministries in office

1939 **Sept:** Outbreak of Second World War

Oct: Resignation of Congress ministries

1942 **Apr:** Gandhi drafts 'Quit India' resolution

Aug: Congress adopts 'Quit India' campaign; August Rising

KEY QUESTIONS

- What was the Non-Cooperation movement?
- Why was the Salt March so significant?
- What happened during further Civil Disobedience campaigns?
- Why was the 'Quit India' campaign significant?

Overview

- Between 1920 and 1922 the Indian National Congress organised a Non-Cooperation movement to put pressure on Britain to grant self-government to India within a year: protestors boycotted elections, schools and law courts, refused to pay taxes or buy British cloth, and rejected official honours and invitations.
- The authorities reacted by arresting protestors and banning meetings. Gandhi terminated the campaign after protests turned violent in some areas, but not all Congress members agreed with this controversial decision.
- Gandhi launched the next nationalist campaign – the Civil Disobedience campaign – with the Salt March in 1930. This shrewdly chosen target and carefully planned protest action gained wide publicity in India and abroad.
- The harsh repression of protests at the Dharasana salt works resulted in international condemnation of the British government's policies and actions in India, and sympathy for the Indian nationalist movement.
- Despite the arrest of Congress leaders, thousands more people participated in acts of civil disobedience, on a larger scale than the Non-Cooperation movement of ten years previously. This resulted in falling tax revenues for the government and the halving of cloth imports from Britain.
- The economic effects of the Depression caused hardship and a move to more radical protests in some areas, a factor which alarmed moderate members of Congress.

- The Civil Disobedience campaign was suspended temporarily after the Gandhi-Irwin Pact in March 1931, but reinstated after the failure of constitutional talks. But harsh repression effectively ended the campaign in 1932, although it was only formally called off in 1934.
- When the Second World War broke out in 1939, Britain committed India to fighting in the war without consulting Indian political leaders. Subsequent attempts to get Congress support for the British war effort failed and Congress launched the 'Quit India' campaign.
- In the absence of the restraining influence of the jailed Congress leaders, the 'Quit India' campaign was the most radical and violent of the nationalist campaigns, involving strikes, rural uprisings and acts of sabotage. Harsh measures were used to suppress the campaign and Congress leaders remained in prison until the end of the war.

5.1 What was the Non-Cooperation movement?

After the repressive Rowlatt Acts were introduced in March 1919, Gandhi called for non-violent protests throughout India in the form of *hartals* (work stoppages). This is sometimes referred to as the Rowlatt *satyagraha*. Support for it varied from province to province but, after violent protests in Gujarat and Punjab, Gandhi called off the campaign. Bates suggests that this campaign was unlike the three great nationwide campaigns that followed later as it was calling for the restoration of civil liberties rather than a British withdrawal from India.

The first of the anti-colonial national campaigns was launched the following year after mounting anger about the Amritsar Massacre and, more especially, the British reaction to it. It started after the Indian National Congress adopted Gandhi's proposal for a nationwide campaign of Non-Cooperation with the British authorities in December 1920.

QUESTION

Examine why the British reaction to the Amritsar massacre created so much anger in India.

The start of the Non-Cooperation movement

Until this time Gandhi did not have a strong support base within Congress, but he achieved the necessary approval for his proposal of a campaign of non-violent Non-Cooperation by forming an alliance with the Khalifat movement. By this stage Gandhi had expressed support for the Khalifat movement, and many of its members attended the Congress meeting at Nagpur in December 1920 and gave support to the campaign.

With the addition of their votes, Congress accepted Gandhi's proposal. Bose and Jalal suggest that, by forging an alliance with the Khalifat movement, 'Gandhi succeeded in out-manoeuvring the moderate elements' in Congress. Metcalf argues that without the votes of the pro-Khalifat Muslims the Non-Cooperation proposal would have been defeated.

The Non-Cooperation movement called on participants to:

*   boycott elections to the legislative assemblies (introduced by the new Government of India Act)
*   refuse to buy imported cloth from Britain
*   boycott British schools, universities and law courts
*   reject all honours and titles awarded by Britain
*   refuse to pay taxes
*   refuse to attend official receptions.

Gandhi declared that Indians could achieve *swaraj* (self-government) within one year through these legitimate and peaceful means. At his suggestion, important structural changes to the organisation of Congress were made at the same meeting. Congress set up a Working Committee of 15 members to run the affairs of Congress on a day-to-day basis. Provincial Congress Committees which operated in local languages were established and the Congress membership fee was reduced to enable the poor to become members. By these means, Congress hoped to attract mass support.

The Non-Cooperation movement had some successes. Thousands of students left schools and colleges to attend 'national schools' set up outside the government system. The boycott of the law courts was not as successful, because many lawyers were reluctant to give up lucrative practices, although some prominent lawyers, such as Motilal Nehru and

Nationalism and Independence in India (1919–1964)

C.R. Das, did so. Congress members withdrew as candidates for the provincial legislatures, and large numbers of qualified voters boycotted the elections. As a result, most seats were won by the Liberals and other moderate parties, who now formed the new provincial governments.

The most successful part of the campaign was the boycott of foreign textiles. Protestors made bonfires of foreign clothes and picketed shops which sold them and, as a result, the import figures for foreign textiles halved. The visit of the Prince of Wales (the future King Edward VIII) to India in 1921, provided a focus for many of the protests. According to Mridula Mukherjee he was 'greeted with empty streets and downed shutters wherever he went', and Indians boycotted official receptions held in his honour.

Figure 5.1: Participants in the Non-Cooperation movement collect clothes to be burned as part of the protests.

The British reaction to the Non-Cooperation movement

At first the British authorities tried to ignore the movement as they did not want to make martyrs of the protestors and in this way intensify the protests. Metcalf explains some of the dilemmas facing the British:

SOURCE 5.1

For the British, Gandhi's turn to non-cooperation posed a seemingly intractable dilemma. Over the years the British had devised ever more effective strategies for dealing with nationalists. The moderates among them could be conciliated, or ignored; the revolutionary terrorists could be clapped in jail and kept there for years on end. But Gandhi's non-cooperation was a baffling novelty, and the British did not initially know how to respond. The Conservatives at home, along with the military in India, argued for outright repression by force. But the Indian government, loath to face more Amritsar massacres, and anxious to get some support for the new dyarchy constitution… did not want to risk policies that would antagonise still more of the Indian people. Furthermore, they realised that to club and jail vast numbers of peaceable demonstrators would make the government, if not the British as a whole, look like bullies in the eyes of the world, and even to themselves. Indeed, Gandhi had contrived his style of agitation in part with this objective in mind – by claiming the moral high ground for himself, he wanted to appeal to the British conscience, and so to make them feel that they were violating their own principles if they moved forcibly against him.

Metcalf, Barbara and Metcalf, Thomas. 2006. **A Concise History of Modern India Second Edition.** *Cambridge: Cambridge University Press. pp. 181–2.*

Nationalism and Independence in India (1919–1964)

What, according to Source 5.1, were the options and dilemmas facing the British government in dealing with the Non-Cooperation movement?

However, in December 1921, the British authorities arrested 30 000 protesters, banned public meetings and assemblies, restricted newspaper coverage and conducted raids on Congress and Khalifat offices. In response to the increased repression, Congress planned to launch a campaign of mass civil disobedience, more far-reaching than the Non-Cooperation campaign.

The end of the Non-Cooperation movement

However, the campaign was never instituted because in some places Non-Cooperation protests got out of control and protesters turned to violence. In protests in Bombay there was looting and burning in which 53 demonstrators were killed and hundreds injured.

In February 1922, when a violent mob burned 22 Indian policemen to death by setting the police station alight in the north Indian village of Chauri Chaura, Gandhi immediately called off the Non-Cooperation campaign. He concluded that many people were not ready to apply the tactics of *satyagraha* as he intended they should be. He decided to withdraw from political agitation and focus instead on social welfare work.

Many Congress members were angered by Gandhi's termination of the campaign and felt a sense of betrayal. It led to a split in the Congress movement. Mridula Mukherjee explains some of the reactions to Gandhi's decision in Source 5.2:

SOURCE 5.2

Gandhiji's decision to withdraw the movement in response to the violence at Chauri Chaura raised a controversy whose heat can still be felt in staid academic seminars and sober volumes of history. Motilal Nehru, C.R. Das, Jawaharlal Nehru, Subhas Bose, and many others have recorded their utter bewilderment on hearing the news. They could not understand why the whole country had to pay the price for the crazy behaviour of some people in a remote village. Many in the country thought that the Mahatma had failed miserably as a leader and that his days of glory were over.

Many later commentators… have continued to condemn the decision taken by Gandhiji, and seen in it proof of the Mahatma's concern for the propertied classes of Indian society. Their argument is that Gandhiji did not withdraw the movement simply because of his belief in the necessity of non-violence. He withdrew it because the action at Chauri Chaura was a symbol and an indication of the growing militancy of the Indian masses, of their growing radicalization, of their willingness to launch an attack on the status quo of property relations. Frightened by this radical possibility and by the prospect of the movement going out of his hands and into the hands of radical forces, and in order to protect the interests of landlords and capitalists who would inevitably be at the receiving end of this violence, Gandhiji cried halt to the movement.

Chandra, B., Mukherjee, M., Mukherjee, A., Mahajan, S. and Pannikar, K.N. 2012. **India's Struggle for Independence 1857–1947.** *London. Penguin. Digital edition: Location 3304–3314.*

To counter the arguments which she summarises in Source 5.2, Mridula Mukherjee suggests instead that Gandhi called off the campaign because he did not want the British to use the incident at Chauri Chaura as justification for suppressing the whole nationalist movement, and he was therefore 'protecting the movement from likely suppression and the people from demoralization'. Mukherjee argues further that the Non-Cooperation Movement was losing momentum at the time and Gandhi's decision gave Congress the opportunity to 'retreat with honour, before the internal weaknesses of the movement became apparent enough to force a surrender or make the retreat look like a rout.'

Nationalism and Independence in India (1919–1964)

Copland offers a similar view and suggests that, because the movement had not achieved what was intended, Gandhi realised that he had miscalculated and so 'mixed pragmatism with high-mindedness and called a halt while the movement's structure and morale remained intact'. He goes on to suggest that Congress emerged from the Non-Cooperation movement greatly strengthened, with an increase in membership over wide areas, making it, for the first time, a mass organisation.

Bates takes an opposite view about the effects of Gandhi's action. He suggests that Gandhi seriously miscalculated by calling off the campaign publicly without consulting other Congress leaders because he risked alienating them. He calls Gandhi's action in this instance as 'little short of catastrophic' because after this the Congress Party split, its membership declined rapidly, and members left to join other political organisations.

DISCUSSION POINT

Which of these theories is the most convincing to explain Gandhi's decision? Discuss any other factors that may have played a part.

Within weeks of the announcement, Gandhi was arrested, charged with sedition, and sentenced to six years in prison. He used the opportunity presented by the trial to address the court and explain the purpose behind the Non-Cooperation movement.

Theory of Knowledge

History and ethics

Gandhi believed that the authorities could be forced to give in, by the firm yet peaceful demonstration of the justice of a cause. Is *satyagraha* a historical term or an ethical concept? How could *satyagraha* be an effective moral force to bring about political change? Can you think of other contexts in 20th-century history where non-violent resistance has been used effectively?

SOURCE 5.3

In my opinion, non-co-operation with evil is as much a duty as is co-operation with good. But in the past, non-co-operation has been deliberately expressed in violence to the evil-doer. I am endeavouring to show to my countrymen that violent non-co-operation only multiplies evil, and that as evil can only be sustained by violence, withdrawal of support of evil requires complete abstention from violence. Non-violence implies voluntary submission to the penalty for non-co-operation with evil. I am here, therefore, to invite and submit cheerfully to the highest penalty that can be inflicted upon me for what in law is deliberate crime, and what appears to me to be the highest duty of a citizen. The only course open to you, the Judge and the assessors, is either to resign your posts and thus dissociate yourselves from evil, if you feel that the law you are called upon to administer is an evil, and that in reality I am innocent, or to inflict on me the severest penalty, if you believe that the system and the law you are assisting to administer are good for the people of this country, and that my activity is, therefore, injurious to the common weal.

Taken from **Mahatma, Vol. II,** *(1951) pp. 129–33, quoted in* **Selected Works of Mahatma Gandhi, Vol. VI. The Voice of Truth Part I Some Famous Speeches,** *pp. 14–24.*

QUESTION

With reference to its origin, purpose and content, discuss the value and limitations of Source 5.3 to historians researching the role of Gandhi in the Indian independence movement.

Although Gandhi was released from prison after two years for health reasons, he abstained from direct political activity until 1929. During this period, he abandoned any political action and withdrew to fast and to meditate. He called for a 'constructive programme' of local hand–weaving industries and social programmes to promote self-reliance. During this period, he also fought for greater rights for the untouchables and managed to negotiate some reforms to the caste system in the province of Travancore, allowing freedom of movement. By championing their cause, Gandhi encouraged social integration and, critically, sent out a signal that postcolonial India would be a modern state based on the values of social equality for all.

5.2 Why was the Salt March so significant?

Between 1922 and 1930 the national movement used meetings and constitutional methods to advance its aims. But it resumed a programme of civil disobedience after the failure of these. This started with the Salt March in 1930, an event which Bose and Jalal say 'had an electrifying effect across the subcontinent'.

The background to the Salt March

The exclusion of Indian representation on the Simon Commission in 1927 reunited the different factions in Congress once more. At its annual meeting in Calcutta in December 1928 Congress called on Britain to leave India by the end of 1929, failing which Congress threatened mass civil disobedience. A year later, at its 1929 meeting in Lahore, Congress adopted *Purna Swaraj* (complete independence) as its goal and nominated 26 January 1930 as 'Independence Day'. The working committee authorised Gandhi to initiate a civil disobedience campaign, leaving the details about the form that it should take to Gandhi himself. Gandhi was mindful of the violence which had ended the Non-Cooperation movement eight years earlier, and so he was cautious about starting another mass campaign which might get out of control and end in similar violence. Therefore, he carefully considered the strategies for the next campaign.

In January 1930 Gandhi sent a letter to the viceroy, outlining the problems facing the peasantry and containing an 11-point list of demands for change. One of these demands was the abolition of the salt tax and the government's monopoly of the production and sale of salt. When there was no response from the government, Gandhi chose this issue to be the focus for the launch of a new civil disobedience campaign.

Bates calls the decision to boycott the salt tax a 'brilliant choice of target, both tactically and symbolically'. According to Arnold, it 'provided the single issue focus in which *satyagraha* excelled'. Kulke and Rothermund suggest that Gandhi had 'engineered a perfect symbolic revolution: one that pitted the Indians against the British but did not create a conflict of Indian interests'. Everybody could participate in it and it had no socially divisive implications like a boycott of rents.

The production and sale of salt was a government monopoly and even the possession of salt which did not come from government sources was illegal. The tax proceeds from salt amounted to less than 4% of the government's revenue in 1929 to 1930, so it was not a major source of revenue. But it was a symbol with which everyone could identify: salt was crucial to life and was abundantly available but the law prevented people from using it freely. It could only be made under government licence and taxed. The salt tax affected the whole population of India, especially the poor. Many critics condemned the tax on a basic necessity of life as immoral, and the issue had been raised in the Imperial Legislative Assembly for many years, but nothing had been done to change it.

DISCUSSION POINT

All forms of taxation are usually unpopular, but most people accept that taxes are necessary to fund the running of a country. Which forms of taxation can be considered just and fair and which ones 'immoral'?

The march itself

As well as the astute choice of the salt tax as the target of protest action, Gandhi also planned the actual march to maximum effect. In March 1930, with a selected group of 78 volunteers, he set off from his *ashram* in Ahmedebad to walk to Dandi on the coast of Gujarat, a journey of 400 kilometres (240 miles). Covering about 20 kilometres a day, it took 24 days to complete the march.

The marchers were welcomed as heroes in countless rural villages along the way and thousands more joined the march. When it reached the coast, Gandhi symbolically picked up pieces of dried salt from the beach, clearly and publically breaking the law. The authorities made no attempt to stop this, so powerful was the message that the protest action sent out to millions of Indians, and to people around the world.

Figure 5.2: Gandhi leading the Salt March, 1930, with Sarojini Naidu, the poet and political activist, who was the first Indian woman to become president of Congress.

Gandhi's example was followed by thousands of people in other parts of India, where protests widened to include a boycott of alcohol (also a source of tax revenue for the government) and foreign cloth as well. The scale of the protests presented the authorities with an 'unprecedentedly well-orchestrated and non-violent campaign', according to Arnold.

Gandhi had planned that the next step in the campaign would be a march to the Dharasana salt works, close to Dandi. Although Gandhi himself was arrested before this took place, the march went ahead as planned in May 1930. The non-violent protestors were brutally struck down by Indian soldiers under British command.

The event received worldwide media coverage and helped to turn public opinion against British rule in India. Vithalbhai Patel, a Congress leader who had taken charge of the Civil Disobedience campaign after the arrest of Gandhi and Nehru, witnessed the scene and made the following statement (Source 5.4). Patel had been leader of the Imperial Legislative Council but had resigned his seat in support of the Civil Disobedience campaign.

SOURCE 5.4

All hope of reconciling India with the British Empire is lost for ever. I can understand any government's taking people into custody and punishing them for breaches of the law, but I cannot understand how any government that calls itself civilised could deal as savagely and brutally with non-violent, unresisting men as the British have this morning.

Quoted in Carey, John (ed). 1987. **Eyewitness to History**. *New York. Avon. p. 504.*

ACTIVITY

The Salt March was one of several historic marches that took place in the 1920s and 1930s. Others include Mussolini's 'March on Rome' in 1922, the Long March undertaken by the Chinese Communist Party in 1934–35, and the 'Jarrow Crusade' of unemployed workers from Jarrow to London in 1936. Research one of these and compare its significance with that of the Salt March.

Significance: Write two sentences to show the significance of each of these:

- the choice of the salt tax as the focus for the start of the Civil Disobedience campaign
- the worldwide publicity which the Salt March elicited
- the events at the Dharasana salt works on 21 May 1930.

The significance of the Salt March

Historians agree that the Salt March had immense symbolic significance in the struggle for independence in India. Metcalf and Arnold discuss the propaganda impact of the march in Sources 5.5 and 5.6.

SOURCE 5.5

The Salt March was a stroke of genius. Gandhi's frail figure, striding forward staff-in-hand to confront British imperialism over access to a basic commodity, fast became the focus of sympathetic attention not only throughout India but around the world, above all in the United States where the salt march first brought Gandhi to public attention. The powerful visual imagery of the march was further enhanced by its ranks of khadi-clad demonstrators, including for the first time marching women… More disciplined in its organization, if less apocalyptic in its expectations, than its predecessor a decade before, the civil disobedience movement spread rapidly throughout India.

Metcalf, Barbara and Metcalf, Thomas. 2006. **A Concise History of Modern India (Second Edition)**. *Cambridge. Cambridge University Press. pp. 191–2.*

SOURCE 5.6

If Indians were to demonstrate that the salt of India belonged to them, not to their foreign rulers, it was a symbolic way of declaring that they no longer owed them loyalty or recognised them as lawful rulers. Salt... was non-sectarian: it offended no religion but provided a moral issue on which all classes and communities, women and men, could unite...

The march caught the imagination of millions in India and abroad. A watching world was held in suspense while a 60-year-old man, clad in his loincloth and bamboo staff in hand, marched briskly towards his goal... With the government watching anxiously from the sidelines, Gandhi was able to win almost unfettered publicity for his cause, and, for all his personal aversion to modern technology, to exploit the vast potential of the media in India and abroad. Three Bombay cinema companies filmed the march, and newspaper reports, photographs and newsreels carried the story of his long march to freedom in words and pictures around the world. Ironically... Gandhi was as much a beneficiary as Hitler, Stalin and Mussolini of the rise of the mass media, of the new technologies of the radio and cinema, that enabled political leaders to appeal directly to the masses.

Arnold, David. 2001. **Gandhi.** *Harlow. Pearson Education. pp. 146–7.*

QUESTION

Compare and contrast what Sources 5.5 and 5.6 suggest about the propaganda value of the Salt March.

DISCUSSION POINT

Discuss how effectively Sources 5.5 and 5.6 make use of emotive language to influence the reader's attitude towards the march.

5.3 What happened during further Civil Disobedience campaigns?

The Salt March was only the first action in the Civil Disobedience campaigns carried out between 1930 and 1934. As the protests spread, the authorities reacted by arresting Gandhi and other Congress leaders as well as thousands of participants. Between March 1930 and March 1931 (when the campaign was temporarily suspended), 90 000 people were arrested and 100 killed by the police. The British reaction only served to damage their credibility as rulers of the subcontinent still further.

The nature of Civil Disobedience

Unlike the earlier Non-Cooperation movement, the Civil Disobedience campaign was organised at a regional rather than centralised level. The main targets were salt, foreign cloth and land taxes, but the protests were sometimes adapted to meet local circumstances and grievances. For example, in some provinces the campaign took the form of opposition to existing forest laws, which prevented local peasants from cutting down trees or grazing their animals in restricted areas. In this way a far wider range of people became involved in protest actions.

Even after Gandhi's arrest in May 1930, the Civil Disobedience campaign continued because Congress had better organisational structures in place than it had ten years before. It could also draw on the support of the middle classes and wealthier peasants, many of whom became dedicated activists and supporters of the campaign. Arnold notes that it was also more disciplined than the earlier campaign: 'In 1921–22 there had been a whiff of revolution in the air, the possibility of peasant insurrection, and a growing fear of uncontrolled change among the propertied classes. In 1930–31 India seemed bent on a far less dangerous course.'

Support for the Civil Disobedience campaign was initially helped by the Great Depression. Farmers were struggling to pay inflexible land taxes as prices for their crops fell, and so they were eager to join in rents boycotts. Traders were more willing to support *hartals* (work stoppages) during the economic slump than they would have been when business was good. However, as the effects of the Depression became worse, some of those who were worst affected were drawn to more radical acts of civil disobedience. Bates observes that as their situation became more desperate, they became more likely to resort to violence. There were bomb attacks, violent demonstrations and attempts to assassinate government officials, as well as attacks on the armoury in Chittagong and on the Writers' Building, the seat of government in Calcutta.

In some places the economic distress and political tensions led to communal attacks. According to Bose and Jalal, by the end of 1930 'the movement showed signs of flagging in some regions and a tendency towards increasing radicalism in others'. Increasingly alarmed by the violence, some moderate members of Congress, especially industrialists and business leaders who gave financial backing to the organisation, called on Gandhi to end the campaign.

The British authorities reacted to the campaign by arresting large numbers of people and introducing emergency laws that enabled them to detain suspects without laying charges against them. They also tried to ban any political activity throughout the country. By 1931, however, the economic effects of the campaign were beginning to take effect. Foreign cloth imports into India had halved and the British administration was affected by the loss of land revenue and reduced income from taxes on salt and alcohol. According to Arnold 'the economic impact of the movement was beginning seriously to alarm the British and to increase the pressure for a more conciliatory approach to the nationalist campaign'.

QUESTION

Examine why both Congress and the British authorities were willing to negotiate an end to the Civil Disobedience campaign by 1931.

The Gandhi-Irwin Pact and the second phase of the campaign

By 1931 it suited both Gandhi and the British authorities to reach an agreement. The result was the Gandhi-Irwin Pact of March 1931, in which Gandhi agreed to suspend the Civil Disobedience campaign.

Once again many in the nationalist movement were surprised and angry that Gandhi had once again called off a *satyagraha* campaign, as he had in 1919 and again in 1922. (You can refer back to the reactions to the Gandhi-Irwin Pact in Chapter 3.) However, after his attendance at the Second Round Table Conference in London and the lack of progress made there, Gandhi called for a resumption of the Civil Disobedience campaign in January 1932.

This time the British authorities clamped down heavily on the protests. They had taken the opportunity of the suspension of the campaign to increase their troops in India, and they introduced more repressive measures designed to suppress resistance quickly. These prevented the Civil Disobedience campaign from regaining its former momentum.

Gandhi was arrested on his arrival back in India and imprisoned without trial, and tens of thousands of Congress leaders and activists were imprisoned once again. As a result of this clampdown, the campaign had effectively been subdued by the end of 1932, although it was only formally called off in April 1934.

ACTIVITY

Compare the reasons why Gandhi called off the Non-Cooperation movement in 1922 and the Civil Disobedience campaign in 1931.

The significance of the Civil Disobedience campaign

Historians have different views about what was most significant about the Civil Disobedience campaign. In Source 5.7, Copland makes some comparisons between the Non-Cooperation movement of 1920–22 and the Civil Disobedience campaign inaugurated by the Salt March. Bates comments on the participation of different groups of people in the campaign in Source 5.8.

SOURCE 5.7

With this symbolic act of civil disobedience on the Arabian seashore, Congress began its second campaign to topple the Raj. Lasting in total over four years, the Civil Disobedience Movement was undoubtedly a more titanic event than its predecessor. It was substantially bigger, very much more intense, and affected far more of the subcontinent. Yet in one respect it compared unfavourably with the former movement. This time around there was little participation from Muslims.

Copland, Ian. 2001. **India 1885–1947: The Unmaking of an Empire.** *Harlow. Pearson Education. p.52.*

SOURCE 5.8

Part of the significance of the civil disobedience movement is that it involved many poor and marginal social groups, in substantial numbers, who had never previously joined in the nationalist struggle... [E]ven though the Muslim League was not involved, large numbers of Muslims joined in the Congress's civil disobedience campaign, especially in the North-West Frontier Province under the leadership of Abdul Ghaffar Khan, as well as, of course, in north India.

Another new departure in the 1930 civil disobedience movement was the involvement of significant numbers of women... Perhaps the highlight of women's participation was the nomination of **Sarojini Naidu** in May 1930 to lead the raid on the Dharasana salt works. She was imprisoned for this, but her role inspired many hundreds of women to take part in street demonstrations, and to join pickets attempting to persuade shopkeepers to trade only in *swadeshi* goods.

Bates, Crispin. 2007. **Subalterns and Raj: South Asia since 1600.** *London. Routledge. pp. 143–5.*

QUESTION

Compare and contrast the views expressed in Sources 5.7 and 5.8 about the significance of the Civil Disobedience campaign.

Sarojini Naidu (1879–1949):

Naidu was a poet and political activist who was educated at Kings College, London and Girton College, Cambridge. She became involved in the nationalist movement and was a supporter of Gandhi's Non-Cooperation movement. She became the first Indian woman to become president of Congress in 1925. She participated in the 1930 Salt March and was a leader of the attack on the Dharasana salt works. She attended the second Round Table Conference with Gandhi. She was actively involved in the Civil Disobedience campaign and served several terms in prison. After independence she became the first woman to be appointed as a state governor.

Figure 5.3: A significant feature of the Civil Disobedience campaign was the involvement of large numbers of women as marchers and speakers.

5.4 Why was the 'Quit India' campaign significant?

After the Civil Disobedience campaign was called off in 1934, the nationalist movement worked within the constitutional framework provided by Britain, by participating in the 1937 elections and taking office in the provincial legislatures. However, this cooperation came to an end in 1939 after Britain decided to involve India in the Second World War without any consultation with Indian political leaders.

In response to British policies and actions during the war, Congress embarked on its final campaign of non-cooperation in the nationalist struggle – the 'Quit India' campaign. (You will read more details about the impact of the Second World War on the situation in India in Chapter 7.) Historian Crispin Bates compares 'Quit India' with the previous campaigns in the nationalist struggle:

SOURCE 5.9

Quit India was the last of the three great nationwide anti-colonial nationalist satyagraha campaigns instigated by Gandhi – the civil disobedience campaign preceding it in the 1930 to 1932 period and the non-cooperation campaign from 1920 to 1922… While non-cooperation was urban-based, and supported mostly only by richer peasant groups in the countryside (especially in Gujarat), the civil disobedience campaign was far more widespread, involved many more poor peasants, and was radicalised by the impact of the depression. Quit India was the most radical and violent of them all, and was conspicuously supported by the poor and labouring classes, who were the most hard-hit by wartime inflation and food shortages.

Bates, Crispin. 2007. **Subalterns and Raj: South Asia since 1600.**
London. Routledge. pp. 159–160.

ACTIVITY

Draw up a three-column table to compare the three nationalist campaigns against British rule between 1920 and 1942. Use the information in Source 5.9, as well as in the rest of this chapter, to fill in categories such as: dates; causes; methods of protest; consequences; significance.

The background to the launch of the 'Quit India' campaign

After the viceroy's announcement that India was at war, the Congress ministries resigned in protest. The British government took over the government of the provinces once again, except in Punjab and Bengal, where Muslim coalition governments were in control. Although most (but not all) Congress politicians supported an Allied victory in the war, they did not want to commit India to full support for Britain without some commitment from Britain about a meaningful transfer of power. They were mindful of their disappointment after the First World War when loyalty and cooperation had not been rewarded.

In December 1941, Japan entered the war on Germany's side with a series of successful military strikes across East Asia. The Japanese rapidly overran European colonies in Indochina, the Malayan peninsula and Burma, bringing their armies to the border of India, and severely denting Britain's military and imperial prestige.

As a result, the British government urgently needed to gain the support of Indian leaders in the fight against Japan. Churchill, the British prime minister, was prompted too by pressure from the US government to reach conciliation with the Indian nationalist movement.

In March 1942, the British government sent Stafford Cripps, a member of the cabinet, to India to negotiate with the nationalist leaders. Cripps made the commitment to grant India independence but only after the war was over. In return, Congress was to commit itself fully to the British war effort.

Gandhi famously referred to the Cripps offer as a 'post-dated cheque on a failing bank' and Congress rejected the offer. It accepted that, in the long term, a Japanese victory in Asia would simply replace one form of colonial domination with another; however, the postponement of independence seemed unreasonable.

The 'Quit India' campaign

After it rejected the offer by the Cripps Commission, Congress began to campaign actively for immediate independence from Britain. In April 1942, Gandhi drafted a resolution, demanding that the British 'Quit India' immediately.

In August 1942, this resolution was adopted by Congress which also called for a mass campaign of civil disobedience to force Britain to leave. Britain reacted immediately by imprisoning Congress leaders, and closing down their offices and printing presses.

The arrest of Gandhi, Nehru and other Congress leaders did not stop the campaign but, in their absence, participants found that there was 'little or no guidance available and they were left to their own initiative', according to Bates.

Kulke and Rothermund, suggest that 'the younger nationalists who had resented Gandhi's restraining influence now unleashed a violent offensive'. This reaction which is sometimes referred to as the 'August Rising' or 'August Revolution', included many acts of violence:

* strikes by factory workers in Bombay, Calcutta and other cities, and attacks on police stations by militant workers and students
* rural uprisings, especially in the province of Bihar, where peasants attacked and destroyed symbols of British authority, such as police stations, post offices and administrative offices – in some districts British authority collapsed entirely
* acts of sabotage in which telegraph poles were pulled down and telegraph wires cut, railways stations attacked and railway lines and bridges destroyed
* non-violent but symbolic acts of defiance such as the placing of Congress flags on government buildings, as well as Women's 'Quit India' marches in Calcutta and other cities.

Nationalism and Independence in India (1919–1964)

Figure 5.4: Women as well as men participate in a 'Quit India' march in Bombay in 1942.

Is violence ever justified? Discuss whether one can draw a distinction between violence used to achieve liberation and violence used to maintain law and order.

The British reaction

Britain suppressed the rising quickly and ruthlessly, making use of additional troops stationed in India for the war. Martial law was imposed in places, demonstrators were machine-gunned from the air, and whole villages were destroyed. Within six weeks most of the revolution was over, although guerrilla activity continued in parts for some time. Over 1000 people were killed, and 3000 wounded, in British attempts to control the increasingly dangerous situation. As Britain's repressive policy took hold, almost 100 000 Indians, including Gandhi and Nehru, were detained without trial.

In prison, Gandhi embarked on another fast in protest against British accusations that he was responsible for the August Rising, but was released from prison in May 1944 because of his health. Most other Congress leaders remained in prison until the end of the war. This seriously affected Congress structures and organisation, leaving it in a weakened position at the end of the war.

KEY CONCEPTS QUESTION

Change and continuity: To what extent did the three mass-protest movements in the nationalist struggle (the Non-Cooperation movement, the Civil Disobedience campaign and the 'Quit India' campaign) represented change or continuity in Congress tactics?

The significance of the 'Quit India' campaign

Historians agree that the 'Quit India' campaign was a hugely important event but they have different interpretations of its significance. Bose and Jalal suggest that it forced the British government 'to fall back on its coercive foundations' and that it gave Congress 'an emotive issue around which to rejuvenate its electoral fortunes at war's end'.

Mridula Mukherjee describes it in heroic terms as a 'legendary struggle' in which 'the common people of the country demonstrated an unparalleled heroism and militancy'. Metcalf examines the nature of the protest actions in Source 5.10, as well as explaining how the campaign came to be viewed in future years. In Source 5.11, Bates, too, examines the nature of the struggle and also suggests reasons why the campaign has not received as much attention from historians as other nationalist campaigns.

SOURCE 5.10

Unlike the earlier Gandhian campaigns of 1920–22 and 1930–32, that of August 1942 was not a disciplined movement of civil disobedience. Rather, from the start, in part because the Congress leadership were peremptorily jailed, the movement erupted into uncoordinated violence, as low-level leaders, students, and other activists took matters into their own hands. Within days this August 'rising' had become the gravest threat to British rule in India since the revolt of 1857. The mystique of Gandhian non-violence has often obscured the unique character of this upheaval. Indeed, Gandhi's role in this movement has itself been the subject of controversy…

Nevertheless, in part perhaps because it was the last mass movement of the colonial era – for independence came five years later without further Non-Cooperation – 'Quit India' took on for many, as they looked back in later years, a mystic stature as a remembered moment of idealism and sacrifice.

Metcalf, Barbara and Metcalf, Thomas. 2006. **A Concise History of Modern India Second Edition.** *Cambridge. Cambridge University Press. pp. 205–7.*

Theory of Knowledge

Historical interpretation

Re-read the information in Chapter 1 about the historiography of the nationalist struggle in India. Into which group of historians would you classify Crispin Bates? What does Source 5.11 suggest about the selection of information and the writing of history? What is the difference between selection and bias?

SOURCE 5.11

Quit India was... by far the most popular, radical, and violent of the anti-colonial campaigns. However, for many years the events between August 1942 and early 1943 remained veiled in obscurity; and little was written about it in depth until more than forty years later when secret documents became available and subaltern and other historians began to consider the topic...

Quit India was... very much a movement of the subaltern classes. No political leader or party could directly take credit for it, and therefore few national leaders have discussed it in detail in their memoirs. The Gandhians least of all wished to draw attention to an uprising that was so very un-Gandhian in its form and content. The British on the other hand were unwilling to report events that constituted the surest proof that the Indian independence movement was a mass campaign founded on profound discontent, especially since British over-reaction and repression itself appears to have provoked much of the violence... Both British colonialist and Indian nationalist accounts have therefore paid slight attention to the actual events of 1942: despite the fact that the Quit India struggle possibly had more impact on the British imperial machine than any previous satyagraha, demonstrated more activism at a grass-roots level than any other anti-colonial campaign, and played an important part in the British decision eventually to leave India at the end of the war.

Bates, Crispin. 2007. **Subalterns and Raj: South Asia since 1600.** *London. Routledge. pp. 164–5.*

ACTIVITY

'Although it was not the kind of disciplined and non-violent protest that Gandhi had always championed, the Indian National Congress benefitted from the Quit India campaign'. Using the quotations and sources from different historians above, as well as your own knowledge, to what extent do you agree with this statement?

Paper 3 exam practice

Question

To what extent was the Civil Disobedience campaign of 1930–32 more effective than the Non Cooperation movement or the 'Quit India' campaign in the nationalist struggle for independence in India?
[15 marks]

Skill

Writing an introductory paragraph

Examiner's tips

Once you have planned your answer to a question (as described in Chapters 2 and 3), you should be able to begin writing a clear introductory paragraph. This needs to set out your main line of argument and to outline *briefly* the key points you intend to make (and support with relevant and precise own knowledge) in the main body of your essay.

Remember: 'To what extent…?' and 'How far…?' questions clearly require analysis of opposing arguments – and a judgement. If, after writing your plan, you think you will be able to make a clear final judgement, it's a good idea to state in your introductory paragraph what overall line of argument or judgement you intend to make.

Depending on the wording of the question, you may also find it useful to define in your introductory paragraph what you understand by **key terms** – such as 'civil disobedience', non-cooperation' and 'Quit India'.

For this question, you should:

- clarify the differences between the three campaigns
- evaluate the effectiveness of each
- write a concluding paragraph that sets out your judgement about whether the Civil Disobedience campaign was more effective than the other two.

You need to cover the following aspects of each campaign:

- **Context:** What was happening in India at the time?
- **Aims:** What were the specific aims of the campaign?
- **Methods:** What forms of protest were used?
- **Support:** How much support was there for the campaign? Who participated in it?
- **Effectiveness:** What was the impact of the campaign? Did it achieve its goals?

Setting out this approach in your introductory paragraph will help you focus on the demands of the question. Remember to refer back to your introduction after every couple of paragraphs in your main answer.

Common mistakes

A common mistake (which might suggest to an examiner that the candidate has not thought deeply about what is required) is to fail to write an introductory paragraph at all. This is often done by students who rush into writing *before* analysing the question and making a plan.

The result may well be that they give a detailed narrative description of each campaign without evaluating its effectiveness or without comparing it with the other two. Even if the answer is full of detailed and accurate own knowledge, this will *not* answer the question, and so will not score highly.

Sample student introductory paragraph

The Civil Disobedience Campaign of 1930–32 was one of three great protest campaigns against British rule by the nationalist movement in India. The Non-Cooperation movement of 1920–22 involved a boycott of British cloth, schools and other institutions and a refusal to participate in elections and official ceremonies. The Civil Disobedience campaign of 1930–32 started symbolically with a refusal to pay the salt tax but grew to involve many other forms of protest as well. The 'Quit India' campaign of 1942 called for immediate independence and involved strikes, sabotage and a rural uprising. Support for the Civil Disobedience campaign was more widespread than it was for the other two and a wide range of people from different social classes participated in it.

It also received international media attention and resulted in falling tax revenues and imports from Britain. So in this sense it was more effective than the other two, although it did not achieve its objective of getting the British to grant immediate self-government.

EXAMINER'S COMMENT

This introduction focuses on the essay question and demonstrates a good understanding of the topic. It sets out a clear and logical plan, and shows how the candidate intends to structure the answer. It suggests that the candidate has sound knowledge of the differences between the three protest movements. Although the last sentence leaves some doubt as to whether the candidate intends to argue that the Civil Disobedience campaign was not all that effective, it also shows an understanding of the complexity of the issue. This indicates that the answer – if it remains analytical and is well-supported – is likely to be a high-scoring one.

Activity

In this chapter, the focus is on writing a useful introductory paragraph. Using the information from this chapter and any other sources of information available to you, write introductory paragraphs for **at least two** of the following Paper 3 practice questions.

Remember to refer to the simplified Paper 3 mark scheme in Chapter 10.

Paper 3 practice questions

1 Discuss the extent to which Muslim participation in the Non-Cooperation movement of 1920–22 was significant.

2 'Gandhi's decision to call off the Non-Cooperation movement in 1922 was a pragmatic and calculated decision rather than a blunder, as some historians have portrayed it.' To what extent do you agree with this statement?

3 Evaluate the significance of the Salt March in the independence struggle against British rule in India.

4 Compare and contrast the reactions of the British authorities to the three nationalist campaigns between 1920 and 1942.

5 Discuss the reasons for and consequences of the 'Quit India' campaign of 1942.

6 | The growth of Muslim separatism

Introduction

Although Muslim emperors had ruled India for many centuries, in colonial India Muslims lost their power and influence. They formed barely 20% of the population and feared for their future in a Hindu majority state. These concerns led to the emergence of 'Muslim separatism', the idea that Muslims were a threatened minority which needed protection. In the 1930s, this view developed into the 'Two Nation' theory, the idea that India was a land of two separate nations. This concept was behind the proposal for the creation of Pakistan as a separate state for India's Muslims, support for which was confirmed in the 1940 Lahore Resolution. This chapter examines the reasons for the growth of Muslim separatism, the development of the 'Two Nation' theory and the significance of the Lahore Resolution.

Timeline

1858 British government abolishes the Mughal Empire

1881 First official census in British India

1906 **Oct:** Simla Deputation

Dec: Establishment of the All-India Muslim League

1916 **Dec:** Lucknow Pact between Muslim League and Congress

1920–22 Non-Cooperation movement

1927–29 Unsuccessful attempts to reach compromise agreement between Congress and Muslim League

1930 **Dec:** Muhammad Iqbal's call for the creation of a separate Muslim homeland

1933 Chaudhri Rahmat Ali's proposal for the creation of 'Pakistan'

1937 **Feb:** Provincial elections

1937–39 Congress ministries spark Muslim fears of Hindu dominance; growing support for Muslim League

1940 **Mar:** Lahore Resolution

KEY QUESTIONS
- What was the background to the growth of Muslim separatism?
- When and how did the 'Two Nation' theory develop?
- How significant was the Lahore Resolution?

Overview

- The growth of Muslim separatism had significant political implications, and led ultimately to the partition of India and the creation of a separate Muslim state in Pakistan.
- The Hindu and Muslim religions, culture and traditions had existed and developed side by side in India for many centuries, sometimes harmoniously and sometimes not. However, there were growing tensions between the two communities in the late 19th century.
- Muslims faced two distinct disadvantages in British India: they formed only about 20% of the population and they were reluctant to accept the English system of education which gave access to influential positions in colonial society.
- They formed the All-India Muslim League to represent and protect Muslim interests. A key aim was to secure constitutional protection in the form of separate electorates as well as reserved seats for Muslims in any future democratic reforms.
- There was initial cooperation between the League and the Indian National Congress, but growing communal tensions in the 1920s and a failure to agree on the issue of separate representation led to a rift between the two organisations.
- During the 1930s the idea that Muslims were a separate community developed into the idea that India was a land of two nations – one Hindu and the other Muslim – and a scholar coined the name 'Pakistan' for the latter. But the concept did not initially receive political support from the Muslim League.

- The poor showing of the Muslim League in the 1937 elections revealed the electoral dangers that Muslims faced as part of a single state. After this the League worked hard to unite Muslims throughout India and promote the recognition of Muslim rights. Their determination was strengthened by fears of Hindu dominance after the success of Congress in the elections.
- At its annual conference in Lahore in 1940, the League formally declared its support for the notion that India was a country of 'two nations' and called for the creation of a separate Muslim state. This became known as the Lahore Resolution (or the Pakistan Resolution).

6.1 What was the background to the growth of Muslim separatism?

The Hindu and Muslim religions, culture and traditions had existed and developed side by side in India for many centuries. In some parts there had been intermarriage and conversion between the two communities and they shared the same language, but in others there were differences and tensions. These differences became more acute in the late 19th century. In the 20th century, Muslims increasingly started to see themselves as a separate 'nation' and this had significant political implications for India. It led ultimately to the partition of India and the creation of a separate Muslim state in Pakistan.

Indian Muslims, however, were not a united and homogeneous community. Although they shared the same religion, there were ethnic, regional, class and language differences among them. Some were descended from the original Arab, Afghan, Turkish and Persian invaders of India, while the majority of Indian Muslims were those whose ancestors had been Hindu converts to Islam. Many of the landowners and better educated élite came from the former group, while many of the latter were peasant farmers, labourers, traders and skilled artisans. According to historians Ian Talbot and Gurharpal Singh, it was from the former group (mainly in the area known as the United Provinces or UP) that the main supporters of Muslim separatism came because 'they were the ones who stood to lose most from a future Hindu-dominated India'.

The position of Muslims in colonial India

When the British took over the government of India in 1858, they disbanded the Muslim empire of the Mughal emperors. As a result of this, according to the Pakistani scholar, Akbar S. Ahmed, Indian Muslims 'lost their kingdom, their Mughal Empire, their emperor, their language, their culture, their capital city of Delhi, and their sense of self'.

According to the American political scientist, Stephen Philip Cohen, in British India 'the fundamental political, social and economic structure of India was reordered in a fashion that gave the Muslims little social space and no political power'. Cohen goes on to suggest that Hindus adapted more quickly than Muslims to the new political and social order of the British Raj.

Copland notes in particular the issue of education: 'Having taken to the new education more slowly and reluctantly than their Hindu equivalents, Muslim élites in north India found themselves increasingly muscled out of lucrative and influential bureaucratic jobs.' Talbot and Singh see clear links between this and the growth of Muslim separatism: 'The Muslims' relative educational backwardness was to be a major factor in shaping the emergence of a separatist Muslim political platform and was to gain further strength in communities which experienced relative decline in colonial India and also possessed memories of former rule.' They go on to suggest that these sentiments were especially strong among the Urdu-speaking Muslim élite in the United Provinces (UP) who formed the 'backbone of the demand for Pakistan', even though they formed only 15% of the population of UP.

DISCUSSION POINT

To what extent would a Western education be an advantage to people in colonial societies?

Another disadvantage of which Indian Muslims were acutely aware was the fact that they formed a minority. The first formal census undertaken by the British was in 1881. This showed that Muslims constituted about 20% of the population, far smaller than the Hindu majority which was 75%.

The size of the Muslim minority varied from province to province, with the largest numbers in the north-west and the north-east. The British used the census as the basis for classifying the population into rigidly defined religious communities. Historians see the division of India into separate and sometimes hostile communities as being partly due to British policies.

SOURCE 6.1

Having unified India, the British set into motion contrary forces. Fearing the unity of the Indian people to which their own rule had contributed, they followed the classic imperial policy of divide and rule. The diverse and divisive features of Indian society and polity were heightened to promote cleavages among the people and to turn province against province, caste against caste, class against class, Hindus against Muslims, and the princes and landlords against the nationalist movement. They succeeded in their endeavours to a varying extent, which culminated in India's Partition.

Chandra Bipan, Mukherjee, Mridula and Mukherjee, Aditya. 2000. **India after Independence: 1947–2000.** *New Delhi. Penguin. p. 18.*

QUESTION

What is meant by a policy of 'divide and rule'? Explain how and why the British used this policy in India.

Nationalism and Independence in India (1919–1964)

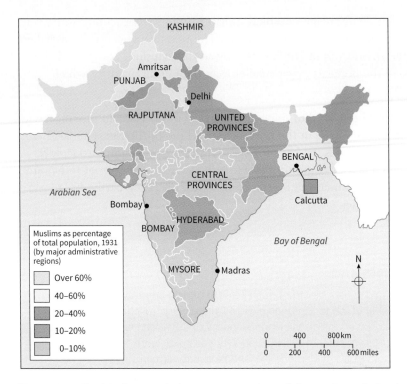

Figure 6.1: The Muslim population as a percentage of the total population in different parts of India in 1931.

QUESTION

Using the information in Figure 6.1, to what extent do you think it is surprising that the leaders of the Muslim separatist movement came from the United Provinces?

Under autocratic colonial rule the population numbers were not that important, but once Britain contemplated constitutional reforms which would give Indians representation in legislatures and government, the numbers became highly significant. Cohen examines one view of the implications of British policies towards Indian Muslims in Source 6.2.

SOURCE 6.2

Many Pakistani scholars and publicists see the dislocation of the Muslim community after 1857 as the *original* source of Muslim discontent, and they attribute it to malevolent anti-Muslim sentiments of the British. By favouring Hindus in education, administration, and other spheres, they tilted against Muslims culturally, economically, and politically. And by promoting democratic institutions, liberal British authorities inadvertently bestowed a permanent minority status on Muslims in greater India, as they would always be outnumbered by the larger Hindu community.

Cohen, Stephen Philip. 2004. **The Idea of Pakistan.** *New Delhi. Oxford University Press. p. 24.*

QUESTION

Source 6.2 suggests that the British had 'malevolent anti-Muslim sentiments' and that they 'favoured' Hindus. To what extent would you consider this a biased view? Discuss which other sources you would need to consult to reach a balanced conclusion about this issue.

There were tensions between Hindus and Muslims regarding their religious practices and festivals and these tensions sometimes spilled over into violence. The growth of Hindu revivalist movements in the 1890s was a matter of special concern to Muslims and a source of friction. Hindu organisations such as the Arya Samaj adopted a militant approach by openly criticising Islam and actively trying to win converts to Hinduism.

As cows were considered sacred to Hindus, they formed 'Cow Protection Societies', a move that created conflict with Muslim butchers and Muslim religious practices which at times required the ritual slaughter of animals. Hindu militants also pushed for Hindi to replace Urdu (the language spoken by many Muslims in north India) as the main language for administrative records. Threatened by this militant Hinduism, Muslims formed their own organisations to consolidate their position and protect their community, religion and language.

Often the tensions between the two communities ended in communal violence. Historian Ian Copland comments on the effects of this: 'By the end of the century, Hindu–Muslim relations had become so soured by this deadly roundabout of blood-letting, grief and revenge that it would have taken a mighty concerted effort by the leaders of the two communities to repair the breach. This effort was never forthcoming.'

The role of the Muslim League

Muslims could not alter their numerical disadvantage in British India so they looked for ways to protect their interests by showing that they were a separate community with its own needs and aspirations. This was the background to the Simla Deputation in October 1906, when representatives of the Muslim community met the British viceroy at Simla and stressed the view that Muslims were a distinct community which needed separate representation for its own protection. They received assurances from the viceroy that Britain would safeguard the political interests of Muslims in any future constitutional reforms.

Although the Indian National Congress claimed to be secular and represent all Indians regardless of religion, several leading Muslims discounted this claim. The most influential of them was **Saiyid Ahmad Khan**. Apart from seeing Congress as an essentially Hindu organisation, he also opposed its support for democratic constitutional reform, which he believed would undermine the position of the Muslim élite. Partly on account of his influence, support for the concept of a separate organisation to represent and uphold Muslim interests began to grow.

Saiyid Ahmad Khan (1817–1898):

Saiyid Ahmad Khan was a reformist and moderniser who saw advantages for the Muslim community in extending education, especially Western knowledge and culture, and in promoting loyalty to Britain. He established schools and, in 1875, the Aligarh Oriental College, which attracted the sons of the Muslim élite. It developed into the Aligarh Muslim University, which later produced the scholars and leaders of the Pakistan movement. In 1888 he was knighted by the British government. Although he promoted the concepts of a distinct Muslim identity and a separate status for Muslims, he never actually advocated the creation of a separate Muslim state. However, his ideas were later taken up by supporters of this movement.

In December 1906, Muslim leaders meeting in Dhaka formed the Muslim League to represent Muslim interests. Its main aim was to secure constitutional protection for Muslims in the form of separate electorates and reserved seats. The assurances which the Simla Deputation had received bore fruit in the Morley-Minto reforms of 1909 which provided for Indian representation in central and provincial legislative councils. Muslims were given separate representation – separate electorates and reserved seats – to ensure that the minority Muslims would have a voice in these councils. This established the principle of separate communal representation and shaped future political developments.

Early relations between the Muslim League and Congress

Initially the Muslim League was dominated by conservative pro-British loyalists but later a younger radical group, the Young Party, emerged. It was more willing to seek an alliance with Congress in a broad nationalist alliance to press for self-government. A key figure in breaching the divide was Mohammad Ali Jinnah, who was a member of Congress as well as the League. In 1915 and 1916, the annual meetings of Congress and the League were held in the same city – Bombay in 1915 and Lucknow in 1916 – which facilitated greater cooperation between the two organisations.

Nationalism and Independence in India (1919–1964)

In 1916, Congress and the Muslim League signed an historic agreement – the Lucknow Pact. In it they agreed that Muslims would have a fixed proportion of seats in any future Indian parliament, and extra seats in areas in which Muslims were in a minority. This in effect meant that Muslim concerns about separate representation to safeguard their interests had been addressed. As a result, Muslims felt no need to promote the concept of separation any further at this stage.

The high point of Hindu-Muslim cooperation came with Gandhi's support for the Khalifat movement and the latter's substantial participation in the Non-Cooperation movement. The common aim shared by the two movements was their opposition to British imperialism. However, this collaboration did not include the Muslim League, many of whose leaders did not support the Khalifat movement. The alliance between Congress and the Khalifat movement came to an end after Gandhi's suspension of the Non-Cooperation movement in 1922, and Turkey's decision to establish a secular republic, thus ending the whole purpose behind the Khalifat movement. Nevertheless, some links between Congress and the Khalifat movement remained. For example, the Khalifat leader Muhammad Ali was elected as president of Congress in 1923. In Source 6.3 he comments on the conflicting sense of identity he felt as a Muslim in India in the 1920s:

SOURCE 6.3

I have a culture, a polity, an outlook on life – a complete synthesis which is Muslim. Where God commands I am a Muslim first, a Muslim second, and a Muslim last, and nothing but a Muslim... But where India is concerned, where India's freedom is concerned, where the welfare of India is concerned, I am an Indian first, an Indian second, an Indian last, and nothing but an Indian.

Quoted in Bose, Sugata and Jalal, Ayesha. 1998. **Modern South Asia: History, Culture, Political Economy.** *London. Routledge. p. 143.*

What, according to Source 6.3, was the dilemma facing Muslims in India at that time?

The growth of communal tensions in the 1920s

A disturbing development in the mid-1920s was the growth of tension and violence between religious communities. This was partly due to the emergence of a politicised form of Hinduism, called *Hindutwa*, which promoted an anti-Muslim message. A political party which supported this stance was the Hindu Mahasabha which criticised efforts by Congress to integrate Muslims as members, as well as its willingness to engage in dialogue with the Muslim League. Although the Mahasabha remained weak in the 1920s, Congress leaders were always mindful of the attraction of these ideas to right-wing members of Congress and this in turn influenced decisions.

According to Copland, some Congress politicians 'insisted on playing the Hindu card at the polls in order to checkmate the potential appeal of the Mahasabha'. *Hindutwa* – the promotion of Hindu values and the creation of a state modelled on Hindu beliefs and culture – was also the aim of a militant Hindu nationalist group, the Rashtriya Swayamsevak Sangh (RSS), which was formed in 1925. Tensions between the two communities were heightened in some regions by economic factors: in many – but certainly not all – provinces, many of the landlords and traders were Hindu; while the Muslims were peasant farmers or poor workers.

Use the internet and any other sources available to you to find out more about *Hindutwa*. Discuss whether it was a political or cultural movement, how strong the support for it was in the 1920s, and whether it is still a significant force in India today.

Nationalism and Independence in India (1919–1964)

Not all Muslims had supported the Non-Cooperation movement. Many, like Jinnah, rejected the activism involved and preferred to use constitutional methods to bring about change. As a result, he resigned from Congress. Many Muslims were also uncomfortable with Gandhi's style of leadership. In his biography of Gandhi, David Arnold examines his role in the rise of Muslim separatism in Source 6.4:

SOURCE 6.4

The rise of Muslim separatism had many causes, not a few of them predating Gandhi's rise to all-India leadership, but there is no doubting that, despite his inclusive understanding of Indian nationalism and his frequently professed faith in Hindu-Muslim unity, he unwittingly contributed to it. Gandhi appeared, in many eyes, an increasingly Hindu figure during the 1920s and 30s – in the manner of his speech and dress, in the religious symbolism he employed, and in the way in which, for example at the time of the 'epic fast' in 1932, he presented himself as a leader with a special responsibility for the Hindu community. Despite having many Muslim associates, and despite his evident differences with the Hindu right, he seemed to many Muslims to epitomise the Congress as an essentially Hindu organisation. Moreover, he could not shed his basic conviction, expressed in *Hind Swaraj* ['*Indian Home Rule*', a book written by Gandhi] in 1909, that India was not just a nation but a civilisation, and that essentially an ancient Hindu civilisation, into which other religions and cultures had over time been assimilated. There was no room within this civilisation for any other 'nation'.

Arnold, David. 2001. **Gandhi.** *Harlow. Pearson Education. p. 217.*

QUESTION

How, according to Source 6.4, did Gandhi 'unwittingly contribute' to the rise of Muslim separatism? With reference to its origin and purpose, assess the value and limitations of this source as evidence of Gandhi's role in the rise of Muslim separatism.

Despite the differences that had emerged, Jinnah continued to try to promote cooperation between Congress and the League. In 1927, the League offered to end its support for separate electorates in exchange for an agreement that Muslims could fill one-third of the seats on the Central Legislative Council.

Some historians suggest that this proposal represented a significant attempt at cooperation and reconciliation by the Muslim League. However, under pressure from Hindu nationalists, Congress turned it down. Instead it accepted the Nehru Report which rejected separate electorates for Muslim voters, a reversal of the agreement reached in the Lucknow Pact. The League made another attempt to reach an agreement with Congress in 1929 which was also rejected by Congress. Jinnah's attempts to promote a compromise solution between the viewpoints of the two organisations had failed.

After this, there was very little cooperation between the League and Congress. Jinnah temporarily retired from politics and moved to London to work as a lawyer, referring to the situation as the 'parting of the ways'. However, in Source 6.5, Metcalf suggests that, although the concept of a separate Muslim identity had emerged, there was, as yet, no proposal for a separate Muslim 'nation'.

SOURCE 6.5

The distrust was never subsequently to be overcome. The way forward, however, as the Muslim leaders wrangled among themselves, was for a long time unclear. They never sought to institute Islamically based policies, but rather to identify strategies to protect the interests of India's Muslims. Their disagreements turned upon the most effective constitutional means to secure that end. There was, in those years, no vision of a separate Muslim state.

Metcalf, Barbara and Metcalf, Thomas. 2006. **A Concise History of Modern India Second Edition.** *Cambridge: Cambridge University Press. p. 191.*

QUESTION

What message is conveyed by Source 6.5?

ACTIVITY

Create a diagram to summarise the different factors that contributed to the growth of Muslim separatism before 1930.

6.2 When and how did the 'Two Nation' theory develop?

During the 1930s the idea that Muslims were a separate community developed into the idea that India was a land of two nations – one Hindu and the other Muslim. This came to have significant political consequences.

The proposal for a Muslim 'homeland'

The first proposal for the practical application of the 'Two Nation' theory – a separate Muslim political entity – was made in 1930 by the Urdu poet and philosopher, Muhammad Iqbal. At a session of the Muslim League in Allahabad, he spoke about a Muslim 'homeland' in the north-west of India, which would still be part of a united India. His poetry and writings drew support for the concept of a separate state, although at this stage it was not part of the political agenda of the Muslim League. According to Bose and Jalal, Iqbal's ideas 'were ignored by most Muslim politicians but gained some momentum in the informal arenas of politics through the medium of the popular press'.

Stephen Philip Cohen, an American political scientist, explains his view of the significance of Iqbal's role.

SOURCE 6.6

Iqbal turned the idea of a separate homeland for India's Muslims into a mass movement, drawing intellectuals, professionals, and community leaders into the fold. He heightened community pride – the community being defined as the Muslims of India – and credibly argued that this community desired and needed a separate state in which it could establish a South Asian counterpart of the great Islamic empires of Persia and Arabia. For Iqbal, this state – he did not call it Pakistan – would not only solve India's Hindu-Muslim puzzle, it would awaken and recreate Islam… At first Iqbal did not advocate a separate country, but one or more distinct components in a federated India; if that was not possible, he declared in his 1930 presidential address to the Muslim League, then Indian Muslims should seek a completely separate state via 'concerted political effort'.

Cohen, Stephen Philip. 2004. The Idea of Pakistan. *New Delhi. Oxford University Press. p. 30.*

QUESTION

What, according to Source 6.6, was the significance of Muhammad Iqbal's role in the development of the 'Two Nation' theory?

In 1933 Chaudhri Rahmat Ali, an Indian student studying at Cambridge, together with a group of fellow Indian students, came up with a plan for a federation of ten Muslim states which he called Pakistan. The name means 'land of the pure' in the Urdu language, and was also an acronym of the names of the Muslim-majority provinces of Punjab, the Afghan border area (the North West Frontier Province), Kashmir, Sind and Baluchistan. However, at this stage there was no active political support in India for this idea which was instead 'disdainfully ignored by the Muslim political leadership', according to Copland.

The impact of the 1937 elections

The events that changed the attitude of the Muslim League leadership and had significant political repercussions were the 1937 elections and the subsequent policies of Congress provincial legislatures. Although the League had fared badly in the elections, Jinnah hoped that it could form part of coalition governments in the provinces that had large Muslim minorities. Having won the elections so convincingly, however, Congress was not prepared to compromise with the League in this way. It turned down Jinnah's offer of cooperation, although it did appoint some of its own Muslim members to provincial governments. Metcalf observes that 'this high-handed treatment did not reassure Muslim opinion'. In some provinces, Muslim leaders complained of favouritism towards Hindus, and the promotion of Hindu symbols and the Hindi language, although this was never Congress policy. The period of Congress rule from 1937 to 1939, therefore, alienated many Muslims.

Figure 6.2: A meeting of members of the All-India Muslim League in 1938.

These developments caused the League to strengthen its efforts to gain a mass following. Using the slogan 'Islam in danger' as a rallying call, Jinnah tried to unite all Muslims within the League. According to Bose and Jalal, 'Jinnah's resort to religion had nothing to do with his ideological convictions. This was the most practical way of mobilising a community divided by politics but defined by religion.' Support for the idea that India's Muslims were a distinct nation entitled to a separate state gained ground, especially as the election results had revealed the electoral dangers that Muslims faced as part of a single state. Copland explains the change in attitude by the League towards the 'Two Nations' concept in Source 6.7:

SOURCE 6.7

By the end of the decade, however, the League's high command had substantially modified its position on the homeland issue. Perhaps the major reason was Congress intransigence. It is easy to see why Congress after the [1937] elections declined to take up Jinnah's power-sharing offer. The two parties differed on many issues, especially land reform; the League was a communal party and the Congress ostensibly a secular one; holding comfortable majorities in six provinces, Congress did not need the League's support to form a government. Nevertheless, with the benefit of hindsight, one can see that this was a strategic mistake. Besides, the negotiations were badly handled by the Congress leadership. Instead of simply rejecting the offer, the Congress Working Committee came back with a counter-offer: that the League's legislators should resign and join the Congress. This was tantamount to telling the League to disband. Jinnah never forgot or forgave this humiliation.

Copland, Ian. 2001. India 1885–1947: The Unmaking of an Empire. Harlow. Pearson Education. p. 61.

Theory of Knowledge

Hindsight and the writing of history

Discuss the advantages and disadvantages of hindsight to historians when they write about the past. To what extent is it difficult to understand the significance of an event that you are witnessing?

Nationalism and Independence in India (1919–1964)

Cause and consequence: Examine the causes and consequences of the rift between the Muslim League and Congress in the late 1930s.

Not all Muslims supported the call for a 'Two Nation' solution. Some continued to support the goal of a united India, as the statement by Maulana Azad, the Muslim president of Congress in 1940, in Source 6.8 shows:

SOURCE 6.8

I am proud of being an Indian. I am proud of the indivisible unity that is Indian nationality... Islam has now as great a claim on the soil of India as Hinduism. If Hinduism has been the religion of the people here for several thousands of years, Islam has also been their religion for a thousand years. Just as a Hindu can say with pride that he is an Indian and follows Hinduism, so also we can say with equal pride that we are Indians and follow Islam.

Statement by Maulana Azad, president of the Indian National Congress, 1940, quoted in Metcalf, Barbara and Metcalf, Thomas. 2006. A Concise History of Modern India Second Edition. *Cambridge. Cambridge University Press. p. 198.*

Compare and contrast the views expressed in Sources 6.3 and 6.8. Discuss how supporters of the 'Two Nation' theory would have reacted to these statements by Muhammad Ali and Maulana Azad, and also how a supporter of *Hindutwa* would respond.

Theory of Knowledge

Generalisations and stereotyping

What can we learn from the statements by Muhammad Ali (Source 6.3) and Maulana Azad (Source 6.8) about the dangers of making generalisations and creating stereotypes when we write about history?

6.3 How significant was the Lahore Resolution?

The outbreak of the Second World War in 1939 created political opportunities for the Muslim League. When the provincial Congress ministries resigned, the League declared it to be a 'day of deliverance' from the 'tyranny, oppression and injustice' of Congress rule. The League resolved to support the British war effort and this strengthened its position in future constitutional talks.

Figure 6.3: Delegates at the meeting of the All-India Muslim League in Lahore, 1940. Jinnah is in the centre of the front row.

Nationalism and Independence in India (1919–1964)

In March 1940, at its annual conference held in Lahore, the Muslim League formally passed a resolution declaring its support for the notion that India was a country of 'two nations' and called for the creation of a separate Muslim state. This became known as the Lahore Resolution (or the Pakistan Resolution), although the name 'Pakistan' was not actually used in the document.

SOURCE 6.9

It is the considered view of this Session of the All-India Muslim League that no constitutional plan would be workable in this country or acceptable to the Muslims unless it is designed on the following basic principles, viz., that geographically contiguous units are demarcated into regions which should be so constituted, with such territorial readjustments as may be necessary, that the areas in which the Muslims are numerically in a majority as in the North-Western and Eastern zones of India should be grouped to constitute 'Independent States' in which the constituent units shall be autonomous and sovereign.

…[A]dequate, effective and mandatory safeguards should be specifically provided in the Constitution for minorities in these units and in the regions for the protection of their religious, cultural, economic, political, administrative and other rights and interests, in consultation with them; and in other parts of India where the Muslims are in a minority, adequate, effective and mandatory safeguards should be specifically provided in the Constitution for them and other Minorities for the protection of their religious, cultural, economic, political, administrative and other rights and interests in consultation with them.

Extract from the 'Lahore Resolution' passed at the Lahore Session of the All-India Muslim Congress, March 1940, from Gwyer, M. and Appadorai, A. (eds). 1957, **Speeches and Documents on the Indian Constitution 1921–47 Volume II**, *Bombay, Oxford University Press, p. 443. Quoted in Copland, Ian. 2001.* **India 1885–1947. The Unmaking of an Empire.** *Harlow. Pearson Education. p. 109.*

Jinnah's presidential address at the Lahore session of the All–India Muslim League is seen as a highly significant statement. By depicting Hindus and Muslims as two distinct and irreconcilable communities, it provided justification for the 'Two Nation' theory:

SOURCE 6.10

If the British Government is really in earnest and sincere to secure the peace and happiness of the people of this sub-continent, the only course open to us all is to allow the major nations separate homelands by dividing India into 'autonomous national states.'

The Hindus and Muslims belong to two different religious philosophies, social customs, and literature[s]. They neither intermarry nor interdine together, and indeed they belong to two different civilisations which are based mainly on conflicting ideas and conceptions. Their perspectives on life, and of life, are different. To yoke together two such nations under a single state, one as a numerical minority and the other as a majority, must lead to growing discontent, and final destruction of any fabric that may be so built up for the government of such a state.

Muslim India cannot accept any constitution which must necessarily result in a Hindu majority government. Hindus and Muslims brought together under a democratic system forced upon the minorities can only mean Hindu Raj.

Address by Quaid-i-Azam Mohammad Ali Jinnah at Lahore Session of Muslim League, March, 1940 from Islamabad: Directorate of Films and Publishing, Ministry of Information and Broadcasting, Government of Pakistan, Islamabad, 1983, pp. 5–23.

185

Change and continuity: To what extent did the Lahore Resolution represent change rather than continuity in the policies of the Muslim League?

Writing from a revisionist perspective, Ayesha Jalal argues in *The Sole Spokesman: Jinnah, the Muslim League and the demand for Pakistan* (1985), that Jinnah did not envisage Pakistan as a separate state at this stage, but was using it as a bargaining tactic to secure a better position for Muslims in a postwar settlement. Metcalf, in *A Concise History of Modern India* notes, however, that the idea of a separate Pakistan became 'a compelling attraction for fearful Muslims' and also for the British who wanted Muslim support during the war.

With reference to its origin, purpose and content, assess the value and limitations of Source 6.10 for historians looking for evidence of Jinnah's attitude towards the partition of India into two separate states.

Views of the Lahore Resolution

Historians agree that the Lahore Resolution represented a change in the politics of the Muslim League: it was the first time that it officially voiced support for the 'Two Nation' theory. However, they have different views of what exactly was most significant about it. Akbar Ahmed focuses on the appeal of the concept of Pakistan to Indian Muslims at the time (Source 6.11). Bose and Jalal see its main significance as being an assertion by Muslims of their claim to nationalism rather than communalism (Source 6.12). Ian Copland discusses different interpretations of the Lahore Resolution in Source 6.13.

SOURCE 6.11

Pakistan meant all things to all people. For some it was theology…
To others it was sociology. Many Muslims, including those who had
little time for orthodox practice, were concerned about preserving
their culture and language. Yet for others it meant economics; it meant
escape from the powerful Hindu commercial and entrepreneurial
presence emerging all over India. Yet to others it was an expression of
the Hindu-Muslim confrontation that had been taking place for centuries;
it was a challenge to those Hindus who believed they could dominate
Muslims and impose Ram Raj on them. But for everyone Pakistan meant
something in terms of their identity. This is what made the movement
work.

Ahmed, Akbar. 1997. **Jinnah, Pakistan and Islamic Identity.** *London.
Routledge. pp. 111–2.*

SOURCE 6.12

The time had come for Muslims to reject the derogatory label of
communalism, once and for all, and advance a vision of nationalism
which was no less valid than that of Congress. Rising from the ashes of
the 1937 electoral debacle, this was Jinnah and the League's attempt
to formally register their claim to speak for all Indian Muslims. An
astonishingly bold stance for a vanquished party to take, it drew strength
from the rising tide of Muslim antipathy to the prospect of Congress rule
at the all-India centre.

Quoted in Bose, Sugata and Jalal, Ayesha. 1998. **Modern South Asia:
History, Culture, Political Economy.** *London. Routledge. p. 175.*

SOURCE 6.13

Was a resolution framed in this open-ended manner intended to be taken seriously? Or was it merely a high-stakes bargaining chip to force the British and the Congress to concede the League's longstanding demand that Muslims be given a special constitutional status? Historians have argued this point for years, and the jury is still out. But there are some good reasons for thinking that the League, at least in 1940–41, was still keeping its options open. One, already mentioned, is the studied vagueness of the Lahore Resolution. A second is the telling evidence gathered by the government's Reforms Commissioner, H.V. Hodson, during his provincial tour of 1941. Almost all the Muslim politicians Hodson spoke to assumed that Pakistan would be part of a larger all-Indian federation. A third is the bitter logic the homeland option posed for the majority of senior League leaders. As the Lahore Resolution frankly recognised, any separate Muslim states would necessarily have to be situated in the north-west and north-east of the subcontinent. But from Mughal times the heartland of Muslim power in India had been the area around Delhi and Aligarh; even in the 1940s most of the League's high command came either from that region or, as in the case of Jinnah, from the Bombay presidency. If the Pakistan scheme ever came to fruition, Jinnah and the millions of other Muslims living in the minority provinces faced the dismal prospect of having to choose between permanent exile in a strange country, or permanent segregation as second-class citizens of 'Hindu' India. No wonder they hesitated.

Copland, Ian. 2001. India 1885–1947: The Unmaking of an Empire. *Harlow. Pearson Education. p. 63.*

QUESTION

Discuss the implications of the terms 'communalism' and 'nationalism' as used in Source 6.12.

Draw up a two column table. Label them as follows:

- The Lahore Resolution as a call for a separate Muslim state
- The Lahore Resolution as a bargaining tactic

Read through all the sources in this section and extract information to back up these claims. Enter it in point form in the appropriate column.

Using the information from these sources and your own knowledge, evaluate the significance of the Lahore Resolution for the growth of Muslim separatism in India.

Paper 3 exam practice

Question

Examine the reasons for the growth of support for the 'Two Nation' theory after 1937. **[15 marks]**

Skill

Avoiding irrelevance

Examiner's tips

Do not waste valuable writing time on irrelevant material. If it is irrelevant, it will not gain you *any* marks. This problem can arise because:

* the candidate does not look carefully enough at the wording of the question
* the candidate ignores the fact that the question requires selection of facts, an analytical approach and a final judgement; instead the candidate just writes down all that they know about a topic (relevant or not), and hopes that the examiner will do the analysis and make the judgement
* the candidate has unwisely restricted their revision, and tries to turn the question into a topic they were expecting instead of answering the question that has been asked; whatever the reason, such responses rarely address any of the demands of the question.

For this question, you will need to:

* explain briefly that the concept of Muslim separatism developed into the theory that India was land of two nations during the 1930s
* examine the growth of support for this after 1937
* analyse the reasons for this.

Common mistakes

One common error with this type of question is for candidates to write about material they know well, rather than material directly related to the question.

Another mistake is to present too much general information, instead of material specific to the actual question.

Finally, candidates often elaborate too much on events outside the dates given in the question.

Sample paragraphs of irrelevant focus/ material

During the 1930s the idea that Muslims were a separate community developed into the idea that India was land of two nations – one Hindu and one Muslim. An Indian scholar proposed the name 'Pakistan' for a Muslim 'homeland'. However, at first there was not much support for this idea and it was ignored by most Muslim politicians, including the Muslim League. This changed after 1937 when the Muslim League, under the leadership of Jinnah, tried to unite all Muslims within the League and support for the 'Two nation' theory began to grow.

Mohammad Ali Jinnah was born in Karachi in 1876 and studied at Bombay University before he went to London in 1892 to train as a lawyer. There he was influenced by British liberal ideas and decided that the Indian independence struggle should use constitutional methods. He joined the Indian National Congress in 1896, but only became active in Indian politics after defending the nationalist Tilak when he was arrested and charged with sedition at the time of the conflict in Bengal in 1905. In 1913, Jinnah joined the Muslim League and in 1916 became its president for the first time. He was largely responsible for the Lucknow Pact between Congress and the League. He was also a member of the Home Rule League which wanted dominion status for India. At first he was moderate in his views but when Britain failed to give independence to India after the First World War he became more radical in his ideas. But he did not support the Non-Cooperation campaign which Gandhi started in 1920, so he resigned from Congress.

[There then follow several paragraphs on relations between Congress and the Muslim League during the 1920s and Jinnah's attempts to reach a compromise agreement between them in 1928 and 1929.]

EXAMINER'S COMMENT

Although the introductory paragraph is good and focused on the question, this is an example of a weak answer. A brief comment on Jinnah's background would be relevant and helpful, but there is certainly no need to go into this much detail. The question also requires an analytical answer, not a narrative account. Thus, virtually all of the material highlighted in blue is irrelevant, and will not score any marks. In addition, the candidate is using up valuable writing time, which should have been spent on providing relevant points and supporting own knowledge.

Activity

In this chapter, the focus is on avoiding writing answers that contain irrelevant material. Using the information from this chapter, and any other sources of information available to you, write an answer to **one** of the following Paper 3 practice questions, keeping your answer fully focused on the question asked. Remember – making a plan *first* can help you maintain this focus.

Remember to refer to the simplified Paper 3 mark scheme in Chapter 10.

Paper 3 practice questions

1   Examine the factors that contributed to the growth of Muslim separatism by 1930.

2   Examine relations between the Indian National Congress and the Muslim League between 1916 and 1929, showing how they moved from a relationship of cooperation to one of alienation.

3   To what extent were the 1937 elections a turning point in the growth of Muslim separatism?

4 Evaluate the significance of the Lahore Resolution in the quest to establish a separate Muslim state.

5 Examine the role played by Mohammad Ali Jinnah in the growth of the Muslim League and the demand for a separate Muslim state.

7

The impact of the Second World War

Introduction

The Second World War brought change to India: it provided economic opportunities for some, but widespread suffering for many civilians. While millions of Indians volunteered to support Britain in the war, a smaller number formed the Indian National Army, with the intention of forcing the British out of India immediately. Britain remained determined to maintain its position in India, but by the end of the war the situation had changed. Britain was seriously weakened by the war – economically, politically and strategically – and this, together with economic problems and growing civil unrest in India, led to a change in policy after the war. This chapter examines how the Second World War and its aftermath changed the relationship between Britain and India and hastened the move towards independence.

TIMELINE

1939 Sept: Viceroy Linlithgow commits India to fighting in Second World War

1941 Aug: Atlantic Charter: statement of Allied war aims

Dec: Japan enters war

1942 Mar: Japan occupies Andaman Islands; Cripps Mission

Aug: Congress adopts 'Quit India' campaign; August Rising

1943 Aug: Start of Bengal famine

Oct: Wavell replaces Linlithgow as viceroy

1945 Apr: Defeat of Indian National Army (INA)

May: End of Second World War in Europe

June: Simla Conference

July: Labour Party wins general election in Britain

Aug: Japan surrenders

Sept: End of Second World War in Asia

Nov: Trial of INA officers begins in Delhi

1946 Jan: General election in India

Nationalism and Independence in India (1919–1964)

KEY QUESTIONS

- How did the Second World War affect India?
- What role did Subhas Chandra Bose play?
- Why did the Cripps Mission fail?
- How did the war affect British power in India?
- What was the situation in India after the war?

Overview

- Over 2 million Indians fought on the Allied side during the Second World War. Japan's military victories in Southeast Asia brought Japanese forces to the borders of India.
- The war promoted industrialisation in India but also created hardships for civilians, including rising prices and serious shortages of food and fuel.
- A devastating famine in Bengal, caused partly by a scorched earth policy and the diversion of food supplies to the military, resulted in widespread suffering and the deaths of over 2 million people.
- Subhas Chandra Bose saw the war as an opportunity to force the British to leave India and led the Indian National Army which was formed among Indian prisoners-of-war and civilians in Southeast Asia. The INA invaded parts of north-eastern India, before being defeated.
- In 1942, under pressure from the US government, Britain sent Stafford Cripps to India to negotiate with nationalist leaders. The mission failed due to the unwillingness of Churchill and other members of the British government to make meaningful concessions.
- A further attempt to reach an agreement at the Simla Conference in 1945 also failed, owing mainly to opposition from Jinnah and the Muslim League about the composition of a proposed interim government.
- Britain was seriously weakened by the Second World War – economically, politically and strategically – and after the war lacked

the resources and will to maintain a large empire. The election of a Labour government hastened Britain's determination to reach a settlement with nationalist leaders in India.

- The wider context of the postwar world also had an impact on British policy: the new superpowers were anti-imperialist; the start of the Cold War made a strong alliance with the USA imperative; and there were growing demands for independence from colonies in Africa as well as Asia.

- After the war the situation in India became more unstable, with economic problems, strikes, a naval mutiny and escalating civil unrest. There was also disagreement between Congress and the Muslim League about the nature and form of a future postcolonial state.

- In the 1946 elections, Congress won an overwhelming majority of the 'open' seats, but the election results showed that the Muslim League now had the support of most Muslims.

7.1 How did the Second World War affect India?

When the Second World War started in September 1939, the British viceroy, Lord Linlithgow, committed India to fight on the Allied side against Germany without consulting Indian political leaders. This act was legal and constitutional, but it emphasised India's subservience to Britain and so alienated Indian opinion.

In December 1941, Japan entered the war on Germany's side with a series of successful military strikes across Southeast Asia. David Ludden suggests that British India immediately 'became critically strategic territory for the Allies and was therefore once again dominated politically by military interests'. Metcalf suggests that the British were 'desperate to retain access to the resources, in men and materiel, as well as the secure bases that India supplied'. The Japanese rapidly overran European colonies in Indochina, the Malayan peninsula and Burma, bringing their armies to the border of India, and shattering the myth of the infallibility of the British Raj.

7

Indian involvement in the war

In spite of the reluctance of Congress to support the war effort, over 2 million Indians volunteered to serve alongside Allied armies, making it the largest volunteer army in history. The size of the army increased tenfold to meet the military threat. Indian soldiers served with Allied troops in Burma against the Japanese, and in North Africa and Italy against the Axis armies. The pay that they received was relatively good and most soldiers managed to send money to their families back home. For the first time, many Indians were promoted into positions of command in the army. The Indian navy and air force also made important contributions to the Allied war effort.

Figure 7.1: Indian soldiers serving alongside the British 8th Army in Italy during the Second World War.

The speed of the Japanese advance took many people by surprise and brought the Japanese army to the borders of India. Over 600 000 Indian refugees fled from Burma into India. In March 1942, the Japanese occupied the Andaman Islands and subjected the local Indian civilian population to a brutal regime of forced labour, torture and public executions. In 1942, Japanese planes bombed cities in eastern India, and 3500 people were killed. Thousands of Indians left coastal towns in panic and moved inland, as did civil servants from Calcutta.

At the outbreak of war, the government passed emergency decrees: it outlawed political activities, censored the press and interned anyone suspected of undermining the war effort. It also launched a propaganda campaign directed against the Japanese and the Nazis.

QUESTION

Compare India's involvement in the Second World War with its role in the First World War.

The economic impact of the war

The war created opportunities for the Indian economy. It encouraged industrialisation on a scale unknown before 1939. The Jamshedpur steel complex became the largest producer of steel in the British Empire for the duration of the war, and Bombay became a major centre of light engineering and the manufacture of pharmaceuticals and chemicals. The Indian economy was a significant factor in the final defeat of the Axis powers.

The war also caused intense hardships for ordinary Indians. The government printed more money to pay for wartime supplies, doubling the amount of money in circulation in five years, and causing rapid inflation and rising prices. Many people, especially the rural poor, were unable to purchase essential items. There were also serious shortages, especially of food, kerosene oil and cloth, due partly to the government purchase of supplies for the army. The situation was aggravated by the influx of hundreds of thousands of British, American and African servicemen, which escalated demand. The shortages resulted in hoarding which made the situation even worse. The province which was most seriously affected by food shortages was Bengal.

The Bengal famine

Bengal in the north-east was on the front line against the Japanese army and so orders were issued by the British military authorities to destroy all boats on the rivers of east Bengal and along the coast to halt the advancing Japanese. As a result, over 20 000 boats were sunk, burned or requisitioned, depriving the region of the means to get food to market and also of vital fish supplies. Bridges across the rivers were destroyed as well, severing transport links. This 'scorched earth' policy contributed to a devastating famine in Bengal in 1943 and 1944. The famine was also caused partly by the loss of rice imports from Japanese-occupied Burma, and partly by a British administrative decision to divert food from the Bengal countryside to feed the military instead. Between 2 and 4 million people in rural Bengal died of malnutrition and related diseases.

DISCUSSION POINT

Are scorched earth tactics ever justifiable? Discuss whether, in wartime, a government is justified in overlooking humanitarian concerns for the sake of security and defence.

The severe food shortages drove up prices and the government had to introduce rationing – first in Calcutta and then in other major Indian cities. The authorities used the police and the army to forcibly requisition grain from merchants and rich peasants to support the ration system, but did not provide any rural relief to the starving people of Bengal. Bose and Jalal suggest that 'the deliberate absence of relief measures contributed to one of the more catastrophic, though less publicised, holocausts of the Second [World] War'. The famine and the official reaction to it served to increase public anger against colonial rule: according to Copland the famine 'did irreparable damage to the credibility of British rule'. When Archibald Wavell replaced Linlithgow as viceroy in October 1943 he visited the affected areas and finally instituted relief measures. In a telegram to Amery, the Secretary of State for India, he described his impression: 'The Bengal famine was one of the greatest disasters that has befallen any people under British rule and has done great damage to our reputation here both among Indians and foreigners in India.'

ACTIVITY

Write a definition for each of these terms: requisitioning; scorched earth policy; rationing; relief measures.

KEY CONCEPTS ACTIVITY

Cause and consequence: Discuss the causes and consequences of the Bengal famine.

The economic effects of the war, and the slow response of the British authorities to the situation in Bengal, increased support and sympathy for the nationalist cause.

SOURCE 7.1

The repressive measures imposed by the British, including the forcible requisition of food grain surpluses in rural villages in an attempt to meet the food shortages, encouraged a steady rise in mass politicisation and discontent. Japanese successes in Burma and South-East Asia, and the return of large numbers of refugees and wounded soldiers from the Burmese front, led to widespread rumours of a Japanese invasion and anticipation of the collapse of British power.

Bates, Crispin. 2007. Subalterns and Raj: South Asia since 1600. *London. Routledge. p. 158.*

QUESTION

How, according to Source 7.1, did the Second World War weaken the British position in India?

Many histories of India during the Second World War focus mainly on the impact of the war on nationalist politics, the 'Quit India' campaign or the activities of Chandra Subhas Bose and the Indian National Army. But in a new study of the impact of the war on India, *The Raj at War: A People's History of India's Second World War* (2015), historian Yasmin Khan focuses on the experiences of ordinary soldiers and civilians, and the suffering many of them experienced, often as a result of official negligence and blunders. She comments that the war caused 'seismic processes of economic, cultural and social changes' in Indian society.

7.2 What role did Subhas Chandra Bose play?

Subhas Chandra Bose (1897–1945) was one of the left-wing members of Congress who supported radical social and economic policies and a more militant form of nationalism. In 1939, with the support of the youth, trade union and peasant wings of the party, he was elected Congress president. However, many of the most powerful figures in Congress opposed his election, and the rift threatened to split the party. When Bose realised he would not have the support of the Congress hierarchy, he resigned as president and left to form the revolutionary Forward Bloc Party. When the Second World War started, he saw the war as an opportunity to force Britain to grant independence immediately.

The Indian National Army (INA)

Under the strict wartime regulations, the authorities banned the Forward Bloc Party and placed Bose under house arrest in Calcutta. In 1941 he left India in order to ally himself with the Axis powers against Britain. He fled to Afghanistan and from there to Germany where he signed a pact with Hitler and broadcast anti-British propaganda. He was put in charge of a small force of about 3000 soldiers – the Free India Legion – formed from among Indian prisoners-of-war captured in North Africa. In 1943 the Germans sent him by submarine to Southeast Asia. In Japanese-occupied Singapore he was put in charge of a force called the Indian National Army (the INA, or *Azad Hind Fauj*).

The INA was formed from Indian prisoners-of-war, many of whom had been among the 85 000 Allied troops who surrendered after the capture of Singapore by Japan in 1942. Historian Crispin Bates suggests that for many of them 'the INA was an attractive alternative to the possibility of being forced to labour on the Siam–Burma railway' although 'others undoubtedly joined out of sheer patriotic enthusiasm'. There were also civilian recruits from among Indian plantation workers in Malaya, small traders in Burma and shopkeepers in Thailand. An additional factor influencing their decision might have been their 'resentment at the abandonment of Indian migrants and soldiers in Southeast Asia when the British fled the Japanese advance', which Bates mentions. Mridula

Mukherjee suggests that many saw the INA as 'a means of checking the misconduct of the Japanese against Indians in Southeast Asia' and as 'a bulwark against a future Japanese occupation of India'. According to Bose and Jalal, 'an overwhelming majority of nearly two million expatriates in South East Asia responded with great emotional fervour to Bose's call for "total mobilization"'. However, other historians put the number of soldiers in the INA at between 40 000 and 60 000.

The INA had Hindu, Muslim and Sikh members, working together for a united cause, and it also included a special women's battalion, the Rani Jhansi, named after a legendary leader of the 1857 uprising against EIC rule. Bose set up INA headquarters in Singapore and the Burmese capital Rangoon, and established a 'Provisional Government of Free India' in Rangoon. The INA fought alongside Japanese forces against the Allies in Burma, and invaded and briefly captured parts of north-eastern India, before being defeated in April 1945. According to Mukherjee, the INA soldiers were completely demoralised by the discriminatory treatment they received from the Japanese army, where they were denied rations and arms and made to do menial work. Bose himself was never captured but died in an air crash over Taiwan in 1945 while trying to escape the advancing Allied forces.

KEY CONCEPTS QUESTION

Significance: Discuss the significance of naming the women's battalion of the INA after a leader of the 1857 Indian Uprising.

Although the INA was defeated in military battles in Burma and north-eastern India and its planned march to Delhi was halted at Imphal in 1944, according to Metcalf it 'evoked great pride in India even among those who repudiated its fascist ties'. Bates suggests, however, that the ties between the INA and the Axis powers were not all that strong: 'The Japanese did not trust the INA, regarding it more as a propaganda tool than anything else, as did Hitler the Free India Legion.'

The significance of the INA

Although the INA did not succeed in its quest to overthrow British rule in India, it provided a serious challenge to British perceptions about upholding that power, as Ian Copland explains in Source 7.2. Sugata

Nationalism and Independence in India (1919–1964)

Bose and Ayesha Jalal support this view and also explain other significant features of the INA movement in Source 7.3.

SOURCE 7.2

Although the INA did little actual damage in the field, the fact that thousands of Indian soldiers had seen fit to renounce their oath of allegiance to the King-Emperor raised serious doubts about whether the military could continue to be relied on to enforce imperial authority.

Copland, Ian. 2001. India 1885–1947: The Unmaking of an Empire. *Harlow. Pearson Education. p. 65.*

SOURCE 7.3

A few significant features of this movement of resistance deserve emphasis. First, it attacked the kernel of British imperial power, namely the British Indian army, which was the ultimate instrument of colonial control, and sought to replace the loyalty of Indian soldiers to the crown with loyalty to the nationalist cause. Second, unlike the Quit India movement in which Muslim participation was minimal, the Azad Hind [INA] movement was not only characterised by harmony and unity among various religious and linguistic communities but had a very large, and indeed disproportionate, representation of Muslims and Sikhs within its leadership and ranks. Third, this movement saw widespread participation by women and included a small but significant women's regiment named after the Rani of Jhansi, the legendary leader of the 1857 rebellion.

Bose, Sugata and Jalal, Ayesha. 1998. Modern South Asia: History, Culture, Political Economy. *London. Routledge. p. 162.*

QUESTION

Compare and contrast what Sources 7.2 and 7.3 suggest about the significance of the INA.

The legacy of the INA

Bose and the INA were hailed as heroes in India after the war. There was a sustained public outcry when the British authorities put three INA officers – one Hindu, one Muslim and one Sikh – on trial in 1945 to 1946. The news also sparked a mutiny in the Royal Indian Navy. According to Sucheta Mahajan, the essence of the protests was not about whether the men were right or wrong, but about whether the British had the right to decide a matter concerning Indians. Eager to tap into the public mood, Congress, the Muslim League and other political groups voiced their support for the men. Congress made its release part of their political platform for the 1946 elections, even though the INA's armed resistance was the antithesis of Gandhi's philosophy and Congress policy about non-violent resistance. The three men were sentenced to deportation but, under great public pressure, these were changed to suspended sentences.

Figure 7.2: Subhas Chandra Bose reviews soldiers of the Indian National Army in 1944.

Even today Bose is remembered as a hero. According to Kulke and Rothermund, his 'heroic endeavour still fires the imagination of many of his countrymen'. Metcalf examines the reality of this heroic image of Bose in Source 7.4.

SOURCE 7.4

His romantic saga, coupled with his defiant nationalism, has made Bose a near mythic figure, not only in his native Bengal, but across India. It is this heroic, martial myth that is today remembered, rather than Bose's wartime vision of a free India under the authoritarian rule of someone like himself.

Metcalf, Barbara and Metcalf, Thomas. 2006. **A Concise History of Modern India (Second Edition)**. *Cambridge. Cambridge University Press. p. 210.*

QUESTION

What message is conveyed by Source 7.4?

Theory of Knowledge

History, terminology and bias

Some historians describe Bose as a terrorist and a traitor. Others see him as a nationalist hero. In what ways can terminology reflect bias in History? Is there a more neutral term to describe him?

7.3 Why did the Cripps Mission fail?

In August 1941, before the United States entered the war, the British prime minister, **Winston Churchill**, and the American president, Franklin D. Roosevelt, signed the Atlantic Charter. This was a statement of Allied war aims which declared support for the right of all people to political self-determination. However, shortly afterwards, Churchill told the British parliament that this provision did not apply to India. It was clear that the British attitude towards India had changed little by 1941 and Indian nationalists were outraged by this turn of events.

Winston Churchill (1874–1965):

Churchill served in the British army on the North West Frontier in India in the 1890s and later went into politics. He was outspoken in his opposition to the Indian nationalist movement and he regarded Gandhi as a dangerous troublemaker. He resigned as an MP in protest against the 1935 Government of India Act and formed the India Defence League to campaign against any form of self-government for India. In May 1940 he became head of a wartime coalition government in Britain and remained determined not to make any concessions to Indian independence. He is quoted as saying: 'I have not become the King's First Minister in order to preside over the liquidation of the British Empire.'

By 1942, however, Japan's sweeping victories in Asia forced Churchill to change his position. He recognised the urgent need to gain the support of Indian leaders in the fight against Japan. He was prompted too by pressure from the US government to reach conciliation with the Indian nationalist movement. Roosevelt had made it clear to Churchill that the US government was not fighting the war to preserve the British Empire. He urged cooperation with Indian nationalists and a commitment from Britain to move towards independence for India. Roosevelt was concerned too about the war situation and the need to ensure Indian support for the Allied war effort against Japan. There was also support for the Indian nationalist cause from Labour members of Britain's wartime coalition government.

QUESTION

Discuss the reasons why the US government put pressure on the British government to negotiate with Indian nationalists, and also why Britain complied.

In March 1942, the British government sent Stafford Cripps, a Labour member of the cabinet, to India to negotiate with the nationalist leaders. Cripps was a friend of Nehru and personally sympathetic to the nationalist movement, so he was optimistic of success. However, the viceroy, Linlithgow, a diehard imperialist, supported Churchill's view that no real concessions should be made to the nationalists. The offer made by Cripps on behalf of the British government was that:

- India would be granted full dominion status as soon as the war was over
- also at the end of the war, Indians would elect a Constituent Assembly to draw up a new constitution (although representatives from the princely states would be nominated by the rulers)
- provinces or princely states that did not want to be part of a united India would not be forced to join the new state
- in the interim, there would be increased Indian representation on the viceroy's executive council during the war, but the British government would remain in control.

The proposal that states could opt out of a united India was unacceptable to Congress. They were also unhappy about the restricted powers of the wartime government, especially as the position of defence minister would remain in British hands. In the end they rejected the proposals and Churchill was not prepared to make any further concessions. In his view, he had satisfied the Americans by trying to reach a compromise agreement with Congress, and he could now blame Congress for the failure of the attempt.

Reasons for the failure of the Cripps Mission

Historians seem to be unanimous in the view that the Cripps Mission failed because members of the British government, especially Churchill, were not committed to reaching a settlement. Bose and Jalal suggest that Churchill *wanted* the mission to fail: 'It is now clear from British documents of this period that both Churchill and Linlithgow… wanted to see the Cripps Mission fail.' Bates claims that Churchill was 'delighted' by the failure of the mission because 'American opinion was placated; and the British government in India could return to the business of war without any further worries about democracy'. According to Arnold, Cripps' offer was 'hedged about with many conditions unacceptable to the Congress and fatally undermined by Churchill's determination not to grant any additional concessions'.

Other historians spread the responsibility for the failure of the mission more widely. Chandra suggests that an important reason for it was 'the incapacity of Cripps to bargain and negotiate' as he had been ordered not to make any further concessions. Chandra also claims that Churchill, Amery (the Secretary of State), Linlithgow, and Wavell (the Commander-in-Chief of the army in India) 'did not want Cripps to succeed and constantly opposed and sabotaged his efforts to accommodate Indian opinion'. Metcalf believes that the Cripps Mission failed because 'the level of suspicion was simply too high, and too many influential figures did not want the negotiations to succeed'. They suggest further that 'in the eyes of a beleaguered Britain the control of India during the war was essential for victory'. According to Kulke and Rothermund, Linlithgow 'sabotaged the mission at its decisive stage' by writing to Churchill to complain that Cripps 'intended to deprive him of his constitutional powers'. They claim further that Cripps returned to London 'embittered and disappointed' because he was 'peeved at the pusillanimity [lack of courage or resolution] of the Congress leaders'.

ACTIVITY

In his biography of Gandhi, David Arnold claims that Churchill had an 'almost fanatical determination to resist constitutional change in India' (Arnold, David. 2001. *Gandhi*. Harlow Pearson Education. p. 153). To what extent do think that this was the key reason for the failure of the Cripps Mission?

Theory of Knowledge

The writing of history

Churchill once wrote: *'History will be kind to me, for I intend to write it.'* Examine what this statement suggests about the writing of History. Use the internet or other resources to find out whether Churchill subsequently wrote histories, and how they were critically received.

7.4 How did the war affect British power in India?

The Second World War was a critical factor in bringing British rule in India to an end. Britain was seriously weakened by the war – economically, politically and strategically – and after the war lacked the resources and will to maintain a large empire. Towards the end of the war, the British government renewed efforts to reach a settlement in India.

The Simla Conference, 1945

By June 1945, with the war in Europe over and the end of the war against Japan in sight, the British government was anxious to reach an agreement with Indian political leaders. It authorised the viceroy, Wavell (who had replaced Linlithgow), to arrange a conference to present proposals about the way forward, and Congress leaders were released from prison so that they could attend.

In June 1945, 21 political leaders – including Gandhi, Nehru and Jinnah – met at Simla. Wavell proposed an equal representation of Hindus and Muslims on his executive council, to function as an interim government to tackle India's immediate postwar problems and to plan future constitutional developments. Although Congress was not satisfied with the proposed composition of the council, it was prepared to participate. However, the conference reached a deadlock over Jinnah's insistence that all 15 Muslim members of the council had to be nominated by the Muslim League. This would exclude any Muslim members of Congress (including the Congress president Maulana Azad), as well as the Muslim Unionist Party, which had strong support in Punjab. As a result, the Simla Conference ended in failure. Historian Lawrence James comments on the significance of this: 'The League had wrecked the chances of a ministry which offered some hope of national cohesion in what would turn out to be a period of unprecedented trauma in India's history.' Metcalf notes the implications of Jinnah's position: 'That the British let Jinnah wreck the Simla conference, rather than proceed without him, was testimony to the leverage the League had secured by its wartime collaboration with the imperial government.'

With its failure to secure an agreement at Simla, Britain now faced the reality of dealing with the postwar situation in India, where political unrest and demands for independence were escalating. At the same time Britain was forced to face the realities of its changed status in the postwar world and the impact of this on British power in India.

ACTIVITY

Draw up a two-column table, to compare the Cripps Mission and the Simla Conference. Include information on: the date of the talks; the main participants; the proposals discussed; and the reasons for failure.

The economic impact of the war on Britain

The Second World War had a negative impact on the British economy. Although the Allies had won the war, the burden of sustaining the war effort for six years had proved costly for Britain and, by 1945, it was in a weak position economically. There were urgent problems to be addressed at home: wartime bombing had destroyed thousands of houses and factories which needed to be rebuilt. Food shortages and the continuation of wartime rationing added to the problems facing the government. At a time of severe postwar economic problems, it was becoming apparent that it would be impossible to maintain a global empire.

In addition, the nature of the economic relationship between Britain and India had changed. British investment in and trade with India had declined substantially over the previous decades. In some cases, British imports were replaced by locally manufactured products as India became more industrialised. The USA and Japan had also become major suppliers of goods to the Indian market, in many cases challenging Britain's position as India's main trading partner.

The war itself transformed India's economic relationship with Britain. Before the war, India had been in debt to Britain. However, during the war, Britain's need to fund the war forced it to borrow heavily from India – so much so that by 1945 the economic relationship between the two had been reversed, with Britain owing India huge sums of money.

Political changes and their implications

In a general election in Britain in July 1945, the Conservative Party, along with it Britain's wartime leader, Winston Churchill, was defeated in a surprising result. The election victory of the Labour Party under Clement Atlee brought about a new direction in British policy as Labour did not share the imperial ambitions of many Conservatives. The Labour government was also anxious to focus on domestic reforms to create a welfare state. Many people in Britain felt that the maintenance of an empire was consuming too much money and attention.

Atlee had been a member of the Simon Commission and had also chaired the India Committee of the wartime coalition government. Over the years the Labour Party had forged links with the Indian National Congress and it was committed to a transfer of British power in India, although it but did not have a fixed plan of how this would happen. Bates examines the significance of the Labour Party victory in Source 7.5.

SOURCE 7.5

At the end of the war there was no serious proposal on the table for further constitutional reforms. However, the ball began to roll in the direction of British withdrawal with the victory of a Labour Party administration in elections held in July 1945 in Britain. The change in government was not solely responsible for a change in policy, but it was responsible for a sudden recognition of realities. Everyone in the wartime government knew that with the end of the war and demobilisation of the British army, Britain would not be able to hang on to the Indian empire. But Churchill himself was resolutely opposed to the idea of negotiation. With the election of a Labour government the determination was made to grasp realities.

Bates, Crispin. 2007. **Subalterns and Raj: South Asia since 1600.** London. Routledge. p. 171.

QUESTION

How, according to Source 7.5, did the Labour Party election victory in 1945 contribute to a change in British policy towards India?

There were changing attitudes in India too. Indian politicians were highly critical when Britain planned to send Indian troops to Southeast Asia to fight uprisings in the Dutch East Indies and French Indochina. They did not want Indian forces to be used to prop up other unpopular colonial regimes. There had been a change too in the composition of the Indian Civil Service: the former instrument of British control now had a predominantly Indian staff. Metcalf examines the impact of the war on attitudes in Britain and India in Source 7.6.

SOURCE 7.6

Though victorious in the war, Britain had suffered immensely in the struggle. It simply did not possess the manpower or the economic resources required to coerce a restive India. For the British public, the jobs and housing promised by the new socialist government took precedence over a costly reassertion of the Raj. In India itself, a naval mutiny in Bombay in 1946 underscored the fact that the allegiance of the subordinate services could no longer be relied upon. Further, the élite Indian Civil Service, the 'steel frame' of the Raj, had by 1945 become over one-half Indian, and these men, though still loyal, had begun to look ahead to service under a national government. By 1946, all that Britain could hope to do, as men like Wavell realised, was to arrange a transfer of power to those whom 'the Indian people have chosen for themselves'. This was not to be an easy or straightforward task.

Metcalf, Barbara and Metcalf, Thomas. 2006. **A Concise History of Modern India (Second Edition).** *Cambridge: Cambridge University Press. p. 212.*

QUESTION

Source 7.5 refers to a 'sudden recognition of realities'. Using the information in Sources 7.5 and 7.6 and your own knowledge, discuss what these realities were.

Britain's changing position in the world

Until the Second World War Britain had been one of the major powers, but in the postwar world, the United States and the Soviet Union were the new superpowers. In their competition to gain allies in the wider world, neither superpower was prepared to support unpopular imperial rulers. This reality, and the start of the Cold War, forced the British government to reassess its priorities. The United States and the Soviet Union were rivals for power and influence, and the development of a Western alliance to contain the Soviet Union was crucial. Unresolved colonial disputes could threaten Britain's good relationship with the United States.

QUESTION

Examine how the start of the Cold War affected Britain's relationship with the United States.

The postwar world was also the beginning of an era of decolonisation: the war had stimulated demands for independence in many Asian and African colonies. With the possibility of drawn-out colonial struggles in other parts of its empire, the time seemed right for Britain to make good its promises of independence and negotiate with the nationalist leaders in India. At the same time Britain was trying to extricate itself from a situation of escalating violence in the British mandate of Palestine, which was also placing a strain on British manpower and resources.

ACTIVITY

1. Draw up a table to compare the impact of the Second World War on India and on Britain, using the example below as a model. Use the internet or other resources available to you to find out additional information.

The impact of the Second World War		
	India	Britain
Political		
Economic		
Social		
Military		
Strategic		
Morale		
Other		

2. 'The Second World War had a more negative impact on Britain than on India.' To what extent do you agree with this statement?

7.5 What was the situation in India after the war?

After the end of the Second World War, anti–British feelings in India intensified. The situation was aggravated by postwar economic problems and rising communal violence.

Economic problems, strikes and growing civil unrest

At the end of the war India faced economic problems including continuing food shortages, rising inflation and unemployment. The demobilisation of millions of soldiers added to the problems, as did the switch to peacetime production in industry, which cost many people their jobs. In the armed forces there was anger at the proposal to send Indian troops to help the French in Indochina. A naval mutiny in Bombay which started over racist remarks and the quality of food soon spread to other ships and naval bases, with the mutineers demanding the release of all political prisoners. The Communist Party organised a workers' strike in Bombay, in support of the mutineers, and over 200 civilians were killed in the violent suppression of the strikes. There were further strikes and student protests in Calcutta and other Indian cities, as well as police strikes, a postal strike and the threat of a national rail strike. Massive public protests about the trial of INA soldiers added to mounting civil unrest. Faced with a rapidly deteriorating situation, the British government realised the importance of reaching a settlement in India urgently.

Figure 7.3: Protesters blockade rail traffic, one of many acts of civil resistance in India in 1945 and 1946.

The situation was further complicated by differences of opinion over the specific form of a postcolonial state. Congress wanted the creation of a single, secular state, in which religious affiliation would not be significant. In contrast to this, as you read in Chapter 6, Muslims feared that their interests would be neglected in a Hindu-dominated India. They wanted the country to be divided, with the creation of a separate Muslim state in the northern part of the subcontinent, where most Muslims lived.

The organisational structures of Congress had been weakened by government suppression of the 'Quit India' movement and the imprisonment of Congress leaders during the war. The Muslim League, on the other hand, had given full support to the British war effort. In return, Britain had started to give serious consideration to a 'two-state solution' to the problem. The League was therefore in a strong negotiating position at the end of the war.

ACTIVITY

'The Muslim League emerged from the Second World War in a far stronger position than it had been in 1939.' To what extent is this an accurate assessment of the position of the Muslim League?

The 1946 elections

In 1946, elections were held for the central and provincial assemblies. These were the first elections to be held since 1937, when the Muslim League had fared so badly at the polls. Historian Ramachandra Guha analyses the contrast between the election messages of Congress and the League in the 1946 election in Source 7.7.

QUESTION

To what extent does Source 7.7 give a biased view? How could one establish whether it is an accurate and reliable interpretation of the situation? Discuss how the language used in a source can contribute to bias.

SOURCE 7.7

The world over, the rhetoric of modern democratic politics has been marked by two rather opposed rhetorical styles. The first appeals to hope, to popular aspirations for economic prosperity and social peace. The second appeals to fear, to sectional worries about being worsted or swamped by one's historic enemies. In the elections of 1946 the Congress relied on the rhetoric of hope. It had a strongly positive content to its programme, promising land reform, workers' rights, and the like. The Muslim League, on the other hand, relied on the rhetoric of fear. If they did not get a separate homeland, they told the voters, then they would be crushed by the more numerous Hindus in a united India.

Guha, Ramachandra. 2007. **India after Gandhi: The History of the World's Largest Democracy. London.** *Macmillan. p. 28.*

DISCUSSION POINT

Historian Ramachandra Guha claims that political parties use two types of approaches to attract voters – the rhetoric of hope and the rhetoric of fear. Discuss whether this analysis can be applied in a contemporary context, using a general election in your own country as an example.

Congress won 90% of the votes for the 'open seats' in the central legislature, as well as majorities in eight of the 11 provinces. The Muslim League fared very well in the 'reserved seats' for Muslim voters, winning all 30 in the central legislature, and 442 out of 500 in the provincial legislatures. These results lent support to Jinnah's claim that the Muslim League represented all Muslims in India. The British government had to recognise this when they reopened negotiations for the transfer of power in 1946 and 1947.

Paper 3 exam practice

Question

Evaluate the threat posed by Subhas Chandra Bose and the Indian National Army to British control in India.
[15 marks]

Skill

Avoiding a narrative-based answer

Examiner's tips

Even once you have read the question carefully (and so avoided the temptation of giving irrelevant material), produced your plan and written your introductory paragraph, it is still possible to go wrong.

By 'writing a narrative answer', history examiners mean providing supporting knowledge that is relevant (and may well be very precise and accurate) *but* that is not clearly linked to the question. Instead of answering the question, it merely **describes** what happened.

The main body of your essay and argument needs to be **analytical**. It must not simply be an answer in which you just 'tell the story'. Your essay must **address the demands and key words of the question**. Ideally, this should be done consistently throughout your essay, by linking each paragraph to the previous one, in order to produce a clear 'joined-up' answer.

> ### EXAMINER'S COMMENT
>
> You are especially likely to lapse into a narrative answer when answering your final question – and even more so if you are getting short of time. The 'error' here is that, despite all your good work at the start of the exam, you will lose sight of the question and just produce an **account,** rather than an analysis. So, even if you are short of time, try to write several analytical paragraphs.

Note that if a question asks you to evaluate the threat or challenge posed by something, it expects you to not simply describe it but to analyse it and show why and how effectively it posed a challenge. Often, such a question gives you the opportunity to refer to different historians' views. (See the activities in Chapter 8 for more on this.)

A good way of avoiding a narrative approach is to refer back to the question continually, and even to mention it now and again in your answer. This should help you produce an answer that is focused on the specific aspects of the question – rather than just giving information about the broad topic or period.

For this question, you will need to analyse the following aspects:

- the actions of Bose and the INA
- how successful they were
- whether they posed a threat to British control.

Common mistakes

Every year, even candidates who have clearly revised well, and who therefore have a good knowledge of the topic and of any historical debate surrounding it, still end up producing a mainly narrative-based or descriptive answer. Very often, this is the result of not having drawn up a proper plan.

The extracts of the student's answer below show an approach that essentially just describes Bose's actions, relating a chain of events, without analysing them or evaluating their effectiveness.

Sample paragraphs of narrative-based approach

This example shows what examiners mean by a narrative answer – it is *not* something you should copy!

At the start of the Second World War, Bose was under house arrest in Calcutta, but he managed to leave India in secret by escaping over the border into Afghanistan. From there he made his way to Germany because he wanted to ally himself with Hitler to fight against Britain. He made propaganda radio broadcasts there and was put in charge of a unit of soldiers who were Indian prisoners-of-war. But then the Axis powers decided that he would be more useful to them in Asia, so they sent him by submarine to Southeast Asia.

There he was put in charge of the Indian National Army which had about 50 000 soldiers. They were mainly Indian-prisoners-or war who had been captured by the Japanese, but there were also some plantation workers. The INA had a special women's battalion called the Rani Jhansi, which was named after a woman who had led resistance against the British in the 1857 Indian Uprising.

Bose set up the headquarters of the INA in Singapore and also in Rangoon in Burma. He also formed a government called the 'Provisional Government of Free India' in Rangoon. The INA fought with the Japanese army against the Allies in Burma. Bose is thought to have died in an air crash in Taiwan in 1945.

[The rest of the essay continues in the same way – there are also plenty of accurate and relevant facts about Bose and the INA. However, there is no attempt to answer the question by evaluating how effective it was and how much of a threat it posed to British control in India. Such an answer would only gain half marks at most.]

Activity

In this chapter, the focus is on avoiding writing narrative-based answers. Using the information from this chapter, and any other sources of information available to you, try to answer **one** of the following Paper 3 practice questions in a way that avoids simply describing what happened.

Remember to refer to the simplified Paper 3 mark scheme in Chapter 10.

Paper 3 practice questions

1 To what extent did the economic impact of the Second World War create hardships for people in India and increase support for the nationalist cause?

2 Evaluate the significance and legacy of the Indian National Army.

3 'The Cripps Mission was doomed from the start because the British government had no intention of making any meaningful concessions.' To what extent do you agree with this statement?

4 Examine the impact of the Second World War on Britain's resolve to maintain its empire in India.

5 To what extent did the postwar situation in India contribute to Britain's decision to reach a political settlement with nationalist leaders?

Independence and partition

8

8

Introduction

The goal of the Indian nationalist movement – independence from British rule – was achieved in August 1947, but it was not the united India that the Indian National Congress had envisioned. Instead, British India was partitioned into two separate states – secular India and Muslim Pakistan. This chapter examines the failed negotiations and the mounting communal violence that led to partition, as well as the bloodshed and refugee crisis that accompanied it. It examines, too, the reasons for partition and the on-going debates among historians about them. Some see the roles of key players – Mountbatten, Jinnah, or Nehru – as being significant factors, while others suggest that a complex interaction of several factors was responsible.

TIMELINE

1946 **Mar:** British Cabinet mission starts visit to India

May: Second Simla Conference

Aug: Direct Action Day; Great Calcutta Killings

Sept: Formation of interim government

1947 **Feb:** Atlee sets date of 30 June 1948 for Indian independence

Mar: Mountbatten arrives as last viceroy of India; he brings date for independence forward by 10 months

June: Partition plan accepted

Aug: Independence of India and Pakistan

Mountbatten becomes governor-general of India, with Nehru as prime minister

Jinnah becomes governor-general of Pakistan, with Liaquat Ali Khan as prime minister

Aug–Nov: Refugee crisis in Punjab

1948 **Jan:** Death of Gandhi

Sept: Death of Jinnah

1971 Secession of East Pakistan to form independent state of Bangladesh

KEY QUESTIONS

- What role did Mountbatten play?
- How did India achieve independence?
- What were the reasons for the partition of the South Asian subcontinent?

Overview

- When the British government sent a Cabinet Mission to India in March 1946, both Congress and the Muslim League initially supported a proposal for a future federal constitution, but agreement collapsed over different interpretations of how it would function.
- A call by Jinnah to the Muslim community for 'Direct Action' triggered communal violence and bloodshed on a vast scale, starting in Calcutta and spreading to other parts of India as well.
- In March 1947 Mountbatten was sent as the last viceroy of India to facilitate the handover of power. His fundamental task was to negotiate a compromise with Indian leaders between the Congress goal of a single united India and the Muslim League's call for a separate Muslim state.
- Mountbatten opted for a 'two-state solution': British India would be partitioned into two separate states – secular India and Muslim Pakistan. The princely states were ordered to join one or other of the two states, thus ending their former autonomy.
- When India and Pakistan became independent states in August 1947, partition was accompanied by waves of violence and bloodshed and a mass population movement of over 15 million refugees. Up to 2 million people were killed.
- The new state of Pakistan was split into two sections, with East and West Pakistan separated by 1500 km (930 miles) of Indian territory. Internal tensions later resulted in the secession of East Pakistan to form the independent state of Bangladesh.

- Imperialist historians used to explain the partition of South Asia into India and Pakistan as inevitable because of irreconcilable differences between Hindus and Muslims, but this view has been challenged.
- More recently, there have been ongoing debates about the reasons for partition. Some historians apportion blame to one or other of the key players. Others think that it was a complex interaction of several factors.

8.1 What role did Mountbatten play?

In early 1946, the new British government decided to reopen negotiations with Indian leaders for a transfer of power. Then, after a high-level Cabinet Mission failed to mediate an agreement between Congress and the Muslim League, and as the violence in India mounted, in 1947 the government sent a new viceroy to India, Lord Louis Mountbatten, to oversee the transfer of power.

The British Cabinet Mission

In March 1946 the British government sent a 'Cabinet Mission' of three members of the government (one of whom was Cripps) to try to break the deadlock between Congress and the League. The mission spent three months in India before presenting its proposals to leaders at a second conference in Simla in May. Their proposals were for a three-tier system of government – the provinces; three regional groupings of provinces; and a federal central government:

- The provinces would control local affairs.
- The three groupings of provinces would be the North East, the North West (both predominantly Muslim areas) and the rest (predominantly Hindu); the provinces in each group would elect their own government to run provincial affairs.
- The central government would run foreign affairs, defence, communications and trade. It would be made up of elected representatives from the three groupings of provinces.

QUESTION

Discuss the significance of the inclusion of Stafford Cripps in the
Cabinet Mission.

Copland describes the proposal as 'an ingenious plan for
accommodating Muslim aspirations within the framework of a unitary
Indian state'. Both Congress and the League initially accepted the plan,
but it soon became clear that they did not share the same vision of
how the system would develop in the future. When Nehru publicly
expressed the opinion that he saw the groupings as transitional rather
than a fixed arrangement, Jinnah interpreted this as an indication of a
Congress plan to dominate the whole structure. As a result, he formally
withdrew the League's acceptance of the proposals and reiterated the
call for the creation of Pakistan as a separate state. Shortly afterwards, the
viceroy went ahead and appointed an interim government of Congress
ministers, under Nehru, to lead India until the British withdrawal.

KEY CONCEPTS ACTIVITY

Cause and consequence: Draw up a table to compare and contrast
the 1945 and the 1946 Simla Conferences, focusing on the
similarities and differences between them, as well as the causes
and consequences of the failure of each of them.

Increasing communal tensions

As negotiations between the British government and Indian
representatives dragged on, tensions mounted. Fearing that Britain
and Congress would push forward with plans for a single state, Jinnah
called for 'Direct Action' in support of the Muslim League's demand for
partition. He wanted to show the other parties that Muslim aspirations
could not be ignored. In his biography of Jinnah, Akbar Ahmed, says
that, in calling for direct action, Jinnah was supporting an act 'which
violated his known principles of upholding the law' but that he was
'frustrated at what he saw as British and Congress perfidy [treachery,
deceit or dishonesty]'. (Refer to the section in Chapter 4 on the role
played by Jinnah to re-read the debate among historians about Jinnah's

call for direct action as the cause of the violence and bloodshed that followed.) Source 8.1 is an extract from Jinnah's statement.

SOURCE 8.1

Never have we in the whole history of the League done anything except by constitutional methods and by constitutionalism. But now we bid goodbye to constitutional methods. Throughout the negotiations, the parties with whom we bargained held a pistol at us, one with power and machine guns behind it, and the other with non-cooperation and the threat to launch mass civil disobedience. We also have a pistol. We have exhausted all reason. There is no tribunal to which we can go. The only tribunal is the Muslim nation.

Part of a statement made by Mohammad Ali Jinnah on 29 July 1946, the day after the Muslim League's call for 'Direct Action'. Quoted in Rees, Rosemary. 2010. **Britain and the Nationalist Challenge in India 1900–1947.** *Harlow. Pearson Education. p. 177.*

QUESTION

What message is conveyed by Source 8.1?

On 16 August 1946, or 'Direct Action Day', there was rioting in Calcutta, which soon turned into widespread communal violence between Muslim and Hindu communities, with both sides committing atrocities. In this Great Calcutta Killing, as it became known, between 4000 and 5000 people were killed, 20 000 seriously injured and hundreds of thousands made homeless. There were violent clashes between Hindus and Muslims in other parts of India as well, and thousands more were killed. The British interpreted the violence as a sign that there were irreconcilable differences between Hindus and Muslims, an interpretation that is questioned by many historians today.

In a desperate effort to restore order, members of the Muslim League were included in the interim government, but this did not stop the escalating violence. In this tense situation, the concept of partition into two separate states increasingly seemed to be the only workable solution, even to reluctant Congress leaders. The violence also exposed the weakness of Britain's position in the subcontinent, and the British government decided to quit India as soon as possible.

KEY CONCEPTS QUESTION

Cause and consequence: Discuss the causes and consequences of Jinnah's call for 'Direct Action'.

The arrival of Mountbatten

In February 1947, the British government set the date of 30 June 1948 as the date for the handover of power, and in March 1947 sent **Lord Louis Mountbatten** as the last viceroy of India to facilitate it. Mountbatten later brought the date forward to 15 August 1947. Therefore, in less than six months, he had to decide whether power would be handed over to one, two or more states, and where the borders between them would be. He also had to negotiate what was to happen to the 'princely states', the large areas of India that had remained under the control of hereditary rulers, with whom the British had signed treaties, recognising their local autonomy. Many historians have commented on the short time frame set to accomplish all of this. In David Ludden's opinion, the British government 'set a precipitous 1947 deadline for its escape from the now politically unbearable burden of empire in South Asia'. According to Copland, it was a 'tacit acknowledgement that the once all-powerful Raj was fast disintegrating'.

> ### Lord Louis Mountbatten (1900–1979):
>
> Mountbatten was a cousin of the king and close friend of the British royal family, and had a successful career in the Royal Navy. During the Second World War he served as the Supreme Allied Commander for Southeast Asia. He was viceroy of India from March to August 1947, and governor-general of independent India from August 1947 to June 1948. Afterwards he resumed his career in the navy and became First Sea Lord of the Admiralty. He was killed in an IRA bomb attack in Ireland.

Some historians are critical of Mountbatten and the manner in which he carried out his brief. They suggest, for example, that he was more sympathetic to Congress and that this was obvious to the Muslim League. Lawrence James suggests that he 'lacked the prestige, authority and resources of his predecessors and, therefore, placed himself in the hands of those who possessed all these assets – Nehru and the Congress high command'. Other historians are more open-minded. Kulke and Rothermund suggest that he was 'dynamic and sociable and immediately established good relations with Indian leaders' but that he did not pay detailed attention to the frequently changing constitutional proposals that were drawn up. Crispin Bates notes that many Indian commentators think that Mountbatten's appointment as viceroy 'was dominated above all by the desire of the British government to save face, and it was for this reason that he pushed Indian politicians so precipitously towards the partition of India'. Another criticism of Mountbatten is that, in the haste to hand over power, he did not make adequate security provisions to cope with the dislocation caused by the abrupt partition of India, resulting in violence and bloodshed on an unprecedented scale. According to Copland, many Indian historians believe that the hasty handover in the final few months 'contributed significantly to the chaos' that accompanied partition. He also notes that many Pakistani historians have questioned 'whether due process was followed' by the boundary commission set up by the British.

QUESTION

What does the phrase 'due process' mean? How would it apply in the drawing of boundaries in India in 1947?

Figure 8.1: Jawaharlal Nehru with Lord Mountbatten and his wife. The Muslim League viewed the obvious friendship between them with suspicion and they questioned Mountbatten's impartiality.

The partition plan

Mountbatten's initial proposal, Plan Balkan, which suggested transferring power to each province separately, was rejected by Nehru, who was determined to avoid the 'Balkanisation' of India. This would mean the division of the subcontinent into several small states, perhaps hostile to each other, as had happened in the Balkan peninsula in south-eastern Europe after the collapse of the Ottoman Empire.

Mountbatten opted for the Muslim League's two-state solution and created two enclaves in north-western India and eastern Bengal, containing large numbers of Muslims, to become Pakistan. In the atmosphere of escalating violence, the Congress leaders reluctantly came to accept that partition was the only viable solution and that British India would be divided into two separate states. Nehru and Patel indicated to Mountbatten that they would accept the creation of Pakistan as long as the Hindu and Sikh minorities in Punjab and Bengal had the option of being part of India. They also asked him to use his influence with the leaders of the princely states to persuade them to be part of India. The provincial legislatures of Punjab and Bengal subsequently voted in favour of the partition of the two provinces. The leaders of the princely states were informed by Mountbatten that they would have to choose incorporation within either India or Pakistan. Many of them felt betrayed by this abrupt decision and believed that their long record of loyalty to the British crown had gone unrewarded.

DISCUSSION POINT

Discuss whether the decision to partition India should be viewed as an admission of failure or as a creative solution to a complex problem.

In June 1947, Mountbatten announced that India and Pakistan would become independent as dominions within the British Commonwealth on 15 August, just two months away. This did not leave much time for the government to arrange the division of the administrative functions between the two states, or the division of assets and liabilities and the demarcation of the new boundaries. In addition, the ethnic and religious mix of the subcontinent was far more complex than the simple geographic division devised by the British implied. It would be impossible to draw the borders so that all Hindus would be in India and all Muslims in Pakistan. For the partition plan to work, millions of people would have to relocate to one country or the other, depending on their ethnicity and religion. As Independence Day approached, millions of people began to flee their homes, afraid of being caught on the wrong side of the new borders.

ACTIVITY

Four other countries which were partitioned during the 20th century were Ireland (1922), Korea (1945), Palestine (1948) and Vietnam (1954). Choose one of these and do some brief research on it. Compare the circumstances that led to the decision to partition it with what happened in India in 1947.

Change and continuity: Examine the key factors that resulted in change rather than continuity in India between 1945 and 1947.

8.2 How did India achieve independence?

In August 1947, British rule came to an end when the subcontinent became independent as two separate states: India and Pakistan. Independence and partition were accompanied by waves of violence and bloodshed and a mass population movement of desperate refugees.

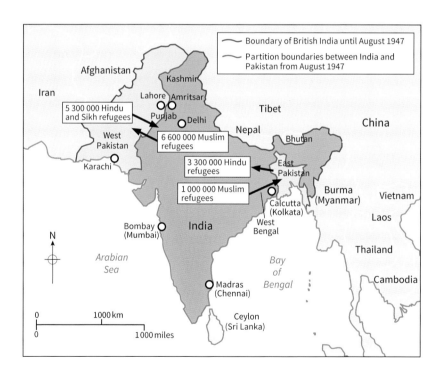

Figure 8.2: The subcontinent after independence, showing the flow of refugees.

Independence Day, 1947

On 14 and 15 August 1947, hundreds of thousands of Indians came to Delhi to celebrate the handover of power and the creation of a new state. They listened to the words of their new prime minister, Nehru, as quoted in Source 8.2.

SOURCE 8.2

Long years ago we made a tryst with destiny, and now the time comes when we shall redeem our pledge, not wholly or in full measure, but very substantially. At the stroke of the midnight hour, when the world sleeps, India will awake to life and freedom. A moment comes, which comes but rarely in history, when we step out from the old to the new, when an age ends, and when the soul of a nation, long suppressed, finds utterance. It is fitting that at this solemn moment we take the pledge of dedication to the service of India and her people and to the still larger cause of humanity.

A speech by Jawaharlal Nehru, the first prime minister of independent India, to the Constituent Assembly in New Delhi, shortly before midnight on 14 August, 1947. From Nehru, Jawaharlal. 1965. **Nehru: The First Sixty Years Volume 2.** *The Bodley Head. p. 336.*

Gandhi himself decided to mark India's independence with a 24-hour fast. He was deeply saddened by the partition and by the widespread violence and bloodshed that accompanied it.

Theory of Knowledge

History and the use of language

Nehru's 'Tryst with Destiny' speech is considered to be a landmark in the freedom struggle in India, and a masterpiece of oratory. To what extent does Nehru use emotion and rhetoric to get his message across? How can an analysis of the language used help us to understand the significance of historical events?

The refugee crisis

Independence and partition led to a desperate migration of millions of people, anxious not to be caught on the wrong side of the new borders. Historians estimate that probably over 15 million people were uprooted in this way. The two areas where partition was most complex were in the provinces of Punjab in the west, and Bengal in the east. Both had very mixed populations, so the decision had been made to divide each of them between India and Pakistan. Matters were further complicated by the fact that the new borders dividing these provinces were announced only a few days after independence. Millions of Hindus and Muslims found themselves on the wrong side of the border and tried desperately to get to safety. They abandoned their homes, fields, livestock and belongings in a panic-stricken scramble to get to the other side. It is estimated that up to 2 million people lost their lives, although the exact number is not known. Talbot and Singh comment on the human tragedy involved: 'Whatever the numbers, immense human suffering occurred in a peace-time situation in which governments demonstrated a lamentable inability to provide basic security for minority communities.'

QUESTION

Who, according to Talbot and Singh, was responsible for the refugee crisis and loss of life at independence?

DISCUSSION POINT

Why is the resettlement of refugees often such a complex and controversial matter? What rights do refugees have? What responsibilities do the countries that they flee to have towards them?

Figure 8.3: A small section of the mass movement of refugees that accompanied partition.

The situation in Punjab was further complicated by the presence of the Sikhs who were scattered throughout the province. Their demands for their own state had been ignored, and they feared that the partition of the province would leave their community powerless and split between two states. When the border was finally announced, they streamed eastwards out of West Punjab, along with millions of Hindus, adding to the violence. At the same time, millions of Muslims were moving westwards towards the border of Pakistan. Law and order broke down entirely, as refugees were killed in communal attacks, with both sides responsible for atrocities. Trains carrying refugees were special targets for attack, with trains being ambushed and derailed and the passengers murdered. Each such attack set off a chain-reaction of revenge and more violence. Bates suggests that some of the looting and murder that took place was 'inspired not by religious emotion or aggressive chauvinism but pure greed' for wealth and land. He goes on to explain that women were the main victims of partition with 'nightmarish violence being perpetrated by men of all three communities as they delighted in their momentary sense of power over vulnerable women'. Hundreds of thousands of women were raped, killed or abducted. Many of them committed suicide, or were killed by their own families, as a desperate means of avoiding the brutal rapes that took place.

DISCUSSION POINT

What do these events suggest about attitudes towards women in South Asia at the time? Is there any evidence that attitudes have changed since then?

As a result of this mass migration of over 15 million people, East Punjab ended up with a population that was 60% Hindu and 35% Sikh, while the population of West Punjab was almost totally Muslim. This process was similar to the 'ethnic cleansing' that we have seen in other countries in more recent times.

ACTIVITY

Ethnic cleansing refers to the expulsion of a population from a certain area, or the forced displacement of an ethnic or religious minority. Use the internet to research an example of ethnic cleansing from the 1990s, for example in Bosnia, Kosovo or Rwanda.

The province of Bengal was also partitioned and millions of Hindu refugees fled from East Pakistan into West Bengal, with Muslim refugees moving in the opposite direction. However, the migration in Bengal was a more gradual process and not accompanied by as much violence and death as in Punjab.

By the end of 1947, the new governments were able to contain the violence and restore order and control. Despite the mass migration, over 40 million Muslims remained in India, and several million Hindus in Pakistan. The resettlement of refugees was a huge financial burden for the new states, which also had to manage the economic consequences of the abrupt partition on existing patterns of communication, infrastructure, agriculture, irrigation and trade.

Some historians think that the reality of partition cannot be understood simply by examining the political events that led up to it or that followed it. They believe that this approach omits the 'human dimension', or the 'history from below' focus.

Urvashi Butalia has constructed a history of partition based entirely on interviews with people who actually experienced it, called *The Other Side of Silence: Voices from the Partition of India* (2000). In a different approach, Gyanendra Pandey investigates the violence that accompanied partition in *Remembering Partition* (2001), and analyses issues such as history and memory and how communities choose to remember (or forget) violent events.

> **DISCUSSION POINT**
>
> Discuss the advantages and disadvantages of using oral evidence in history.

The state of Pakistan

The creation of Pakistan was the result of the 'Two Nation' theory – the idea that India's Muslims were a separate nation who needed their own state. However, although Pakistan itself was a predominantly Muslim country, about 40 million Muslims – roughly one-third of the Muslim population of British India – remained in India, many because of their economic situation and some out of choice.

Pakistan did not have the same continuity of leadership that India had after independence. Jinnah, the founder of Pakistan and its first leader in 1947, died of tuberculosis a year later, and his successor, Liaquat Ali Khan, was assassinated in 1951. Pakistan also lacked the leadership experience that Congress had built up over many years.

The heartland of support for the Muslim League had been in the province of Uttar Pradesh, which was now part of India. Muslims from this region had moved westwards as refugees to Pakistan, but once there they had to compete with local people for access to land and employment, which put them at a disadvantage. There was also resentment against them as they were perceived as dominating positions of power and wealth.

ACTIVITY

Write an obituary for Mohammad Ali Jinnah, evaluating his role in the history of South Asia.

At the time of partition, over 90% of industries in the subcontinent were in India, as well as most of the railways and hydro-electric plants. The largest cities of South Asia – Delhi, Bombay and Calcutta – were all in India. Lahore was the only city of economic and cultural significance in Pakistan. Pakistan's economy was mainly agricultural, there were few exports and most people were poor farmers.

Both countries faced the challenge of settling millions of refugees, but for Pakistan it was particularly difficult, because the refugees formed a larger percentage of the population than they did in India. In addition, many of those coming into Pakistan were unskilled rural labourers, while many who fled from Pakistan to India were professionals, skilled workers and traders. This contributed to a shortage of skills to staff the new administration in Pakistan.

The circumstances of Pakistan's beginnings as an independent state – its weak economy, a dispute with India over Kashmir (which you will read about in Chapter 9), and the belief that its borders were insecure in the face of a strong and hostile neighbour – put the country's military in a strong position. The army frequently justified its intervention in politics on the pretext of stamping out corruption. From the 1950s onwards there were several long periods of military rule, interspersed with interludes of weak civilian government.

Pakistan itself was divided into two parts, East and West Pakistan, separated by 1500 km (930 miles) of Indian territory. There was no corridor linking the two areas as Jinnah had requested. Although the people of East and West Pakistan shared a common religion, Islam, there were vast linguistic and cultural differences between them.

East Pakistanis resented the political and economic dominance of the western part. In 1971 they broke away and formed the independent state of Bangladesh. With help from the Indian army, they successfully fought off an attempt by Pakistan to reunite them.

DISCUSSION POINT

Discuss the implications of the division of Pakistan into two separate countries for the 'Two Nation' theory that had been the dream of Muslim separatists for so long.

8.3 What were the reasons for the partition of the South Asian subcontinent?

There are debates about the reasons for the partition of the South Asian subcontinent into India and Pakistan. Historians have offered different explanations of the causes. British imperialist historians suggested that partition was inevitable because there were irreconcilable differences between Hindus and Muslims in India, but Ian Talbot and Gurharpal Singh reject this explanation in Source 8.3.

SOURCE 8.3

It is important to remember that partition was not the inevitable outcome of entrenched Hindu-Muslim differences. Notions of what constituted a religious community in the subcontinent had always been more plural, flexible and malleable than either census enumerators or religious reformers would countenance. Political separatism based on religion therefore was an ideology which resonated only in particular contexts. Its importance strengthened against the background of several intersecting developments – the fears stoked by democratisation in the 1930s, the Second World War, Congress's anti-war stance, the open declaration by the British in the early 1940s that they would leave India and the near civil war conditions between 1946 and 1947. Even at the height of communal polarisation in 1946–47, there were well-documented cases where people, political parties and national political leaders refused to accept the official registers which defined the political categories of Hindus and Muslims.

Talbot, Ian and Singh, Gurharpal. 2009. **The Partition of India**.
Cambridge. Cambridge University Press. p. 57.

QUESTION

Assess how each of the following could have strengthened 'political separatism based on religion' (which is mentioned in Source 8.3):

- **democratisation in the 1930s**
- **the Second World War**
- **Britain's intention to leave India.**

Other historians offer explanations for partition by apportioning blame to one or other of the key players – Britain, or Jinnah and the Muslim League, or the Congress politicians. Another group of historians have focused on the complex reasons behind partition and have seen it as a combination of various factors.

Historians of the Subaltern Studies group, such as Talbot, Singh, Bates and others, believe that it is not only the constitutional negotiations between Britain and Indian leaders (the 'high politics' of partition) that need to be understood, but the 'human dimension' as well ('history from below'). They suggest that ordinary people should not be seen simply as victims of partition, but also as agents of it, some of whom, for example, saw the economic advantages that could be derived from it.

British policies and actions as a cause of partition

Indian nationalist historians, especially in the decades after independence, saw British colonial policies, which emphasised differences between the Hindu and Muslim communities, as a major factor. Bipan Chandra claims that Britain followed 'a classic imperial policy of divide and rule… to promote cleavages among the people… which culminated in India's partition'. (See Source 6.1 in Chapter 6.) This view also suggests that the path to partition was set in motion as early as 1909 when Britain granted separate representation to Muslims in the Morley-Minto reforms, and then repeated this formula in the Government of India Acts of 1919 and 1935. In this view, Muslim communalism was a force created and promoted by the British to weaken the nationalist struggle against colonial rule.

Other historians have focused on the impact of the Second World War on British policies in India. Talbot and Singh suggest that the fact that Congress was marginalised during the war years, as a result of the 'Quit India' campaign, strengthened the position of Jinnah and the Muslim League and 'ultimately jeopardised the long-term British commitment to a united India'. They also suggest that the demands of the war on Britain 'undermined the long-term colonial capacity for governance'. Another view is that the election of a Labour government in 1945 also played a part because Labour was sympathetic to Congress and both wanted a speedy handover of power to a strong Indian central government: the creation of a separate state of Pakistan seemed in the end to be the best way of achieving this.

Several historians have focused on the role played by Mountbatten and suggested that, by setting such a short timetable for the withdrawal of British rule, he made partition inevitable. Referring to Mountbatten's decision to bring the date for independence forward from June 1948 to August 1947, Stanley Wolpert makes this observation: 'Mountbatten scuttled the last hope of the British Imperial Raj to leave India to single independent government… Those ten additional months of postwar talks, aborted by an impatient Mountbatten, might have helped all parties to agree that cooperation was much wiser than conflict.' Pakistani historians also accuse Mountbatten of being biased towards Nehru and the Congress view and in this way aggravating suspicion and mistrust and making partition seem the only viable option.

Barbara and Thomas Metcalf examine two views of Mountbatten's decision to bring forward the date for the transfer of power in Source 8.4.

SOURCE 8.4

Whether Mountbatten's decision to speed up the transfer of power contributed to the ensuing disorder, has long been a subject of controversy. It could be argued that, had the British held on for a further year, with transitional institutions set up and the army deployed beforehand in troubled areas, a peaceable transfer could have been arranged to governments better prepared to maintain order. But it could be as easily argued that the 'shock treatment' of an early transfer served the purpose of forcing India's squabbling politicians to put an end to talk and accept responsibility for a growing disorder Britain by itself was no longer able to contain.

Metcalf, Barbara and Metcalf, Thomas. 2006. **A Concise History of Modern India (Second Edition)**. *Cambridge. Cambridge University Press. p. 220.*

QUESTION

Why, according to Source 8.4, has Mountbatten's role in the transfer of power in India been a subject of debate?

Once Britain had decided to partition India, it made haste to leave as quickly as possible, and made little effort to ensure that there would be a smooth handover of power. Many historians think that Britain should and could have taken steps to prevent the violence that accompanied partition. For example, the British troops that were stationed in India were confined to barracks with orders that they were only to be used if an evacuation of Europeans became necessary. Bose and Jalal suggest that the speed and manner in which Britain left India 'needs to be signposted… in the historical archive as the clearest admission of the former colonial master's dereliction of duty at the moment of India's gravest crisis'. Another criticism levelled at Britain is the fact that the new boundaries were announced only a few days after independence, so that Britain would not be held responsible for any violent reaction that resulted.

ACTIVITY

Read 'The Hidden Story of Partition and its Legacies', by historian Crispin Bates, on the BBC website. In what ways does he blame the British for the upheavals that accompanied independence in India? According to this article, what are the unresolved issues from the time of partition?

The ambitions and actions of Jinnah and the Muslim League

Many historians have focused on the role of the Muslim League, and especially Mohammad Ali Jinnah, as the reason for partition. However, they have widely different views of the nature of this role.

Pakistani historians generally see the partition of South Asia in a positive light and as the fulfilment of the vision of Muslim separatists that India was a land of 'two nations'. In their view, the establishment of Pakistan was the only means by which they could maintain and defend their separate identity. To them, Jinnah is the hero, the father of the nation and 'great leader' – the *Quaid-i-Azam* – who fought for the partition of India and achieved it through his single-minded devotion to the cause.

Indian nationalist, and British imperialist, historians see Jinnah in an unsympathetic light as a stubborn and austere figure who refused to compromise. This view is reinforced by Mountbatten's description of Jinnah as 'an evil genius'. In his biography of Jinnah, Akbar Ahmed raises the question about whether 'Mountbatten consciously manipulated and propagated a negative image of Jinnah'. Historians who hold a critical view of Jinnah cite his refusal to accept many of the constitutional proposals as the underlying reason for the failure of negotiations. They view his call for direct action in August 1946 as the clear cause of intensified communal violence which ruled out the chance of a united India and made partition inevitable. According to Ramachandra Guha, 'Jinnah and the League hoped to polarise the two communities further, and thus force the British to divide India when they finally quit. In this endeavour they richly succeeded.' Sucheta Mahajan argues that, after the violence which followed Jinnah's call for direct action, the British 'were frightened into appeasing the League by Jinnah's ability to unleash civil war'.

The revisionist interpretation of Jinnah's role which has received a great deal of attention is that of Ayesha Jalal who has argued, some historians believe convincingly, that Jinnah did not want partition but was using the call for a separate Muslim state as a bargaining tool to get a better deal for Muslims in a united India. However, in his biography of Jinnah, Akbar Ahmed suggests that this view ignores how powerful the ideals of religion and culture were in the Pakistan movement.

QUESTION

Examine why the role of Jinnah in the partition of India is the subject of such fierce debate.

The attitude and actions of Congress leaders

Some historians suggest that by rejecting Jinnah's earlier attempts at cooperation in the 1920s and 1930s, Congress leaders unwittingly contributed to partition. They also suggest that the actions of the Congress provincial governments in power between 1937 and 1939 fuelled Muslim fears of Hindu domination in a single India, and led directly to the growth of support for the Pakistan movement.

Other historians believe that Congress politicians should share a more direct responsibility for partition. In the postwar negotiations about independence, Copland blames Nehru for the failure of the Cabinet Mission in June 1946: 'This last chance reprieve for the principle of a united India was destroyed by the thoughtless intervention of a single individual: Jawaharlal Nehru.' This is a reference to Nehru's public announcement that he did not regard the proposed grouping of states (which the Muslim League saw as offering some protection against Hindu domination) as a permanent arrangement. Jalal too suggests that Nehru contributed to partition because he was never really willing to contemplate sharing power with Muslim League politicians. In his diaries, Maulana Azad, a Muslim who served as president of Congress from 1940 to 1946, depicted Nehru as 'overreaching himself, greedy for power and reluctant to compromise', according to Bates. Bose and Jalal suggest that the Congress leaders agreed to partition because they were 'more anxious to acquire power than uphold the nationalist ideals for which so many freedom fighters in the past had sacrificed their lives'.

Theory of Knowledge

History and ethics

Is it the historian's role to apportion 'blame'? To what extent should historians make moral judgements about the past? Discuss whether it is the historian's role simply to relate what happened or to interpret what happened in the past.

Other views of the reasons for partition

There are other factors too that may have played a role in the partition of South Asia.

Bates explains what he refers to as the 'crisis of the state' theory of partition. In this view, partition cannot be blamed on 'the manipulation of Congress politicians or the Muslim League, or on the wheelings and dealings of the British' because none of them 'had the power or ability to deliver on any of their policies', as Source 8.5 explains:

SOURCE 8.5

The British empire was in a debilitated state, the army had been demobilised, and, by 1946, large numbers of civil servants had resigned or had taken early retirement… There were police strikes, a naval mutiny and widespread disaffection. The British state in India was crumbling and, it was widely recognised, could not hope to retain control if an insurrection on anything approaching the scale of Quit India was to be repeated. The Congress Party was also disordered and chaotic and the Muslim League, after Jinnah's Day of Direct Action on 16 August 1946, had lost control of its followers. Widespread civil disturbance and rioting then ensued until 1947.

SOURCE 8.5 *(CONTINUED)*

That this theory has still not been widely circulated in print is an indication that the whole issue of partition still dominates strained relations between India and Pakistan, and it is not really possible at present for commentators, even those on the left, to articulate a view that suggests that partition might not have been the fault of either Jinnah or the British – that what happened was not a division of the spoils but a fracturing of the state in 1947.

Bates, Crispin. 2007. **Subalterns and Raj: South Asia since 1600.** *London. Routledge. p. 168.*

DISCUSSION POINT

Source 8.5 implies that the 'crisis of the state' theory would be rejected by many people in India today. Discuss possible reasons for this.

Some historians believe that it was a complex interaction of various factors rather than one single reason that led to partition, as Sources 8.6, 8.7 and 8.8 show:

SOURCE 8.6

Although great controversy still surrounds Mountbatten's timing of partition and the boundary and security arrangements which accompanied it, there is little evidence for the claim that he imposed partition on reluctant and unsuspecting Indian leaders. Partition was not a 'parting gift' of outgoing imperial masters: it was self-consciously willed by the All-India Congress and Muslim League leaders and, above all, reflected their fears and mistrusts, as well as hopes, that a 'right-sized' state would deliver to them the power to construct a new political, economic and social order in a free subcontinent.

Talbot, Ian and Singh, Gurharpal. 2009. **The Partition of India.** *Cambridge. Cambridge University Press. p. 41.*

SOURCE 8.7

Why the Congress, wedded to a belief in one Indian nation, accepted the division of the country, remains a question difficult to answer... Nehru and Patel's acceptance of Partition has been popularly interpreted as stemming from their lust for quick and easy power, which made them betray the people...

[However] it is forgotten that Nehru, Patel and Gandhiji in 1947 were only accepting what had become inevitable because of the long-term failure of the Congress to draw in the Muslim masses into the national movement and stem the surging waves of Muslim communalism... This failure was revealed with stark clarity by the 1946 elections in which the League won 90 per cent [of the] Muslim seats. Though the war against Jinnah was lost by early 1946, defeat was conceded only after the final battle was mercilessly waged in the streets of Calcutta... The Congress leaders felt by June 1947 that only an immediate transfer of power could forestall the spread of Direct Action and communal disturbances. The virtual collapse of the Interim Government also made Pakistan appear to be an unavoidable reality...

There was an additional consideration in accepting immediate transfer of power to two dominions. The prospect of balkanisation was ruled out as the provinces and princes were not given the option to be independent – the latter were, in fact, much to their chagrin, cajoled and coerced into joining one or the other dominion. This was no mean achievement. Princely states standing out would have meant a graver blow to Indian unity than Pakistan was.

Chandra, B. et al. 2012. **India's Struggle for Independence 1857–** *1947. London. Penguin. Digital edition: Chapter 37: 'Freedom and Partition', Location 8871–8887.*

SOURCE 8.8

All the while, it is arguable, the subaltern factor was the main issue forcing the hand of the British. They were desperate to get out and to hand over power to a respectable successor before events overtook them. The moral and physical incapacity of the British raj by the end of 1946, and the failure of Nehru and Jinnah to agree on any alternative, led to the solution of partition. Whether this intransigence may be laid at Nehru's or Jinnah's door, or whether indeed all players were relatively powerless in the face of the state's collapse, will remain a subject of continuing debate.

Bates, Crispin. 2007. Subalterns and Raj: South Asia since 1600. *London. Routledge. p. 178.*

ACTIVITY

Using the information in Sources 8.6 to 8.8, design a spider diagram to illustrate the factors leading to the partition of South Asia. Use colour coding to differentiate the different categories of factors (such as those relating to Britain, to Jinnah and the Muslim League, to Congress, or any other catagories that you think appropriate).

QUESTION

'In the end, Indian leaders accepted partition because it offered certain benefits as well as a solution to the crisis facing India in 1947.' Using Sources 8.6 to 8.8 and your own knowledge, to what extent do you agree with this statement?

Paper 3 exam practice

Question

To what extent did British policies and actions contribute to the partition of South Asia and the violence that accompanied it?
[15 marks]

Skill

Using your own knowledge analytically and combining it with awareness of historical debate

Examiner's tips

Always remember that historical knowledge and analysis should be the *core* of your answer – aspects of historical debate are desirable extras. However, where it is relevant, the integration of relevant knowledge about historical debates and interpretations, with reference to individual historians, will help push your answer up into the higher bands.

Assuming that you have read the question carefully, drawn up a plan, worked out your line of argument and approach and written your introductory paragraph, you should be able to avoid both irrelevant material and simple narrative. Your task now is to follow your plan by writing a series of linked paragraphs that contain relevant analysis, precise supporting own knowledge and, where relevant, brief references to historical debate interpretations.

For this question, you will need to:

- give a brief explanation of the historical context – the situation in India after the Second World War
- supply an outline of the steps which led to independence and partition in 1947
- provide a consistently analytical examination of Britain's role, as well as those of other key players and factors.

Such a topic, which has been the subject of some historical debate, will also give you the chance to refer to different historians' views.

Common mistakes

Some students, being aware of an existing historical debate (and knowing that extra marks can be gained by showing this), simply write things like: 'Historian X says… and historian Y says…' However, they make no attempt to evaluate the different views (for example, has one historian had access to more or better information than another, perhaps because he or she was writing at a later date?); nor is this information integrated into the answer by being pinned to the question. Another weak use of historical debate is to write things like: 'Historian X is biased because she is American.' Such comments will not be given credit. What is needed is explicit understanding of historians' views and/ or the application of precise own knowledge to *evaluate* the strengths and weaknesses of these views.

Sample paragraphs containing analysis and historical debate

British policy and actions certainly played a part in the partition of South Asia into Muslim Pakistan and India which was predominantly Hindu. The colonial policy of classifying the population into different religious communities and providing separate representation for Muslims was one of the factors that need to be examined. British actions during and after the Second World War were also significant, given the short timetable which Britain set for their withdrawal. However, there were other factors that need to be taken into account, such as the actions of Jinnah and the Muslim League, as well as Congress politicians, and the unstable situation in India itself by 1946–47.

India had been a British colony since 1858 and, as part of its system of colonial rule, British administrators classified the population into different religious and other communities. This emphasised differences between Hindus and Muslims. This separation was reinforced when Britain granted separate representation to Muslims in the Morley-Minto reforms in 1909 and repeated this formula in the Government of India Acts of 1919 and 1935. By recognising Muslims as a separate community, Britain encouraged the growth of Muslim separatism which ultimately resulted in calls for a separate Muslim state. **Indian historians, such as Chandra,** *believe that it was done as part of the colonial policy of 'divide and rule' to weaken the nationalist struggle against colonial rule and that this laid the foundation for partition.*

British policy towards India during the Second World War also played a part. The British government was unwilling to make any concessions to Indian nationalists. Most historians accept that the failure of the Cripps Mission was due to this, especially the attitude of Churchill towards India. After this Congress launched the 'Quit India' campaign and, as a result, became marginalised during the war. This strengthened the position of Jinnah and the Muslim League. **Talbot and Singh** *think that this influenced British policy towards India as they came to accept the view that partition might be preferable. After the war Britain was in a weak position economically and the newly elected Labour government wanted a speedy handover of power and so was anxious to reach an agreement quickly.*

The actions of Mountbatten, the last British viceroy, also played a part. He set a very short timetable for the withdrawal of British rule, bringing the date forward by 10 months. Historians such as **Wolpert** *think that this made partition inevitable, as the extra time might have made it possible for a peaceful agreement instead of violent partition.* **Ahmed** *also thinks that Mountbatten was biased in favour of Nehru and the Congress and that this aggravated suspicion and mistrust among Muslim politicians, making them more determined to press for partition.*

Once Britain had decided to partition India, they wanted to leave as quickly as possible, and made little effort to ensure that there would be a smooth handover of power. **Bose and Jalal** *think that Britain should and could have taken steps to prevent the violence that accompanied partition. Another criticism of British actions is the fact that the new boundaries were announced only a few days after independence, so that Britain would not be responsible for any violent reaction that resulted.*

However, there are other views of the reasons for partition…

[There follow several paragraphs examining other views – that Jinnah and the Muslim League were responsible, or the actions of Congress politicians, or the collapse of authority in India at the time, as well as a complex combination of various factors.]

Examiner's comment

This is a reasonable example of how to use historians' views. The *main* focus of the answer is properly concerned with using precise own knowledge to address the demands of the question. However, although the candidate has also provided some brief but relevant knowledge of historical debate, which is **smoothly integrated** into the answer, there is no evaluation of different views. Consequently, such an answer would probably be awarded a mark at the bottom rather than the top of Band 2.

Activity

In this chapter, the focus is on writing an answer that is analytical and well supported by precise own knowledge, and one which – where relevant – refers to historical interpretations and debates. Using the information from this chapter, and any other sources of information available to you, try to answer **one** of the following Paper 3 practice questions using these skills.

Remember to refer to the simplified Paper 3 mark scheme in Chapter 10.

Paper 3 practice questions

1 Examine the reasons for the failure of the 1946 Simla Conference and the impact of its failure.

2 Discuss the reasons for and consequences of Jinnah's call for 'Direct Action' in August 1946.

3 To what extent did Mountbatten's decision to speed up the transfer of power contribute to the disorder and death that accompanied partition?

4 Evaluate the complex interaction of factors that led to the partition of South Asia in 1947.

5 Examine the debate among historians about Jinnah's role in the partition of India.

9 | Post-independence India

Introduction

Independence had been achieved, but the new government faced significant political, economic and social challenges, some caused by the abrupt partition of South Asia. The princely states were successfully incorporated but communalism and conflicts relating to ethnicity and separatism posed threats to unity. Nevertheless, India became a stable, secular democracy, the largest in the world, although an on-going conflict with Pakistan over Kashmir created tensions at times.

The government implemented ambitious economic policies to create a more equitable distribution of wealth and resources, and introduced social reforms to end discrimination based on gender and caste. However, these measures were not always successful. This chapter examines the challenges facing post-independence India and evaluates its achievements between 1947 and 1964.

TIMELINE

1947 **Aug:** Independence and Partition

Nov: Indian army occupies princely state of Junagadh

1948 **26 Jan:** Official Independence Day: India becomes a sovereign democratic republic

30 Jan: Assassination of Gandhi

Dec: Constituent Assembly completes work

1949 **Jan:** UN arranges ceasefire in Kashmir

Sept: Indian army occupies princely state of Hyderabad

1950 Indian Planning Commission established

1951–56 First Five Year Plan

1952 First general election

1953 State of Andhra Pradesh created

1954 France hands over Pondicherry to India

1955 Hindu Marriage Act

1956 Hindu Succession Act; reorganisation of states along linguistic lines

1956–61 Second Five Year Plan

1957 Second general election

1960 Bombay split into Gujarat and Maharashtra

1961–66 Third Five Year Plan

1961 **Dec:** India annexes Goa from Portugal
1962 Third general election
1964 Death of Nehru

KEY QUESTIONS

- What ethnic and religious conflicts did India face?
- How were the princely states incorporated?
- Why was there conflict with Pakistan over Kashmir?
- To what extent were Nehru's domestic policies successful?

Overview

- The new government faced threats from communalists who opposed the establishment of a secular state. Gandhi was assassinated by a member of a militant Hindu nationalist group angered by his conciliatory policy towards Muslims.
- Conflicts linked to ethnicity and language included a Sikh separatist movement in Punjab, a Teluga language movement in Andhra Pradesh and a struggle by the Naga people for greater autonomy. Several state boundaries were redrawn to accommodate the demands of protesters.
- The incorporation of over 550 princely states was in most cases a peaceful process when their rulers gave up their autonomy in return for generous pensions and the right to retain wealth and privilege. Two exceptions were Junagadh and Hyderabad which the Indian army annexed by force.
- A third exception was Kashmir which was claimed by both India and Pakistan. It was eventually partitioned between them by the UN, a situation which did not satisfy either side. The dispute over Kashmir remains unresolved, and the tensions between India and Pakistan remain high.

- The first task facing the new government was to cope with the crises created by the abrupt partition of the subcontinent. These included the search for abducted women and the resettlement of millions of refugees.

- At the same time the government took steps to consolidate India's status as a unified, secular democracy. In 1950 a new constitution was adopted, making India, with a population of over 300 million people, the largest democracy in the world. The Congress Party gained a convincing victory in the first general election in 1952.

- The government introduced policies to promote economic growth and address poverty, unemployment, landlessness and the unequal distribution of resources. Despite impressive levels of growth, poverty and inequality remained significant problems.

- The government also introduced social policies to extend education, improve health services, provide social welfare, and end discrimination based on gender and caste. But progress was offset by rapid population growth and conservative traditional attitudes.

- Jawaharlal Nehru, the first prime minister, led India until his death in 1964. He is widely admired for his commitment to democracy and secularism, and for his role in establishing a united and democratic India.

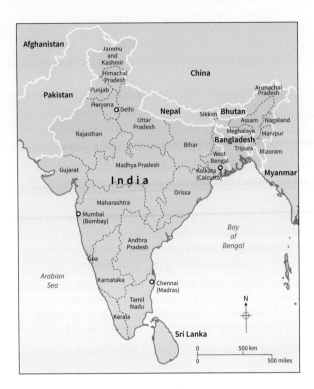

Figure 9.1: Modern India.

9.1 What ethnic and religious conflicts did India face?

Many of the challenges faced by the new government of India were linked to what historian Ramachandra Guha has called the 'axes of conflict' in Indian society: religion, language, caste, class and gender. Partition did not put an end to religious conflict, and independence did not solve the tensions over language and caste, nor end the inequalities resulting from class and gender. Ethnicity in India was inextricably linked to issues of language and religion. All three created conflicts that were complex and difficult to resolve and resulted, at times, in acts of political extremism, posing a threat to secular democracy.

Threats posed by communalism and Hindu nationalism

Less than six months after independence, the government faced a crisis caused by right-wing Hindu nationalism. A right-wing group, the Rashtriya Swayamsevak Sangh (RSS), opposed the creation of a secular state in India. Its members were openly anti-Muslim and portrayed Muslims as a hostile and alien element in Indian society. They had a vision of India as a land of, and for, Hindus. Although they claimed to be a cultural rather than a political organisation, they formed uniformed paramilitary cells. At the time of independence, they drew support from students, refugees and the urban lower middle classes. According to Guha, Nehru believed that they were responsible for much of the violence that accompanied partition. They were opposed to Gandhi's efforts to reduce communal violence and his conciliatory gestures towards Muslims. They promoted a campaign of hatred against Gandhi, accusing him of being a traitor.

In January 1948, Gandhi was assassinated by Nathuram Godse, an active supporter of the RSS, who was incensed by Gandhi's protection of the Muslim community in Delhi. For some months before his death, Gandhi had been in Delhi, trying to stop the communal violence there. The remaining local Muslim population was living in fear in strongholds and refugee camps, after the occupation of their homes by Hindu and Sikh refugees who had fled from Pakistan. Gandhi visited them in their camps, and had meetings with local Hindu, Sikh and Muslim leaders, trying to find a way of ending the violence. He also announced his intention of visiting Pakistan. Talbot suggests that the main reason for his assassination was his public fast to force the Indian government to pay Pakistan its share of the assets of British India.

On 30 January 1948, Nehru broadcast the news of Gandhi's death to the shocked nation. An extract from the broadcast appears in Source 9.1.

Figure 9.2: Mourners surround the body of Mahatma Gandhi as it lies in state after his assassination in January 1948.

SOURCE 9.1

The light has gone out of our lives and there is darkness everywhere. I do not know what to tell you and how to say it… A madman has put an end to his life, for I can only call him mad who did it, and yet there has been enough of poison spread in this country during the past years and months, and this poison has had an effect on people's minds. We must face this poison; we must root out this poison… We must hold together and all our petty troubles and difficulties and conflicts must be ended in the face of this great disaster. A great disaster is a symbol to us to remember all the big things of life and forget the small things of which we have thought too much. In his death he has reminded us of the big things of life, the living truth, and if we remember that, then it will be well with India.

Nehru, Jawaharlal. 1965. Nehru: The First Sixty Years Volume 2. *The Bodley Head. pp. 364–5.*

Discuss the techniques that Nehru uses in this speech to combat communalism and promote unity.

With reference to its origin, purpose and content, assess the value and limitations of Source 9.1 for historians investigating the circumstances surrounding Gandhi's death.

The shock of Gandhi's death strengthened the hand of secularists in the government, and helped to calm communal tensions within the new Indian state. The government banned the RSS and arrested most of its leaders. It blamed them for their support for communalism and violence and generating an atmosphere of hatred towards Gandhi and secularism. The ban was lifted, however, in July 1949, after the RSS renounced violence and secrecy, and agreed to restrict itself to cultural rather than political matters.

To what extent can the manner of Gandhi's death be considered both tragic and ironic?

When British India was divided, Pakistan was created as a specifically Muslim state, with Islam as its official religion. In contrast to this, India became a secular state. The Congress Party had always promoted secularism. The constitution adopted in 1950 established India as a completely secular state, with a separation of religion and state, and no official state religion.

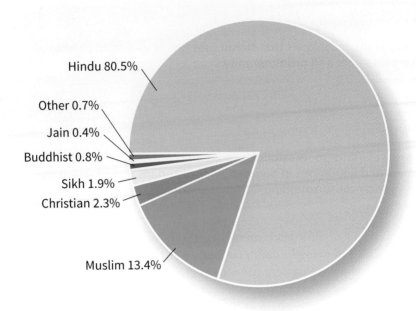

Figure 9.3: Religious affiliation in India, according to the 2001 census. Although the population is over 80% Hindu, there are sizeable religious minorities in India, including 138 million Muslims, 24 million Christians and 19 million Sikhs. There are almost as many Muslims in India as there are in Pakistan.

However, over 80% of the population of India was Hindu, and Hindu nationalists and communalists believed that India should be a Hindu state. This is where pressure groups such as the RSS, and political parties such as the Bharatiya Jan Sangh (BJS), found their support. The BJS was a Hindu nationalist party, which challenged the secular nature of the Indian state. It promoted Hindu culture, religion and traditions and, using the slogan 'one country, one culture, one nation', attempted to unite all Hindus. The party treated India's Muslims with suspicion, questioning their loyalty to India. However, in the 1952 general election, the BJS won only 3% of the vote, indicating that there was little support for a communalist Hindu party at that stage. However, although it did not play a significant role during Nehru's lifetime, the rise of Hindu nationalism and communal violence in later decades once more became a feature of Indian politics.

Conflicts relating to ethnicity and separatism

The Sikhs made up a distinctive religious group, numbering about 10 million at the time of independence, with their own history, culture and identity, as well as their own language, Punjabi. Many of them resented the fact that, while Hindus and Muslims had been accommodated in the partition plan, Sikh demands for their own state were ignored. When partition came, millions of them left their farms and villages in West Punjab and fled to India as refugees. By 1951, they formed one-third of the population of Indian Punjab, and held prominent positions in politics, business and the army.

The main Sikh political party was the Akali Dal ('Army of the Immortals'), which wanted more control for the Sikhs in Punjab. Some even wanted an independent Sikh state, to be called Khalistan, but Nehru was firmly opposed to the creation of any separate state based on religious grounds. In 1955 the Akali Dal held mass demonstrations demanding greater autonomy for the Sikhs. To stop the protests, the government ordered the army to invade the Golden Temple in Amritsar, the Sikhs' most sacred holy place, which the government believed was the centre of the protests.

Although Nehru resisted Sikh demands, in 1965, a year after his death, the Indian government finally agreed to create a smaller Punjab state where Sikhs would be in the majority, after the Sikh leader, Sant Fateh Singh, threatened to fast to death unless the government recognised Sikh demands. Punjab was split into a new state called Haryana (which was mainly Hindu) and a smaller Punjab, where Sikhs formed slightly more than half of the population. The reorganisation of state borders was ostensibly made along linguistic rather than religious lines, with Hindi and Punjabi as the respective official languages.

However, the position of the Sikhs remained unresolved, and led to problems for future Indian governments. In the 1980s, a violent campaign for the creation of a separate Sikh state led to the assassination of the Indian prime minister, **Indira Gandhi**.

> **Indira Gandhi (1917–1984)**
>
> Nehru's daughter, Indira Gandhi, was Prime Minister from 1966 to 1977 and from 1980 to 1984, when she was assassinated by her Sikh bodyguards after she had ordered troops to storm the Golden Temple at Amritsar to arrest the leader of a militant Sikh separatist group. Thousands were killed in the process. After her death, at least 2000 Sikhs were murdered and many more made homeless in anti-Sikh riots in Delhi and elsewhere.

Conflicts about language

There were many hundreds of languages in India, and part of the colonial legacy was the use of English as the language of government, the law courts and of higher education, as well as that of the middle and upper classes.

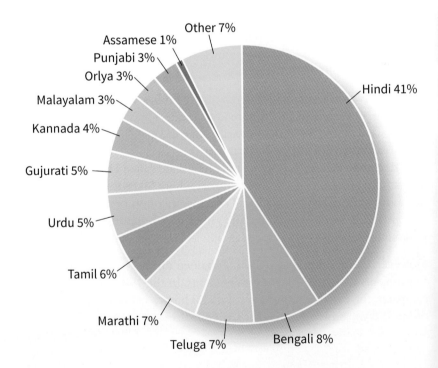

Figure 9.4: The percentage of speakers of the official languages in India, according to the 2001 census. (Kashmiri, Sindhi and Sanskrit, which also have official recognition, are included in 'Other').

The most widely used language was Hindi, spoken in the north, but it was used by only half of the people in India. The constitution recognised 14 major languages, and made Hindi and English the official languages. The constitution also allowed the Indian parliament to alter state boundaries, and this opened the way for different language speakers to press for changes to the provincial borders.

Some of the people involved in struggles for the reorganisation of state boundaries along linguistic lines saw themselves as separate groups with their own history, culture and identity, as well as their own language. The people of southern India were the first to press for changes, so that their own languages could have official recognition within their states. Gandhi had supported the idea of separate states for different language groups, but the experience of partition made Nehru uneasy about further sub-divisions. He had seen the country divided on grounds of religion; he did not want further divisions on grounds of language. He initially opposed all suggestions about redrawing boundaries and this resulted in violent opposition.

The Teluga-speaking Andhras were the first to campaign for a state of their own. In 1952, **Potti Sriramulu**, one of their leaders, fasted to death in protest against the government's refusal to create a province for Teluga-speakers. There were riots following his death, and in 1953 a Teluga-speaking state, Andhra Pradesh, was created from part of the state of Tamil Nadu, which at the same time was recognised as a Tamil-speaking state.

Potti Sriramulu (1901–1952):

Sriramulu was a veteran of the 1930 Salt March and a leader of the Teluga-speaking Andhra people. His death by fasting led to the creation of the state of Andhra Pradesh and, ultimately, to the redrawing of the map of India along linguistic lines. He is regarded as a hero and martyr in Andhra Pradesh for his self-sacrifice.

The government also appointed a States Reorganisation Commission to investigate the whole issue. As a result of its recommendations, some state boundaries were reorganised in 1956, to create 14 states on the basis of language. However, this did not satisfy every language group, so further changes were made later. There were violent riots in the state of Bombay over language issues, and in 1960 it was split into Gujarat and

Maharashtra, to satisfy the demands of Gujarati and Marathi speakers respectively. The division of Punjab into two provinces was also based on language.

Metcalf examines the significance of the reorganisation of some states along linguistic lines in Source 9.2.

SOURCE 9.2

States reorganisation encouraged a new regional linguistic politics, yet at the same time, by peaceably accommodating an intensely felt popular sentiment, the move helped stem separatist enthusiasm. Indeed, throughout much of India, Congress, like the Indian nation itself, emerged stronger for having successfully met, in democratic fashion, this challenge to its authority.

Metcalf, Barbara and Metcalf, Thomas. 2006. A Concise History of Modern India (Second Edition). *Cambridge. Cambridge University Press. p. 241.*

QUESTION

How, according to Source 9.2, did India benefit from the reorganisation of state boundaries along linguistic lines?

Another linguistic issue was opposition to the use of Hindi as the sole official language. The constitution had made provision for the phasing out of English as an official language and for Hindi to become the main official language by 1965. Nehru was always aware of the importance of retaining English as an official language, partly as a means of satisfying the non-Hindi-speaking south, and also because of its value as an international language. After his death, Tamil-speakers in southern India protested violently against the use of Hindi, and several protesters burned themselves to death. As a result, English was retained, not as an official language, but as the main language of inter-regional communication, business and higher education. The continued use of English perpetuated another division in Indian society, between the educated élite who spoke it and the rest of the population.

Theory of Knowledge

History and language

There is a saying that 'language is power'. Discuss the reasons why people whose language is not officially recognised feel disempowered. Evaluate the advantages and disadvantages to a country of having a large number of official languages.

Rural protests by tribal communities and peasant farmers

The 'tribal communities' made up about 7% of India's population. Most of them lived in isolation in small communities, mainly in the hills and forest areas, and their cultures, traditions and languages differed from those of surrounding communities. Some of them wanted greater autonomy and recognition of their languages and cultures. One such group were the half a million Naga people in the north-east. The 1950 constitution recognised the Naga Hills as part of the province of Assam, but the Nagas rejected this and declared their independence. When the Indian government refused to recognise it, Naga guerrilla fighters launched a campaign against the Indian army, which was sent in to crush resistance in 1955. After a long struggle, the Naga-speakers of the north-east became the separate state of Nagaland in 1963. However, the dissatisfaction of other 'tribal communities' remained unresolved, and later Indian governments faced further violent acts of protest.

Another form of rural conflict was a peasant uprising in the Telangana region of Hyderabad from 1947 to 1950. Large estates were seized from landlords and redistributed among landless peasants, and the system of forced labour was abolished. The leaders of this rebellion were activists from the Communist Party of India, who hoped it would lead to a nationwide revolution. However, it was suppressed by the police and the army, and thousands were killed in the process.

DISCUSSION POINT

Discuss the links between political extremism and issues relating to religion, ethnicity and language in Indian politics.

9.2 How were the princely states incorporated?

At the time of independence there were over 550 'princely states', under the nominal control of hereditary rulers who had signed treaties with Britain. Their territory occupied about 40% of British India (See Figure 2.1 in Chapter 2). In theory they were free to decide their own futures once the British left. In practice, however, there were strong pressures on them to give up their independent status. They were tied economically to the surrounding areas that were now part of either India or Pakistan. In addition, Indian nationalists were opposed to the idea that independent India should be a patchwork, broken up by hundreds of tiny autonomous states. With Mountbatten's support, the issue was given to Patel, Nehru's deputy, to resolve. He did so successfully, using a combination of persuasion and, in a few cases, force. Many Congress leaders regarded the integration of so many small states as an important feature of nation-building for the new state.

All except three of the princes voluntarily decided to join either India or Pakistan, in return for generous pensions, and the right to use their titles and palaces, and to keep some of their extensive personal holdings. Talbot observes that 'the bitter pill of the ending of the old princely order had been sugared by tax-free pensions linked to the former state's revenue levels and by making some of the rulers of large states governors of the new administrative entities'. Two of the exceptions were Junagadh and Hyderabad, where Muslim princes ruled over large Hindu populations, in states that were surrounded by Indian territory. The ruler of Junagadh actually elected to join Pakistan at the time of partition, but was then subjected to an economic blockade before being 'liberated' by India in November 1947. The following year the Indian army invaded Hyderabad which subsequently became part of India. Although these annexations by force were against the wishes of the Muslim rulers, they were generally welcomed by the people of these states. The third exception was the state of Kashmir, which presented a special problem. (You will read about it later in this chapter.)

The addition of the princely states added 90 million people and over a million square kilometres (about half a million square miles) to India, which compensated to some extent for the losses at the time of partition. However, levels of political and economic development in many of these states were very low, and some were the most socially conservative parts of the subcontinent.

With the exception of the unresolved issue of Kashmir, the consolidation of India was completed with the final withdrawal of other European colonial powers which had held small parts of India. France agreed to withdraw from Pondicherry and other small French enclaves in 1954. And, when Portugal was reluctant to hand over control of Goa, the Indian army invaded and united Goa with the rest of India by force in 1961.

QUESTION

Examine why the existence of independent princely states and remaining colonial enclaves was unacceptable to Indian nationalists. Discuss how they would justify using force to unite them with India.

9.3 Why was there conflict with Pakistan over Kashmir?

Kashmir was a large state, strategically placed in the north–west, and bordering on both India and Pakistan (see Figure 2.1 in Chapter 2). At the time of independence, it had a Hindu prince ruling over a predominantly Muslim population. Initially he hoped to retain the independent status of Kashmir. However, when irregular soldiers from Pakistan came to the aid of Muslim tenants rebelling against their Hindu landlords in Kashmir, he feared a full-scale invasion by Pakistan and appealed to India for military help. The price of this assistance was to join the Indian Union. Indian troops were airlifted to Kashmir, where they fought against forces from Pakistan for control of the province. The war lasted from December 1947 until January 1949, before the United Nations arranged a ceasefire and divided Kashmir between the two countries, a result that satisfied neither side, nor the people of Kashmir. A UN peacekeeping mission remained in Kashmir to monitor the border between the two sides.

Nationalism and Independence in India (1919–1964)

Historians Ian Talbot and Barbara and Thomas Metcalf explain the significance of Kashmir to India and Pakistan in Sources 9.3 and 9.4.

SOURCE 9.3

A number of writers have linked India's unyielding stance on the Kashmir dispute to the fear not only of Balkanisation if the region became independent or went to Pakistan, but to the importance for India's secular self-image of having this sole Muslim majority state safely within the Union. It could be argued, however, that the Kashmir issue has been far more important to Pakistani than Indian nationalism. because it has provided a rallying point in an otherwise fractious political environment.

Talbot, Ian. 2000. India and Pakistan. *London. Arnold. p. 168.*

SOURCE 9.4

Kashmir mattered not so much because it possessed rich mineral or other resources, nor because it was the original home of the Nehru family, but rather because for both sides it raised issues central to their self-definition as nations. For Pakistan, the critical fact was Kashmir's overwhelmingly Muslim population...

From the Indian perspective other issues were at stake. Nehru, and with him the Congress, although obliged to accept the creation of Pakistan, had never accepted the 'Two Nation' theory. India was not, in this view, a 'Hindustan' or land of Hindus. In a major defeat for Jinnah, Nehru maintained that his state was the legitimate successor of the British Raj...

In the view of the Congress, India was not only successor to the Raj, but also a secular state, in which Muslims, with all other minorities, stood, in principle, on equal footing with their Hindu fellow citizens. Millions of Muslims, remaining behind after partition by choice or necessity, already lived within India. The addition of the residents of Kashmir would only further testify to the inclusive nature of the new state.

Metcalf, Barbara and Metcalf, Thomas. 2006. A Concise History of Modern India (Second Edition). *Cambridge. Cambridge University Press. pp. 224–5.*

QUESTION

Compare and contrast what Sources 9.3 and 9.4 say about the links between the dispute over Kashmir and issues of religion and national identity in post-independence India.

Since then, India and Pakistan have fought two more wars over Kashmir – in 1965 and 1999. As both states became nuclear powers in the 1990s, the ongoing conflict over Kashmir became an issue of grave concern to the international community. The dispute over Kashmir remains unresolved, and the tensions between India and Pakistan remain high.

9.4 To what extent were Nehru's domestic policies successful?

After independence, India was dominated by the figure of its first prime minister, Jawaharlal Nehru, who led the country until his death in 1964. During this period India emerged as a stable democracy – a notable achievement given the large size of the country and its population, the legacies of colonial rule and the difficulties encountered during the progress towards independence. The government also faced significant economic and social challenges.

Problems arising from partition

Even before India's constitution was drawn up, the new state had to cope with crises created by the abrupt partition of the subcontinent.

The women affected by partition

An immediate problem facing the new government was the issue of the 'abducted women'. During partition, thousands of women had been killed, raped, abandoned or forcibly married to their abductors. An estimated 75 000 Hindu, Muslim and Sikh women on both sides of the new borders had been forcibly taken from their communities.

The Indian and Pakistani governments came to an agreement that the abducted women should be returned to their own communities. Nehru spoke out strongly in support of this, urging respect for the women and promising assistance.

By mid-1948, the Indian authorities had located 12 500 women and restored them to their families. Tragically, however, for many women the restoration programme was yet another ordeal. They awaited an uncertain reception and many were rejected by their own communities. The policy of forcible repatriation was abandoned in 1954.

DISCUSSION POINT

Is it justifiable to criticise the policy of forcible repatriation? Discuss how else the Indian government could have dealt with the issue.

The resettlement of refugees

Agriculture, in which over 75% of India's workforce was involved, was the sector of the economy most seriously affected by partition. The government had to deal urgently with the considerable disruption to existing patterns of farming, irrigation systems, roads and settlements in rural areas. It also had to find a means of livelihood for the millions of refugees resulting from partition.

The problem was most acute in Punjab, where Hindu and Sikh refugees had abandoned 2.7 million hectares (6.67 million acres) of farmland in West Punjab when it became part of Pakistan. The Indian government began a massive resettlement programme, using the land and villages abandoned by Muslim refugees after their flight into Pakistan. With government loans for seed and equipment, millions of refugees were resettled in villages where they could begin farming again. However, not all the refugees were farmers: there were also artisans, traders and workers. About half a million of them went to Delhi, where they initially lived in makeshift camps set up all over the city, until many of them were allocated land or houses in new townships and satellite towns built to accommodate them outside the city. In time, many of them came to play a dominant role in trade and commerce. By the early 1950s, most refugees in Punjab had found employment and homes.

The situation was more difficult for the more than 3 million refugees who fled into West Bengal from East Pakistan, many of them to the city of Calcutta. Unlike the mass exodus of refugees who flooded into Punjab in the weeks after partition, the flow of refugees into West Bengal went on at a steady pace for years. It was difficult to provide the people with work and shelter. Most of them had previously been involved in agriculture, but there was no land available on which to settle them, as there had been in Punjab. Some of them ended up living on the streets of Calcutta, while others formed informal settlements on vacant land, building their own houses and roads. Providing employment for such an influx of refugees proved to be an impossible task.

QUESTION

To what extent were the problems arising from partition extremely complex issues for the government to resolve?

The establishment of democracy

At the same time, the government was taking steps to consolidate India's status as a unified, secular, democratic state. The first government of independent India was a coalition, dominated by the Congress Party but designed to be as inclusive as possible. Its main task was to rule India until a new constitution was written and the first elections could be held. The government was led by Jawaharlal Nehru and his deputy was another Congress Party veteran, the conservative **Vallabhbhai Patel**. After Patel's death in 1950, Nehru was able to consolidate his dominant position in the party and push through a more active policy of reform.

Sardar Vallabhbhai Patel (1875–1950)

Patel was a leading member of the Congress Party and a close associate of Gandhi. He served as deputy to Nehru and as home affairs minister in the first government of India, and was responsible for negotiating the successful transfer of the princely states. He played a leading role in drawing up India's constitution.

Nationalism and Independence in India (1919–1964)

The new constitution

India's constitution was drawn up by a Constituent Assembly, which met from December 1946, when India was still under British rule, until December 1948. It consisted of 300 members, 82% of them members of the Congress Party, but the party itself represented a wide range of views. The public was also invited to make submissions, and large numbers were received, on issues ranging from the recognition of local languages and special rights for people from lower castes, to the prohibition of cow-slaughter and special safeguards for religious minorities. The chief architects of the constitution were Patel and the law minister, B.R. Ambedkar.

The constitution came into effect on Independence Day, 26 January 1950. It adopted a British or Westminster form of government, with two houses of parliament, the Lok Sabha (Assembly of the People), and a smaller upper house, the Rajya Sabha (Council of States), chosen by the state assemblies. Elections would be held every five years, using a system of universal suffrage for all citizens of 21 years and older. This made India, with a population of over 300 million people, the largest democracy in the world. The constitution abolished the colonial system of separate electorates for different religious groups, which Metcalf notes had had 'divisive tendencies', and replaced it with a constituency system open to all.

The constitution created a federal structure, with a strong central government, which controlled issues such as foreign affairs and defence, leaving individual states a certain amount of autonomy. This, according to historian Bipan Chandra, met the demands for diversity as well as the need for unity, and allowed for decentralisation but not disintegration.

The constitution was completely secular. This meant that there was to be no state religion, a separation of religion and state, a secular school system, and no taxes to support any religion. It recognised the equality and freedom of religion of all individuals, and any citizen could hold public office. Nehru was deeply committed to secularism. According to Chandra, Nehru defined secularism as keeping the state, politics and education separate from religion, making religion a private matter for the individual, and showing equal respect for all religions and equal opportunities for their followers. He defended it vigorously against communalism, which he saw as a major threat to democracy and national unity.

Change and continuity: In what ways did the new constitution represent change from, rather than continuity with, India's colonial past?

Although India became a republic, with an Indian president as head of state rather than the British monarch, it remained a member of the Commonwealth. This meant that India did not become isolated, despite Nehru's determination to pursue a policy of non–alignment internationally.

Find out what 'non alignment' meant in terms of international relations at the time of the Cold War. Examine how, and why, India became a leader of the Non-Aligned Movement.

The first election

In 1952, India held its first general election. Over 173 million voters, of whom 84% were illiterate, cast their votes for 489 national parliamentary seats, and over 3000 seats in the state assemblies. The election was a triumph for the Congress Party, which won 75% of the seats in the Lok Sabha, despite gaining only 45% of the vote. This was because of the electoral system, which required a simple majority to win each constituency.

The Communist Party became the main opposition. The extremist right–wing BJS, which supported communal interests, won only 3% of the votes. A Turkish journalist, quoted by Guha in *India After Gandhi*, described the election as a victory for secularism, moderation and national unity, and a rejection of communalism and narrow regional interests. The Congress Party also won majorities in nearly all the state assemblies.

Nationalism and Independence in India (1919–1964)

Apart from the illiteracy of most of the electorate, discuss the challenges which faced the organisers of India's first election.

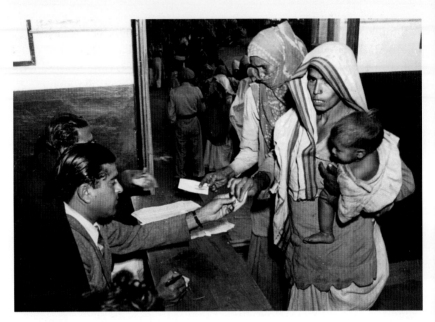

Figure 9.5: Voters in India's 1952 elections receive their ballot papers at a voting booth in outer New Delhi.

The Congress Party managed to win successive elections during Nehru's lifetime and remained in power mainly because the opposition was fragmented. But it faced significant problems relating to political extremism, separatist movements and communalism.

Historian Ian Talbot evaluates the achievements of India's democracy in Source 9.5, while Robert Stern suggests that we need to remember the context in which it was achieved in Source 9.6.

SOURCE 9.5

The Congress system of one-party dominance, as political scientists have termed it, also enabled the interests of newly politicised communities to be articulated under its broad umbrella... The 'exceptionalism' of Indian democracy in the third world was not only increasingly remarked upon by political analysts, but along with secularism and non-alignment constituted India's claim to moral authority and leadership in the developing world...

Democracy, like secularism, was, however, little more than a paper promise for those at the base of society where inequalities arising from gender, class and caste persisted, despite the promises of the constitution and the periodic round of elections.

Talbot, Ian. 2000. **India and Pakistan.** *London. Arnold. p. 170.*

SOURCE 9.6

Political development in India has been most notably of parliamentary democracy. In four decades, one of the world's few stable parliamentary democracies has been produced by a society that is more populous and diverse in every way than Europe's, scattered over more than half-a-million localities in a vast subcontinent, largely parochial and illiterate and fundamentally anti-democratic in its traditional institutions and cultural biases.

Stern, Robert. 1993. **Changing India: Bourgeois Revolution on the Subcontinent.** *Cambridge. Cambridge University Press. p. 184.*

QUESTION

Using Sources 9.5 and 9.6, and your own knowledge, evaluate how successfully India developed democratic institutions in the early years after independence.

Economic and social policies

The economic and social policies implemented after independence attempted to address some of the immense challenges facing the country. These included poverty, unemployment, landlessness and an unequal distribution of resources. Literacy levels and life expectancy were low, and there was discrimination based on gender and caste. The new government introduced policies to promote economic growth, extend education, improve health services, provide social welfare, improve the position of women and end the caste system. Underlying all of these was the desire to create a more equitable society and a fairer distribution of wealth.

Policies to promote economic growth

Nehru admired Stalin's achievement of rapid industrial growth in the Soviet Union, and he believed that a similar system of state involvement in the economy was essential for India's economic development. However, unlike the Soviet Union, India favoured a mixed economy, with some centralised planning, but also a large private sector outside direct government control.

In 1950 the government set up the Indian Planning Commission, chaired by Nehru, to formulate plans to promote economic development and improve living standards. It was given wide powers and massive funding to implement a series of Five-Year Plans. The first Five-Year Plan (1951–56) focused on increasing agricultural production; the Second Five-Year Plan (1956–61) emphasised large-scale industrial development; and the Third Five-Year Plan (1961–66) aimed to make India self-sufficient in basic foodstuffs, increase industrial output and decrease dependence on imports. Three giant steel mills were built, with the aid of foreign funding, as well as several large dams and irrigation schemes. In addition to heavy industry, labour-intensive small industries and labour-absorbing rural projects were set up as a means of providing employment. Talbot suggests, however, that an underlying weakness of the three plans was their emphasis on industry rather than agriculture as the key to India's development.

The Five-Year Plans achieved a great deal. Agricultural production grew by 25% during the first five years and a further 20% in the second, and industrial production more than doubled between 1948 and 1964. Although much of the industrialisation was financed from abroad, Nehru was careful to limit foreign influence and avoid the dangers of neo-colonialism, through high tariff barriers and government control of key industries.

Although the Five Year Plans increased agricultural and industrial production, and provided employment to more people in factories and workshops, the problem of unemployment remained critical. This was especially so for millions of landless peasants and for the increasing numbers of jobless people living in the streets, slums or informal settlements of large cities like Calcutta and Bombay.

Policies to create a more equitable distribution of wealth

An important objective of the Five-Year Plans was to eradicate poverty and improve living standards. The underlying assumption was that higher economic growth would help to solve the problem of poverty and would make greater equity possible. Land reform was also seen as a key factor, as well as greater access to education and healthcare, and eliminating the inequalities resulting from gender and caste.

However, according to Bates, only land reform could break the vicious cycle of rural impoverishment and population growth. New land reform legislation freed most of the peasants from the domination of the major landholders, by reducing the amount of land held by the *zamindari* (the landowners of large estates), who were often absentee landlords. However, it was usually the wealthier peasants who benefited most from these reforms. The position of poor peasants, such as sub-tenants and those who were landless, did not really change. Historians suggest that Congress did not want to alienate the richer peasants who were key supporters of the party. Similarly, it was the wealthier peasants who benefited from rural development projects, by ensuring their election to local councils and in this way dominating decision-making and the allocation of funding. Metcalf suggests that, because of these factors, the rural development schemes of the Nehru government did little to eradicate inequality or reduce poverty among the millions of landless villagers in India.

Another problem was regional inequality. There were vast differences between the wealthier areas, such as Bombay and Punjab, and the poorer regions. Although the government recognised this and implemented plans to uplift the poorer areas, regional inequality remained a key feature of the economy. For example, there were huge regional differences in female literacy rates between the better-developed states such as Kerala, and the least-developed such as Rajasthan, where even in the 1990s over 80% of girls in the state had never attended school.

Improvements resulting from economic and social policies were often offset by high population growth rates. As a result, efforts at land reform and rural development schemes had limited success in reducing inequality or poverty. However, although there were shortcomings in the attempts to bring about a more equitable distribution of wealth and resources, historians emphasise the importance of remembering that India's considerable achievements were made within a democratic framework. This was in marked contrast to the force used in totalitarian states such as the Soviet Union and China. In the words of historian Aditya Mukherjee: 'While persisting poverty has been the most important failure in India's post-independence development, the survival of the democratic structure has been its grandest success.'

Policies to extend education

Another challenge facing the new government was the state of education. At the time of independence, only 16% of the total population was literate. The situation was worst in rural areas where on average only 6% of people were literate, very few of them women. Many girls did not attend school at all. Nehru supported the extension of education because he believed that a literate electorate was essential for the survival of democracy. He also saw education as the means to bring about economic and social transformation.

The constitution committed the government to providing free and compulsory education for all children up to the age of 14, and set 1961 as the target date for this to be achieved, but this target was later extended many times. The government allocated large sums of money for the extension of education at primary, secondary and technical level, and during Nehru's term of office there were impressive achievements. Between 1951 and 1961, the number of boys attending primary school doubled, and the number of girls trebled. There was even better progress in the numbers attending secondary school, and thousands of new schools were built.

There were impressive advances in the fields of tertiary and technical education. By 1964, 41 new universities had been established, in which the number of female students enrolled rose to 22% of the total. These included technical universities and higher research establishments, where there was an emphasis on science and technology to sustain the economic policies of industrialisation and modernisation. However, from the late 1950s onwards there was a 'brain drain' of scientists and other highly skilled personnel. Along with the attraction of better pay and working conditions abroad, this was partly due to the bureaucratic and hierarchical organisation of the institutes.

Despite impressive advances, the provision of schooling could not keep pace with the population growth, and by the mid-1960s only 61% of all children, and 43% of girls, were attending primary school. Although there were enough schools in the large cities, in some rural areas there were no schools at all, and even where they existed, the drop-out rates, especially among girls, were high. Rural schools and those in small towns lacked equipment and facilities, and 40% of them had only one teacher to cope with several age-groups at once. As a result, the literacy rate had risen to only 24% by the time of Nehru's death in 1964.

DISCUSSION POINT

Between 1947 and 2010, the average life expectancy in India more than doubled to 66 years, and literacy rates improved dramatically, to 61%. However, in the same time, the population tripled to nearly 1.2 billion people. Discuss the problems that these trends would pose for any government. To what extent could education play a role in helping to solve them?

Critics also believed that, although the government made progress in increasing the number of students attending school, there was insufficient reform of the education system as a whole. Therefore, education failed to help raise the status of the majority of the population, namely the urban poor and those in rural areas.

Historian Bipan Chandra suggests that there was a decline in educational standards because, apart from the technology sector, the education system was not reformed – the content of education remained largely unchanged from the colonial period. Pavan Varma, the director of the Nehru Institute in London, claims that the emphasis on institutes of higher learning was at the expense of primary and secondary education, resulting in substantial numbers of highly skilled engineers, scientists and technologists, but also the world's largest number of children not attending school. He concedes, though, that insufficient resources made it impossible to eradicate illiteracy and to invest in institutions of higher learning simultaneously.

Policies to improve health services

In 1950, India had a population of 350 million, with an average life expectancy of 32 years. Millions of people died each year as a result of epidemics of smallpox, plague, cholera and malaria. Most towns had no modern sanitation, and only the wealthier parts of the big cities did. Health services were poor: in 1951, there were only 18 000 doctors and 113 000 hospital beds in the whole of India, and these were mainly in the cities. Polluted water, overcrowding, poverty and a lack of medicines to combat infection added to the problems.

India's high population growth rate was linked to the incidence of disease and high infant mortality, as Sources 9.7 and 9.8 explain.

SOURCE 9.7

A lack of education and the expectation of high infant mortality – the main consequences of poverty – meant that disadvantaged villagers in rural India continued to have larger families. In the absence of income and savings only family members could provide economic security to the elderly. This was not a relationship that even female education could break, as those at the bottom of the rural hierarchy in social and economic terms were rarely allowed the chance to make use of it, including access to the means of birth control. As death rates fell throughout the twentieth century a further vicious cycle began to develop: poverty was leading to larger families, causing landholdings to become highly sub-divided. The rural population was soon increasing at a rate faster than agricultural growth could accommodate.

Bates, Crispin. 2007. **Subalterns and Raj: South Asia since 1600.** *London. Routledge. pp. 219–220.*

SOURCE 9.8

In Tegu Raghuvir's village in Uttar Pradesh, northern India, there was no hospital and no doctor. 'We used to go running to fetch a herbalist, but by the time we got back the patient would be dead,' he recalls. 'Smallpox, measles, cholera, plague, influenza – these were fatal diseases.' As many babies and children died, people tried to have large families, partly to help supplement the family income. Only six of Tegu Raghuvir's nine children survived. 'Some people had this fear that, "If I just have this one child, and if he dies, then my family will be finished." And some people kept having daughters hoping they would have a son.'

Hodgson, Godfrey. 1996. **People's Century Volume 2.** *BBC Books. p.137.*

QUESTION

How, according to Source 9.7, did a 'vicious cycle' develop? With reference to their origin and purpose, assess the value and limitations of Sources 9.7 and 9.8 for historians researching the reasons for high population growth rates in India.

DISCUSSION POINT

What evidence is there in the interview in Source 9.8 of the clash between science and traditional beliefs and attitudes in developing countries? How can governments in this type of situation solve the problem of high population growth rates?

The government allocated funding to improve health services, train more doctors and nurses and build hospitals and clinics. As a result, the number of hospital beds increased by 165% during the Nehru period. With the help of the World Health Organisation, the government also launched large-scale immunisation campaigns to tackle the spread of disease. Death rates began to decline as a result, but birth rates remained high, so population growth continued to rise, putting more pressure on land and resources.

The government introduced family planning programmes to halt the rapid population growth, which threatened to undermine the progress that had been made. However, a propaganda campaign encouraging people to have smaller families had limited success, in a country with high rates of illiteracy and where large families were a tradition. By the time Nehru died, the population had risen to nearly 500 million. Later Indian governments tried to slow down population growth by offering incentives for people to have smaller families and providing voluntary sterilisation programmes.

Policies to provide social welfare

One of Nehru's goals was to create a welfare state, but he realised that improvements in social welfare could only be achieved through economic development. Nevertheless, the government launched two major programmes in an attempt to lay the foundations of a welfare state at village level. The aims were to improve the quality of life for the people of rural India, and at the same time promote rural development.

On the anniversary of Gandhi's birthday, on 2 October 1952, Nehru launched the first of these, the Community Development Programme. Its aims were to promote improvements in various aspects of rural life, such as agricultural methods, communications, education and health. Trained workers would advise farmers, but the emphasis was on self-help and self-reliance through popular participation at village level. Though it was initially received with enthusiasm and brought about some improvements, it did not achieve one of its fundamental goals, namely that of encouraging self-help. Instead it increased people's expectations of the government and the reliance of villagers on government officials, according to Bipan Chandra. Crispin Bates suggests that the programme was 'ambitious, well-intentioned, but grossly under-funded' and that it failed because it was 'defeated by the sheer scale of poverty in post-colonial rural India and by the opposition of aristocratic privilege and feudal prejudice'.

In 1959, a system of increased self-government in villages was introduced. This was called *Panchayati Raj*, and it was an experiment in democracy at grass-roots level. People elected village councils to run the affairs of their village. These councils drew up development plans for their area and allocated government funds for local projects in each community. In this way villagers were able to participate in making decisions and implementing development programmes. However, the system did not always work effectively because local councils were dominated by richer peasants and capitalist farmers, who often directed the funds to benefit their own farms, while the poorer and landless peasants remained powerless. In addition, many state governments were not enthusiastic about the system, and the success of rural reform relied on state involvement.

DISCUSSION POINT

Discuss the efforts of the government to transform India through a combination of massive industrial projects and simple village-based projects.

Policies to improve the position of women

Traditionally, Indian women in general had a subservient role in society. Male domination was the norm: a man could marry several wives, but a woman had no right to ask for a divorce. Daughters received a dowry when they married, but were excluded from any right of inheritance. As a result, women were always dependent on men and had no rights of their own. In rural areas, a woman moved into the home of her husband's family, where she was subjected to control and often oppression. Few women had access to education: in 1951 fewer than 8% of women were literate, compared with 25% of men.

ACTIVITY

Use the internet to find out how the dowry system functioned in India, why it was outlawed, and whether efforts to eliminate it have been successful.

After independence, there were dramatic changes in the status of women. Women were included among the first ministers and provincial governors. In the 1950 constitution, women were granted complete equality with men and the right to vote. Even so, Nehru, who was a strong supporter of advancing women's rights, knew that further measures were necessary to make equality a reality. In 1950 he and other reformists introduced the Hindu Code Bill in parliament, which outlined reforms to the laws governing marriage, divorce, inheritance and property rights. However, there was strong opposition from Hindu traditionalists, such as the Bharatiya Jan Sangh (BJS) and other communalist groups, who viewed these changes as a threat to Hindu identity and traditions. There was also opposition from conservative members of Congress, including influential leaders like Patel. Faced with this opposition, Nehru withdrew the bill, hoping to mobilise more support for reform.

After Patel's death in 1950, Nehru was able to proceed with his reforms more easily. The Hindu Code Bill was reintroduced and passed as a series of separate laws. The two most significant were the Hindu Succession Act, which gave women equal rights with men in the inheritance and ownership of property; and the Hindu Marriage Act, which abolished polygamy, provided for maintenance for a wife if her husband divorced her, and gave women the right to sue for divorce. A further reform came in 1961, when the dowry system was outlawed. Nehru later stated that he considered his reform of Hindu law to improve the position of women to be his greatest achievement in Indian politics.

Muslim marriages continued to be governed by traditional Islamic law. The government did not want to be accused of tampering with the laws and traditions of a minority. As Kulke and Rothermund note, this exclusion was incompatible with the idea of a secular state in which a civil code should apply equally to all citizens, regardless of their religious affiliation. Talbot suggests that Muslim women were deprived of the equal status provided by the constitution partly because Congress leaders wanted to reassure the Muslim minority and partly because they wanted the vote of the Muslim bloc in elections.

Although the legal position of women improved with the passing of these acts, it was very difficult to change traditional attitudes, especially in rural areas. For example, women were often reluctant to claim the rights of inheritance that the new laws gave them. And, although it had been officially outlawed, the dowry system continued. Metcalf suggests that the new laws did little to change the real position of women, because the lack of resources available to them, and the constraints of traditional rural society, made their application unlikely.

There was a significant improvement during the Nehru years in the number of girls attending school, but most of these improvements were in urban areas, and educational opportunities for girls in rural areas lagged far behind those for boys. Even decades later, the female literacy rate for India as a whole remained much lower than that for males. However, women certainly became more actively involved politically.

By the time of the second general election in 1957, 94% of women were registered as voters, although only about half of them actually exercised their right to vote: the percentage of women voting in the 1962 election was under 47%.

Change and continuity: To what extent did democracy bring both change and continuity for women in India?

Policies to end discrimination associated with the caste system

The Indian government wanted to end the discrimination associated with the caste system as part of its plan to promote equality and civil rights. In Hindu tradition, society was divided into a hierarchy of different levels, according to the caste system. Status, occupation, rights and opportunities in life were all determined by the caste into which someone was born. Outside the caste system were the 'untouchables', who suffered many forms of discrimination. Although it is usually associated with Hindu tradition, according to historian Mridula Mukherjee, the caste system was prevalent among Sikhs, Christians and Muslims too, providing 'legitimation for the unequal access to resources, and to the exploitation and oppression of lower castes'.

Theory of Knowledge

History and terminology

The British colonial administration referred to 'untouchables' as 'the depressed classes'. Gandhi fought for their rights and called them 'harijans' (or 'children of God'). The Indian government used the official term 'scheduled castes', but the people themselves prefer to be called 'Dalits' (which means 'oppressed'). What are the implications of each of these terms? Discuss what this suggests about the use of terminology in the writing of history.

Figure 9.6: In this 1946 photograph, a high-caste Hindu farm-owner fastidiously drops wrapped wages into the hands of his lowly Sudra caste workers, thus avoiding 'pollution'.

Considered even lower than the lowest caste, the 'untouchables', were subjected to many forms of discrimination. They could not own land, enter temples, or use common resources such as village wells or roads. They performed all the menial work, such as carrying water, tanning leather, and working the land, usually as sharecroppers. The number of people regarded as 'untouchable' varied from area to area, with the highest numbers in the north, but, before independence, it probably included between 15% and 20% of the total population of India. Although there is evidence that some aspects of the system were beginning to change in urban areas, there were still social pressures, such as exclusion from hotels and restaurants. Some parts of India even instituted new restrictions in the 1930s, such as prohibiting literacy, and banning the use of certain clothing items, such as umbrellas, by 'untouchables'. Gandhi had spoken out strongly on the issue of 'untouchability', and several movements were formed to fight the various forms of discrimination against them. **Dr B.R. Ambedkar** emerged as their most respected leader. At the time of independence in

1947, the caste system still dominated rural society, and 'untouchability' remained a prominent feature.

B.R. Ambedkar (1891–1956):

Ambedkar was a leading campaigner for the rights of Dalits (untouchables) and formed a political party, the Scheduled Castes Federation, to support their interests. As an Independent in the first government, he served as law minister and played a leading role in drawing up India's constitution. He was also largely responsible for drawing up the Hindu Code Bill, and he resigned when the government withdrew it in the face of conservative opposition. As a rejection of Hinduism and its discriminatory caste system, he converted to Buddhism and focused on persuading his fellow caste members to do the same.

Congress leaders who supported modernisation opposed the caste system as a source of division in Indian society. According to Nehru's biographer, Tariq Ali, Nehru saw it as an outdated practice. But there were others who held conservative views and saw the system as part of a tradition that should not be changed. The 1950 constitution gave equal rights to all, regardless of religion, race, gender, language or caste, and it specifically stated that 'untouchability' was abolished and its practice forbidden. It also reserved 20% of the seats in parliament and in the state assemblies for the former untouchables and the forest tribes, another minority group. They were listed in a special schedule in the constitution, and became known from then on as the 'scheduled castes and scheduled tribes'.

The way lay open for the government to introduce reforms through a programme of social legislation. As well as having equality in law and as voters, the scheduled castes were now free to use the same shops, schools and places of worship as any other citizen. Special funding was set aside in the Five-Year Plans to improve their position by, for example, providing wells for them in villages where fellow villagers still refused to share water with them. They were also given special land allotments, as well as access to housing, healthcare and legal aid. To overcome their low rate of literacy, they were exempt from paying school fees, and given special access to hostel accommodation and scholarships. However, by the early 1960s their literacy rate was still only a third of the average for India as a whole.

In 1955, the practice of treating people as untouchables became a criminal offence, which could result in a fine or prison sentence. However, in reality, few people were prosecuted under this law and the scheduled castes were still frequently prevented from participating in ordinary community life.

Although the constitution put an end to discrimination and made provision to raise the status of the scheduled castes and scheduled tribes, there was no sustained campaign against the caste system. Ambedkar criticised the Congress government for not doing enough. He believed that independence had not meant freedom for the scheduled castes, and he described their situation as a continuation of the tyranny, oppression and discrimination that had always existed. In *India after Independence* (2000), historian Bipan Chandra observes that, although discrimination based on caste was officially outlawed, the government made insufficient effort to eradicate the whole concept of the caste system as an ideology. The new laws and the special aid did not abolish social disadvantages and discrimination, and caste oppression was still common in rural areas, where acts of brutal violence against scheduled castes sometimes occurred. In some cases, these attacks occurred partly because other people resented the preferential treatment scheduled castes received as a result of government policies. In spite of these policies, progress in removing discrimination based on the caste system was slow.

KEY CONCEPTS ACTIVITY

Significance: Write a couple of paragraphs to explain the significance of the caste system in India and the efforts to end it.

Crispin Bates comments on the passing of legislation to reverse discrimination against women and the lower castes in Source 9.9.

SOURCE 9.9

In the 1950s – at least initially – the policy of positive discrimination or 'reservation' in favour of the lower castes had a positive impact, and created a real sense (however illusory) among the élite that they had lived up to their promises to Indian women and to the mass of downtrodden lower castes, whose position they had avowed to improve in the days of the independence struggle.

Bates, Crispin. 2007. Subalterns and Raj: South Asia since 1600. *London. Routledge. p. 216.*

QUESTION

To what extent does Source 9.9 suggest that the attempts to outlaw discrimination based on caste were unsuccessful?

ACTIVITY

Draw a four-column table like the example below to summarise the successes and failures of Nehru's domestic policies. In the first column list issues such as: economic growth; distribution of wealth; education; health; social welfare; position of women; the caste system.

Economic and social issues	What were the challenges?	What policies were implemented?	How successful were they?

9

An assessment of Nehru's role

In January 1964, Nehru suffered a stroke, and in May of that year he died. He had dominated Indian politics for decades, first as a leader of the nationalist movement alongside Gandhi, and then as the first prime minister of independent India. He is widely admired for his commitment to democracy and secularism, and for the role he played in establishing a united and democratic India.

Robert Stern comments on Nehru's legacy to the development of democracy in India in Source 9.10.

SOURCE 9.10

Were we to name a founding father of parliamentary democracy in India and the one-party dominance of the Congress... it would be Jawaharlal Nehru... He might have succumbed easily, as did many of his contemporaries in Asia and Africa, to the self-serving revelation that parliamentary democracy is for any number of reasons inappropriate to a 'third world' country and declared himself chief guide in a 'guided democracy', first person in a 'people's democracy', president-for-life, great helmsman, whatever. But he did not. Instead he led his party in India's first three democratic elections and tutored its electorate in parliamentary democracy, tolerated dissent within Congress, suffered the rivalry of opposition parties – left and right, regional and national, secular and religious; and bore the restraints that democracy imposes on executive power: by cabinet and party colleagues, a lively parliament, an articulate opposition, a free press, an independent judiciary, and an unpoliticised civil service.

Stern, Robert. 1993. **Changing India: Bourgeois Revolution on the Subcontinent.** *Cambridge. Cambridge University Press. pp. 186–7.*

Other historians share similar positive views about the values Nehru prized, his qualities as a leader and his role in establishing a multi-party democracy in India. Metcalf suggests that his unwavering support for democratic processes ensured that these became an entrenched feature of the way democracy functions in India. According to Guha, Nehru represented the voice of democracy against dictatorship, and of secularism against narrow communal interests. Chandra provides a balanced view, describing Nehru as a visionary leader but one who failed to find a way of putting his ideals into practice. He cites some of the areas that were neglected by Nehru's government which created problems for the future. These included the education system, which was not reformed and failed to reach the majority of people; the failure to launch an effective mass struggle against communalism as an ideology; and the inadequate implementation of land reforms, leaving a legacy of economic inequality, social oppression and political violence in rural India.

Some historians, such as Crispin Bates and Nehru's biographer Tariq Ali, believe that Nehru could have achieved his goal of transforming India more successfully if he had not been restrained by the right wing of the Congress Party. The British philosopher Bertrand Russell, who was a great admirer of Nehru, voiced this view in an obituary after Nehru's death (see Source 9.11). Bates suggests that these conservative forces marred 'many of his government's best initiatives'. He attributes the origins of the strength of the right wing to the rightward shift of Congress after 1936 and the 'strong continuities that existed with the pre–existing colonial regime in consequence of the peaceful transition to independent rule'.

SOURCE 9.11

After the independence struggle had been won, Nehru was hampered by the power of the right-wing which increasingly came to dominate the Congress Party. This domination was only held in check by his own leadership and command over the population of India. The price, however, of having to reconcile the powerful economic forces which the Congress comprised with his hopes for democratic socialism, was the emasculation [weakening] of the latter programme. India has a slow growth rate and remains stricken with poverty and disease. Nehru's own efforts to alter this would have succeeded more had his party been forthrightly socialist with an opposition in Parliament representing the very forces which now dominate the Congress.

Bertrand Russell, quoted in Ali, Tariq. 1985. **The Nehrus and the Gandhis: An Indian Dynasty.** *Chatto & Windus, The Hogarth Press. pp. 108–9.*

> ## KEY CONCEPTS QUESTION
>
> **Perspectives:** Compare the different perspectives of Stern, Metcalf, Guha, Chandra and Tariq Ali in their evaluation of Nehru's role. Discuss the reasons why historians hold such different views. To what extent is it important for students of history to evaluate different perspectives?

Paper 3 exam practice

Question

Evaluate the achievements of Nehru's government in ending discrimination based on gender and caste. **[15 marks]**

Skill

Writing a conclusion to your essay

Examiner's tips

Provided you have carried out all the steps recommended so far, it should be relatively easy to write one or two concluding paragraphs.

For this question, you will need to cover, and evaluate, the following aspects of the policies of Nehru's government:

* policies to improve the position of women regarding property, inheritance, marriage and the dowry system
* education policies
* policies to end the caste system
* reserved seats and affirmative action measures.

This question requires you to consider a **range** of different policies and issues, and to support your analysis with **precise and specific** supporting knowledge – so you need to avoid generalisations. Such a question implicitly offers you the chance to consider different views, and to come to some kind of **judgement** about the successes and failures of the Nehru's government in these areas.

Common mistakes

Sometimes, candidates simply rehash in their conclusion what they have written earlier – making the examiner read the same things twice. Generally, concluding paragraphs should be relatively short. The aim should be to come to an overall judgement or conclusion that is clearly based on what has already been written. If possible, a short but relevant quotation is a good way to round off an argument.

Sample student conclusion

The new constitution recognised the equality of all citizens, regardless of gender or caste, and women and 'untouchables' were included among the first government ministers and provincial governors. The Hindu Succession Act recognised women's right to inherit and own property and the Hindu Marriage Act outlawed polygamy and gave women the right to divorce and maintenance. The dowry system was outlawed and great progress was made in increasing the number of girls attending school. The 'scheduled castes' were given reserved seats in parliament, and special access to education, land and village facilities, and the system of 'untouchability' was outlawed altogether.

However, the new measures did not end discrimination against women or untouchables. Although they were equal in law, it was difficult to change traditional attitudes especially in rural areas. Muslim women were not protected by the new laws, and, although it was outlawed, the dowry system continued. Although more girls attended school, female literacy remained far below the average. Despite the efforts to end discrimination based on caste, there was no sustained effort to end the caste system, and untouchables continued to be denied access to ordinary community life. Other people resented the preferential government policies they received and there were sometimes brutal attacks on them. However, Bates suggests that even though the policies did not achieve all that they might have, they had a positive impact and that Congress leaders 'had lived up to their promises to Indian women and to the mass of downtrodden lower castes' whom they had promised to help during the independence struggle.

Examiner's comment

This is a fairly good conclusion because it briefly pulls together the main threads of the argument. In addition, there is an apt final quotation that rounds off the whole conclusion. However, in parts the conclusion is too detailed and there is a tendency to summarise what has already been covered in the essay. Also there is no clear concluding statement.

Activity

In this chapter, the focus is on writing a useful conclusion. Using the information from this chapter, and any other sources of information available to you, write concluding paragraphs for **at least two** of the Paper 3 practice questions. Remember: to do this, you will need to create full plans for the questions you choose.

Remember to refer to the simplified Paper 3 mark scheme in Chapter 10.

Paper 3 practice questions

1   Examine the impact of communalism and Hindu nationalism on the development of secular democracy in India.

2   To what extent did issues relating to ethnicity and language pose a threat to unity in post-independence India?

3   Examine the reasons for and consequences of the dispute between India and Pakistan over Kashmir.

4   To what extent did Nehru's government succeed in promoting economic growth and ending rural poverty and inequality?

5   'Nehru was a visionary leader but he failed to put all his ideals into practice in post-independence India.' To what extent do you agree with this statement?

10 | Exam practice

Introduction

You have now completed your study of the nationalist movement in India between 1919 and 1947, the independence and partition of India, and the challenges facing independent India. You have also examined some of the historical debates and differing historical interpretations which surround these developments.

In the earlier chapters, you have seen examples of Paper 3-type essay questions, with examiner's tips. You have also had some basic practice in answering such questions. In this chapter, these tips and skills are developed in more depth. Longer examples of student answers are provided, accompanied by examiner's comments that should increase your understanding of what examiners are looking for when they mark your essays. Following each question and answer, you will find tasks to give you further practice in the skills needed to gain the higher marks in this exam.

IB History Paper 3 exam questions and skills

If you are following HL Option 3 – *Aspects of the History of Asia and Oceania* – will have studied in depth *three* of the 18 sections available for this HL Option. *Nationalism and Independence in India 1919–64* is one of those sections. For Paper 3, two questions are set from each of the 12 sections, giving 36 questions in total; you have to answer *three* of these.

Each question has a specific mark scheme. However, the 'generic' mark scheme in the IB *History Guide* gives you a good general idea of what examiners are looking for to be able to put answers into the higher bands. In particular, you will need to acquire reasonably precise historical knowledge so that you can address issues such as cause and effect, and change and continuity. This will be required in order to explain historical developments in a clear, coherent, well-supported and relevant way. You will also need to understand relevant historical debates and interpretations, refer to these and critically evaluate them.

Essay planning

Make sure you read each question *carefully*, noting all the important key or 'command' words. You might find it useful to highlight them on your question paper. You can then produce a rough plan (for example, a spider diagram) for *each* of the three essays you intend to attempt, *before* you start to write your answers. That way, you will soon know whether you have enough own knowledge to answer them adequately. Next, refer back to the wording of each question – this will help you see whether or not you are responding to *all* its various demands and aspects. In addition, if you run short of time towards the end of your exam, you will at least be able to write some brief condensed sentences to show the key points and arguments you would have presented. It is therefore far better to do the planning at the *start* of the exam; that is, before you panic if you suddenly realise you don't have time to finish your last essay.

Relevance to the question

Remember, too, that your answers need to be relevant and focused on the question. Don't go outside the dates mentioned in the question, or write answers on subjects not identified in that question. Also, don't just describe the events or developments. Sometimes students simply focus on one key word, date or individual, and then write down everything they know about it. Instead, select your own knowledge carefully, and pin the relevant information to the key features raised by the question. Finally, if the question asks for 'causes' or 'reasons' and 'results', 'continuity and change', 'successes and failures', or 'nature and development', make sure you deal with *all* the parts of the question. Otherwise, you will limit yourself to half marks at best.

Examiner's tips

For Paper 3, examiners are looking for well-structured arguments that:

- are consistently relevant and linked to the question
- offer clear and precise analysis
- are supported by the use of accurate, precise and relevant own knowledge
- offer a balanced judgement
- refer to different historical debates and interpretations or to relevant historians and, where relevant, offer some critical evaluation of these.

Simplified mark scheme

Band		Marks
1	**Consistently clear understanding of and focus** on the question, with **all main aspects addressed**. Answer is **fully analytical, balanced** and **well-structured/ organised**. Own knowledge is **detailed, accurate and relevant**, with events placed **in their historical context**. There is **developed critical analysis**, and **sound understanding of historical concepts**. Examples used are **relevant**, and used effectively **to support analysis/evaluation**. The answer also integrates **evaluation of different historical debates/perspectives**. All/almost all of the main points are **substantiated**, and the answer reaches a **clear/reasoned/consistent judgement/ conclusion**.	13–15
2	**Clear understanding of the question**, and most of its **main aspects are addressed**. Answer is mostly **well-structured and developed**, though, with **some repetition/ lack of clarity** in places. Supporting **own knowledge mostly relevant/accurate**, and events are placed **in their historical context**. The answer is **mainly analytical**, with relevant examples **used to support critical analysis/evaluation**. There is **some understanding/evaluation of historical concepts and debates/perspectives**. Most of the main points **are substantiated**, and the answer offers a **consistent conclusion**.	10–12
3	**Demands of the question are understood** – but some aspects **not fully developed/ addressed**. Mostly **relevant/accurate supporting own knowledge**, and events generally placed **in their historical context**. **Some attempts at analysis/evaluation but these are limited/not sustained/ inconsistent**.	7–9

Band		Marks
4	**Some understanding** of the question. **Some relevant own knowledge,** with some factors identified – but with **limited explanation. Some attempts at analysis,** but answer **lacks clarity/coherence, and is mainly description/narrative.**	4–6
5	**Limited understanding of/focus on** the question. **Short/generalised** answer, with very **little accurate/relevant own knowledge.** Some **unsupported assertions,** with **no real analysis.**	0–3

Student answers

The following extracts from student answers have brief examiner's comments throughout, and an overall comment at the end. Those parts of student answers that are particularly strong and well-focused (such as demonstrations of precise and relevant own knowledge, or examination of historical interpretations) will be highlighted in red. Errors/confusions/irrelevance/loss of focus will be highlighted in blue. In this way, you should find it easier to follow why marks were awarded or withheld.

Question 1

Examine the reasons for, and consequences of, the growth of Muslim separatism by 1947. **[15 marks]**

Skills

- Factual knowledge and understanding
- Structured, analytical and **balanced** argument
- Awareness/understanding/evaluation of historical interpretations
- Clear and balanced judgement

Examiner's tips

Look carefully at the wording of this question, which asks you, essentially, to examine the causes and consequences of the growth of Muslim separatism. This will involve tracing its roots as well as identifying the factors that led to the growth of support for it from the late 1930s. You also need to examine what impact it had. Remember that there may be no clear-cut division between causes and consequences. You will need to take this into account as you plan your essay. All aspects of the question will need to be addressed in order to achieve high marks. Remember – don't just list or describe the various causes and consequences. You need to provide explicit analysis and explanation of them.

Student answer

The growth of Muslim separatism had significant political implications, and led ultimately to the partition of India and the creation of a separate Muslim state in Pakistan. However, the growth of Muslim separatism was a gradual process that developed over many decades, from initial steps to safeguard the position of Muslims within India to calls for a separate Muslim state. The underlying factor behind this was that Muslims formed a minority of the population in British India, and were outnumbered by Hindus by about 4 to 1. As a result, they feared that their identity, culture, religion and interests would not be upheld in a Hindu-dominated state.

EXAMINER'S COMMENT

This introduction is not clear enough. It should focus more directly on key words in the question ('reasons for' and 'consequences of'). It should also provide the examiner with a clear idea of how the essay will be structured. It would be better to include the detail on numbers in the body of the essay.

The roots of Muslim separatism lay in the period of colonial rule when Muslims faced two distinct disadvantages. They formed only about 20% of the population and they were reluctant to accept the English system of education which gave access to influential positions in colonial society. The British were the first to hold a census in India in 1881 and it classified people according to religion. Chandra sees this as part of a colonial policy of 'divide and rule' and thinks that it laid the foundation for the future partition of India. Talbot and Singh think that the education issue was a major factor which led to the growth of separatism. Cohen even suggests that the British deliberately favoured Hindus and that Muslims resented this. Muslims were also concerned about the Hindu revival in the 1890s which they felt threatened their position in India.

EXAMINER'S COMMENT

It is good to make reference to the views of different historians. However, these need to be integrated into the answer and not simply listed. Some of the statements made here require further explanation and analysis.

To protect their interests, they sent a deputation of Muslim leaders to see the viceroy, who assured them that their status as a separate community would be recognised in future constitutional reforms. They also formed the All-India Muslim League to represent and protect their interests. They wanted to make sure that there would be separate electorates and reserved seats for Muslims. This is what happened when the Morley-Minto constitutional reforms were introduced in 1909. At first there was cooperation between the League and the Indian National Congress, and in 1916 they signed the Lucknow Pact. This meant that Muslim concerns about separate representation to protect their interests had been addressed. As a result, Muslims felt no need to promote the concept of separation any further at this stage. But during the 1920s there were growing communal tensions between Hindus and Muslims, and even violence, so Muslims once more became concerned about their future. They were also concerned because attempts by the Muslim League leader, Jinnah, to reach an agreement with Congress failed.

EXAMINER'S COMMENT

This paragraph relies too much on narrative, describing a sequence of events, without explanation or analysis. The information included is accurate but it is too vague in places. For example, what exactly was the Lucknow Pact? Why were there growing communal tensions in the 1920s?

During the 1930s the idea that Muslims were a separate community developed into the idea that India was land of two nations – one Hindu and the other Muslim. This came to have significant political consequences. The proposal was first made in 1930 by Muhammad Iqbal at a Muslim League meeting but, according to Cohen, it wasn't clear whether he wanted separate Muslim states within an Indian federation, or a completely separate country. Either way, Bose and Jalal say that the idea didn't attract much attention from Muslim leaders at the time. But some people supported the 'Two Nation' theory and even suggested a name, Pakistan, for a separate Muslim state. The idea gained more support after the Muslim League did badly in the 1937 elections and Congress governments were voted into power in most of the provinces. Congress refused to include Muslim League members in these governments. This made many Muslims acutely aware of the dangers they would face in the future as a minority in India and was a key reason for the growth of Muslim separatism.

After the 1937 elections, the Muslim League worked hard to get Muslims throughout India to join the organisation. At its annual conference in 1940, the League passed the 'Lahore Resolution' which formally stated that it supported the 'Two Nation' theory and called for the creation of a separate Muslim state. This was a direct consequence of the growth of Muslim separatism.

EXAMINER'S COMMENT

There are some good analytical comments here and attempts to focus more directly on the question. However, there is no mention of different historians' views of the Lahore Resolution, and especially, the debate among historians about whether Jinnah and the League wanted a separate state at that stage of were using it as a bargaining tactic to get a better deal in negotiations.

[There then follow several more paragraphs giving accurate and reasonably detailed facts on the position of the League during the war, the situation in India at the end of the war, the failed negotiations and communal violence in 1946, and the decision to partition India in 1947.]

The reasons for the growth of Muslim separatism had their roots in the Muslim wish to maintain their identity and protect their interests as an outnumbered minority. From initially wanting separate electorates and reserved seats to safeguard these interests, this developed into the 'Two Nation' theory and the call for a separate Muslim state. The consequence of this was the partition of India in 1947 and the creation of Pakistan as a separate Muslim state.

> **EXAMINER'S COMMENT**
>
> This conclusion is adequate as it focuses directly on the 'reasons for' and 'consequences of' that are mentioned in the question and so rounds off the essay appropriately.

Overall examiner's comments

There is accurate own knowledge, with some hints of analysis. However, parts of the essay are descriptive rather than analytical, relating a series of events rather than explaining them. In places, the essay loses focus and the material needs to be more explicitly linked to the question. Although some reference is made to the views of historians, it is rather limited. A good answer would show a much better understanding of historical debate and would integrate it smoothly into the answer. An answer such as this one would probably be placed in Band 3 and earn 9 marks.

Activity

Look again at the simplified mark scheme and the student answer. Now draw up a plan focused on the demands of the question. Then write several paragraphs which will be good enough to get into Band 1, and so obtain the full 15 marks. As well as making sure you address *all* aspects of the question, try to integrate into your answer some references *and* evaluation of relevant historians and historical interpretations.

Question 2

Evaluate the successes and failures of Nehru's domestic policies in creating a more equal society in independent India between 1950 and 1964. **[15 marks]**

Skills

- Factual knowledge and understanding
- Structured, analytical and **balanced** argument

- Awareness/understanding/evaluation of historical interpretations
- Clear and balanced judgement

Examiner's tips

Look carefully at the wording of this question, which asks you to evaluate the successes and failures of Nehru's domestic policies and also provides specific dates for consideration. You will need to start by examining what forms of inequality existed, and then select and explain what policies the government introduced to address them. Finally, you will need to evaluate what successes and failures these policies had and whether they created a more equal society.

Remember to stick closely to the dates given in the question. It is important not merely to describe features and events, but use them to support an argument. In making your plan, you will be able to decide whether you can produce more evidence on one side than the other, and thus decide what that argument will be. It does not matter what view you adopt, as long as you have a 'thesis' and can write analytically and convincingly.

Student answer

One of the immense challenges facing the first government of independent India, led by Nehru, was inequality. There were great extremes of wealth, widespread poverty and landlessness and an unequal distribution of resources in Indian society. There was also discrimination based on gender and caste. After 1950, when the new constitution was adopted, the government implemented policies to address these issues. Despite some impressive achievements, by the time of Nehru's death in 1964, poverty, inequality and discrimination remained significant problems.

EXAMINER'S COMMENT

This is a clear and focused introduction. It indicates some knowledge of the factors which created inequality. It also shows an understanding of the significance of the dates which are mentioned in the question. It is clear from this introduction which line of argument will be followed and that some form of evaluation will be part of it.

When India became independent in 1947, there was a great deal of inequality in Indian society. Millions of people, especially in rural areas were desperately poor, and had no access to land. There was a vast gap between the educated élite and 84% of the population who were illiterate. Women did not have the same rights to property or inheritance as men did, and had little access to education. Male domination was the norm and women were expected to play a subservient role in society. The structure of society was based on the traditional caste system and Untouchables were excluded from many aspects of society. They performed all the menial work and could not own land or use common resources such as village wells or roads. There was also regional inequality, between the wealthier areas, such as Bombay, and the least developed regions such as Rajasthan. There were big differences too between rural and urban areas in terms of access to education and healthcare. The new constitution recognised the equality of all citizens and the government introduced policies to try to make this a reality.

EXAMINER'S COMMENT

This is useful and succinct explanation of the various forms of inequality that existed. It shows a good understanding of the problems and sets the scene for a discussion of the government's attempts to alleviate them. It does not make the mistake of writing too much detail as background here, as the focus should be on evaluating the policies themselves.

[There then follow several paragraphs explaining the policies implemented to promote economic growth and address poverty, unemployment, landlessness and the unequal distribution of resources, including access to education and healthcare.]

The Five Year Plans increased agricultural and industrial production, and provided employment to more people in factories and workshops. There were also impressive advances in the provision of education and healthcare: the number of children attending school rose dramatically, and death rates declined as immunisation programmes tackled the spread of disease. But although literacy levels and life expectancy rose, progress was offset by high population growth rates which put more pressure on land and resources. The problem of unemployment remained critical, especially for millions of landless peasants and for the increasing numbers of jobless people living in the streets or informal settlements of big cities.

Historians have critical views about the effectiveness of the economic and social policies of Nehru's government. Bates believes that only proper land reform could have broken the vicious cycle of rural poverty and population growth, but that the government's policies did not succeed because the people who benefitted most from them were the wealthier peasants. Metcalf believes that the policies did little to reduce inequality or poverty. Mukherjee agrees that the biggest failure of the government was its inability to eradicate poverty. But she also thinks that we need to take into account the fact that the achievements that were made, although not perfect, were made within a democratic framework.

EXAMINER'S COMMENT

These paragraphs show some good understanding of the issues but they are too vague in places. It would be better to supply hard evidence than to use phrases such as 'impressive advances' and 'rose dramatically'. The candidate also shows knowledge of the views of historians about the economic and social policies and has integrated them into the paragraph effectively.

[There then follow several paragraphs explaining the policies implemented to improve the position of women and end discrimination based on gender.]

The legal position of women improved with the passing of the Hindu Succession Act and the Hindu Marriage Act, but it was very difficult to change traditional attitudes, especially in rural areas. For example, women were often reluctant to claim the rights of inheritance that the new laws gave them. And the dowry system continued, even though it had been officially outlawed. Metcalf suggests that the new laws did little to change the position of women, because of the lack of resources available to them and the constraints of traditional rural society. The new laws about marriage and property did not apply to Muslim women. Kulke and Rothermund see this as a failure because, as India claimed to be a secular democracy, laws should apply equally to all citizens, regardless of their religion. Talbot's view is that Congress leaders did not extend these laws to Muslim women because they did not want to tamper with the customs of a religious minority.

Women's lives changed in other ways as well. They became more actively involved politically and, by the time of the second general election in 1957, 94% of women were registered as voters, although only about half of them actually voted. There was also a significant improvement in the number of girls attending school, although most of these improvements were in urban areas. Educational opportunities for girls in rural areas lagged far behind those for boys, and the female literacy rate for India as a whole lagged far behind that for males.

EXAMINER'S COMMENT

Again, the answer shows a good knowledge of historical debate by integrating the views of these historians into the answer. However, when evaluating successes and failures it is important to give a balanced answer. This answer tends to focus more on the failures. For example, it mentions that 'the legal position of women improved' but does not give examples of this.

[There then follow several paragraphs explaining the policies implemented to improve the position of untouchables and end discrimination based on caste.]

After the 1950 constitution abolished 'untouchability' and reserved parliamentary seats for the 'scheduled castes', the legal position of Untouchables improved. They were now free to use the same shops, schools and places of worship as anyone else. The government also set aside special funding to improve their position by, for example, providing wells for them in villages where fellow villagers still refused to share water with them. They were also given special land allotments, as well as access to housing, healthcare and legal aid. To help to overcome their low rate of literacy, they were exempt from paying school fees, and given special access to hostel accommodation and scholarships.

The practice of treating people as 'untouchables' became a criminal offence, which could result in a fine or prison sentence, but few people were prosecuted under this law and the scheduled castes were still frequently prevented from participating in community life. The new laws and the special aid did not abolish social disadvantages and discrimination. Caste oppression was still common in rural areas, where acts of brutal violence against scheduled castes sometimes occurred. In some cases, these attacks occurred partly because other people resented the preferential treatment they received as a result of government policies. In spite of government policies, progress in removing discrimination based on the caste system was slow. Chandra suggests that the government did not make enough effort to eradicate the whole concept of the caste system as an ideology.

EXAMINER'S COMMENT

These paragraphs provide a balanced evaluation of the measures to end discrimination based on the caste system. However, the account needs more explanation and analysis. For example, the answer should suggest reasons why the Congress government didn't do enough to end it – for example right-wing opposition within its own ranks.

Between 1950 and 1964 the Indian government of Jawaharlal Nehru introduced various economic and social policies designed to create a more equal society. However, despite impressive levels of growth, poverty and inequality remained significant problems. Progress in extending education, improving health services, and instituting land reform was offset by rapid population growth. Attempts to end discrimination based on gender and caste were hampered by conservative traditional attitudes.

EXAMINER'S COMMENT

The conclusion is brief and to the point but fails to make a clear judgement about whether India was a more equal society by 1964.

Overall examiner's comments

This answer displays a good understanding of the successes and failures of Nehru's domestic policies and of the policies themselves, addressing all aspects of the question and providing accurate supporting knowledge. There is little that is irrelevant, for example. The essay also shows an awareness of historiography and differing historical interpretations, although there is scope for the range of interpretation to be developed further. The answer is, on the whole, well-structured and there are attempts at evaluation. The essay is not without its faults. It tends to be superficial in places and needs more explanation and analysis, as well as evidence to back up statements. There needs to be more focus on the question itself, especially in the conclusion which is rather bland. However, there is definitely enough here for an award in Band 2, with 11 marks.

Activity

Look again at the simplified mark scheme and the student answer. Now try to draw up your own plan and rewrite the answer in a way that would reach the criteria for Band 1 and so obtain the full 15 marks. You will need to offer a clearer judgement, provide a little more supporting detail and evaluate a greater range of alternative interpretations.

Bibliography

Ahmed, Akbar S. 1997. *Jinnah, Pakistan and Islamic Identity.* London. Routledge.

Arnold, David. 2001. *Gandhi.* Harlow. Pearson Education.

Bates, Crispin. 2007. *Subalterns and Raj: South Asia since 1600.* London. Routledge.

Bose, Sugata and Jalal, Ayesha. 1998. *Modern South Asia: History, Culture, Political Economy.* London. Routledge.

Butalia, Urvashi. 2000. *The Other Side of Silence: Voices from the Partition of India.* Durham. Duke University Press.

Chandra, Bipan, Mukherjee, Mridula and Mukherjee, Aditya. 1999. *India after Independence 1947–2000.* New Delhi. Penguin Books.

Chandra, Bipan, Mukherjee, Mridula, Mukherjee, Aditya, Mahajan, Sucheta and Pannikar, K.N. 2012. *India's Struggle for Independence 1857–1947.* London. Penguin. Digital edition

Cohen, Stephen. 2004. *The Idea of Pakistan.* New Delhi. Oxford University Press.

Copland, Ian. 2001. *India 1885–1947: The Unmaking of an Empire,* Harlow. Pearson Education.

Guha, Ramachandra. 2007. *India after Gandhi: The History of the World's Largest Democracy.* London. Macmillan.

James, Lawrence. 1997. *Raj: The Making and Unmaking of British India.* London. Little, Brown and Company.

Kulke, Hermann and Rothermund, Dietmar. 2004. *A History of India (Fourth Edition).* London. Routledge.

Leadbeater, Tim. 2015. *Indian Independence 1914–64.* London. Hodder Education.

Ludden, David. 2014. *India and South Asia: A Short History.* London. Oneworld Publications.

Metcalf, Barbara and Metcalf, Thomas. 2006. *A Concise History of Modern India (Second Edition).* Cambridge. Cambridge University Press.

Nehru, J. 1946. *The Discovery of India*. London. Meridian Books.

Pandey, Gyanendra. 2001. *Remembering Partition*. Cambridge. Cambridge University Press

Rees, Rosemary. 2010. *Britain and the Nationalist Challenge in India, 1900–1947*. Harlow. Pearson.

Stern, Robert. 1993. *Changing India: Bourgeois Revolution on the Subcontinent*. Cambridge. Cambridge University Press.

Talbot, Ian. 2000. *India and Pakistan*. London. Arnold.

Index

Acknowledgements

The authors and publishers acknowledge the following sources of copyright material and are grateful for the permissions granted. While every effort has been made, it has not always been possible to identify the sources of all the material used, or to trace all copyright holders. If any omissions are brought to our notice we will be happy to include the appropriate acknowledgement on reprinting.

Text Credits

Excerpts from Gandhi by David Arnold, © 2001, published by Taylor & Francis, reproduced by permission of Taylor & Francis Books UK; Excerpts from Subalterns of the Raj: South Asia Since 1600 by Crispin Bates, © 2007, published by Taylor & Francis, reproduced by permission of Taylor & Francis Books UK; Excerpts from India 1885–1947: The Unmaking of an Empire by Ian Copland, © 2001, published by Taylor & Francis, reproduced by permission of Taylor & Francis Books UK; Excerpts from Changing India: Bourgeois Revolution on the Subcontinent by Robert Stern, © 1993 published by Cambridge University Press; Excerpts from A Concise History of Modern India by Metcalf & Metcalf, 2006, © Barbara D. Metcalf and Thomas R. Metcalf 2001, 2006, published by Cambridge University Press and reproduced with permission.

Picture Credits

Front Cover – Dinodia Photos / Alamy Stock Photo; Figure 1.1 – Keystone/Hulton Archive/Getty Images; Figure 1.2 – Renato Granieri/Alamy Stock Photo; Figure 2.3 – Central Press/Getty Images; Figure 2.4 – Branger/Roger Viollet/Getty Images; Figure 2.5 – Print Collector/Hulton Archive/Getty Images; Figure 3.1 – Mary Evans

Picture Library/Alamy Stock Photo; Figure 3.3 - Keystone/Getty Images; Figure 3.4 - Keystone/Hulton Archive/Getty Images; Figure 4.1 - The British Library Board; Figure 4.2 - The British Library Board; Figure 4.3 - Popperfoto/Getty Images; Figure 4.4 - Dinodia Photos/ Alamy Stock Photo; Figure 4.5 -   Pictorial Press Ltd / Alamy Stock Photo; Figure 5.1 - PA Archive/Press Association Images; Figure 5.2 - Bettmann/Getty Images; Figure 5.3 - Mansell/The LIFE Picture Collection/Getty Images; Figure 5.4 - Keystone/Getty Images; Figure 6.2 - Dinodia Photos / Alamy Stock Photo; Figure 7.1 - PNA Rota/ Getty Images; Figure 7.2 - ullstein bild/Getty Images; Figure 7.3 - World History Archive / Alamy Stock Photo; Figure 8.1 – TopFoto; Figure 8.3 - Margaret Bourke-White/The LIFE Picture Collection/ Getty Images; Figure 9.2 - Keystone/Getty Images; Figure 9.5 - Popperfoto/Getty Images; Figure 9.6 - Margaret Bourke-White/The LIFE Picture Collection/Getty Images.